WAR AND SOCIETY
IN NORTH AMERICA

WAR AND SOCIETY IN NORTH AMERICA

Papers presented at the Canadian Association for
American Studies Meeting, Montreal, Fall, 1970

Edited by
J. L. Granatstein and R. D. Cuff

Thomas Nelson and Sons
(Canada) Limited
Toronto, Montreal, Vancouver

©Thomas Nelson and Sons
(Canada) Limited 1971
Printed and bound in Canada
ISBN 0-176-31829-1

Contents

Introduction

War has been studied with care by Canadian and American scholars, novelists and poets. There has always been something stirring, more often something tragic, in the clash of great armies by night. Society, too, has been dissected by academics and writers who search for the motive forces that drive men to greatness or folly. Curiously, however, few North Americans have looked at the effects of *war on society*. This is a strange omission, for in the hothouse atmosphere of war strange aberrations sometimes thrive. War seems to loosen all restraints, and in an atmosphere compounded of patriotism, sacrifice, and excess, people may behave in unusual fashions.

One reason for the absence of serious work in the joint area of war and society may be that North Americans have been relatively isolated from the devastation of conflict. Neither Canada nor the United States has been invaded in modern times, and except for the American Civil War neither state has suffered the terrible battle casualties that France, say, sustained in World War I. Indeed, Americans were freed from the necessity of defence throughout the nineteenth century, and the chief causes of their wars were domestic. On the other hand, for most of its history Canada has felt threatened by the United States. Even if this threat was not usually serious enough to compel Canadians to take adequate measures for their defence, nonetheless it added a significant tone to Canadian life.

No one can doubt the differential impact of war on these two societies, but neither Canadian nor American scholars have tried to analyze this problem. In fact, comparative Canadian-American studies in general are still in their infancy. This is unfortunate, because the essays in this volume show that this is a fruitful area for research. The essays by Professors Bliss and Cuff, for example, suggest that Canadian businessmen may have held different concepts from their American counterparts about the role of the state, and different attitudes toward such values as individualism, competition, and bureaucratic organization. Equally significant, the studies by Professors White and Morton examine institutions — the Canadian and American armies — and reveal both similarities and differences in the way the two forces tried to handle the problem of assimilating minorities. Studies such as these can help us to clarify the glib generalizations that so often dominate discussions and comparisons of Canadian and American national characters. And periods of crisis may well be the best places to begin serious research.

For example, one of the great questions about war and society has to do with its integrative or disintegrative effects, and clearly this has direct relation to the North American scene. Canada came into being in 1867 as a distinctive entity partly because of a supposed American military threat. But in 1940 and after, the pressures of extra-continental menaces forced the increasing integration of North American defences and economies. Who can doubt that the effects of this later integration have seriously undone the work of 1867? At the same time as Canada has been pushed closer to its neighbour, who can deny that the Vietnam War has not been disintegrative in its effects on the United States, effects that, as John Holmes and Dennis Duffy point out, have had their inevitable repercussions on Canada? War as an underlying factor in determining the contours of Canadian and American societies has not yet received the attention it merits.

One of the purposes of these essays is to encourage just this kind of work. These papers were presented at the annual meetings of the Canadian Association for American Studies in Montreal in November, 1970 — a not inapt place to study the effects of near-war on society. The papers have been revised for this volume, and the editors would like to thank the contributors for their speedy cooperation.

J. L. G.
R. D. C.

Business, The State, and World War I: the American Experience

Robert D. Cuff

Creation of a large emergency government was one of the most characteristic features of the war effort in the United States, as it was in every country. But while this bureaucratic explosion bulks large in history, it has received surprisingly little attention in American historiography. Students of the war years have not given this phenomenon nearly the attention it deserves. For the most part, we still derive our understanding of wartime administration from contemporary chronicles, or from works written in the 1940s when war planners looked to World War I for a usable past. Many of the histories of mobilization agencies remain to be written; and these individual stories have yet to be integrated into a general analysis of Wilsonian war government.[1]

Within these larger tasks, one of the most critical problems is to analyze the role played by dollar-a-year men in the federal establishment. It is true that businessmen were only one among several social groups to seek positions in the nation's war apparatus in 1917. Private careers and public offices intersected on a grand scale in these years; elite groups from a variety of private institutions involved themselves in governmental administration. Social scientists,

[1]Frederic L. Paxson's *American Democracy and the World War,* 3 vols. (Boston, 1936-1948), still remains the most comprehensive treatment of the war years. Among the war agencies which still require scholarly analysis are the Food Administration, the War Finance Corporation, the War Trade Board, and the Council of National Defense. One of the best surveys to come out of the re-examination of the 1940s is Harold J. Tobin and Percy W. Bidwell, *Mobilizing Civilian America* (New York, 1940).

social workers, labor leaders, churchmen, and more, flocked to Washington in an unprecedented application of social knowledge to public crisis. Still, none of these groups rivalled the businessmen in government in either numbers or power. After April 6, 1917, all volunteer mobilizers could associate themselves with the powers of a state energized by war, but only the businessmen among them could also tap the enormous power concentrated in large business corporations. Only business administrators could possibly become extensions of both public bureaucratic power and private economic power. They had access to those who controlled the means of production as well as to those who directed the state. It was hoped that as brokers between the economy and society, business volunteers could merge private and public power on behalf of the national interest.

Historians have generally subsumed the recruitment and conduct of businessmen in government under the larger story of state expansion during the war. As a result, the image of the businessman in government has benefited from the general conception of the state as a neutral if not beneficent force in American development. This conception, so prevalent in the older Progressive historiography, has regarded state expansion as essentially the triumph of the people over predatory special interests. Recent research has, of course, seriously altered our conception of business, the state and social change, but the onslaught against the older version has not fully permeated discussion of the war years.[2] Revisionist studies of the Progressive era, for example, should alert us to the importance of unsnarling the complex relationship of business groups to public administration in wartime. For if there is one point which these newer studies make crystal clear, it is that state expansion cannot be regarded as springing solely from a desire to subordinate private power to public need.[3] More specifically, this work should raise serious

[2]The close relationship between business interests and the state in social change is revealed most clearly for the nineteenth century in studies of economic growth. Robert A. Lively has analyzed much of this literature in "The American System: A Review Article," *Business History Review,* XXIX (March, 1955) , 81-96.

[3]Among the studies which reflect on this fact, with varying degrees of success, are Gabriel Kolko, *Railroads and Regulation, 1877-1916* (Princeton, 1965) and *The Triumph of Conservatism* (New York, 1963) ; Robert H. Wiebe, *Businessmen and Reform: A Study of the Progressive Movement* (Cambridge, 1962) ; and James Weinstein, *The Corporate Ideal in the Liberal State* (Boston, 1968) .

questions about the role of a state which located businessmen in strategic positions in its bureaucratic structure. Could public and private interest be merged, even in wartime? Could businessmen in government transform themselves into neutral public officials? What was the public interest for a businessman in government?

In trying to answer these questions, one must first make clear the kind of businessmen in government who will be studied. A useful distinction can be made between those in central policy-making positions and those on the outer rings of the wartime organization: between agency chairmen and division heads, for instance, and business specialists who occupied positions in the administrative exterior. Now it is true, as so many general administrators discovered, that the narrow specialists dominated their specific preserves by virtue of a superior technical knowledge and closer trade connections, but the central administrators possessed the greatest influence over general questions of public policy. It was the central administrators and their advisors who ultimately set the course for their respective agencies. Among those who occupied such positions were Walter Gifford, AT&T executive and Director of the Council of National Defense; Howard Coffin, vice president of the Hudson Motor Company and chairman of the Aircraft Production Board; Herbert Hoover, engineer-entrepreneur and chairman of the Food Administration; Edward Hurley, machine-tool manufacturer and president of the United States Shipping Board; Eugene Meyer, Jr., Wall Street banker and a director of the War Finance Corporation; Bernard Baruch, Wall Street speculator and chairman of the War Industries Board; Robert Brookings, retired millionaire and chairman of the WIB's Price Fixing Committee; and Arch Shaw, business theorist, magazine publisher, and head of the WIB's Conservation Division.

These men came into their positions of central authority in diverse ways, and they exhibited very different styles on their march to high office. Of far more interest than such differences, however, are the qualities they held in common and the remarkable congeniality evident between their prewar habits and their wartime functions. Of the hundreds of businessmen in Washington, why did these particular men arrive in positions of high office? Accident alone does not explain the results.

Clearly, their special position in the prewar social structure, and the kind of values derived from it, prepared these administrative generalists for their functions during the process of mobilization. Some had already found themselves attracted to careers beyond the narrow grooves of business before 1917; and many others discovered this inner wish during the war itself. Taking up positions between economic and political, private and public institutions in the prewar years, they had already begun to identify with causes beyond a single business interest or beyond a single industry. They had begun to consider the needs of America's economic system as a whole. The further they had progressed in this direction in peacetime, the more valuable they became to the Wilson Administration in wartime. In this way not only could they offer a broad grasp of large administrative problems; they could also present themselves as men above special interests and dedicated to the public interest.

Howard Coffin, Bernard Baruch, and Edward Hurley exemplify the prewar transitional trend very well. As president of the Society of Automobile Engineers in 1910 Coffin saw that the fortunes of the Hudson Motor Company were inextricably intertwined with practices in the auto industry as a whole; after August 1914 Coffin made the question of the automobile industry part of the great problem of industrial conversion for war. Coffin launched an industrial preparedness campaign in 1915, determined to fashion the links between the business community and the military establishment and to design the administrative tools of advanced industrial planning. The same restlessness with private career was evident in Bernard Baruch, who found himself attracted to Democratic politics and industrial preparedness in the prewar years. Embarking upon his new role as presidential advisor, Baruch set about to bind business groups closer to the Wilson Administration for reasons of politics and defense, anxious all the while to have a major post in any prospective mobilization. Edward Hurley, like Baruch, found satisfaction in promoting the Wilson candidacy in 1912 and 1916. More fortunate than his colleague, though, Hurley gained a public post for his pains as vice chairman and then chairman of the Federal Trade Commission in 1915.[4]

[4]George V. Thompson, "Intercompany Technical Standardization in the Early American Automobile Industry," *Journal of Economic History,* XIV (Winter, 1954), 1-20; Lloyd N. Scott, *Naval Consulting Board of the United States* (Washington, 1920), ch. II; Magaret Coit, *Mr. Baruch* (Cambridge, 1957) pp. 109-116, 131-147; Bernard M. Baruch, *My Own Story* (New York, 1957), pp. 176-182, 188,

These businessmen had confronted general questions of public policy before 1917, and they had already made personal attempts to overcome obstacles in the way of binding together military, business and government institutions. They appreciated the associational values so characteristic of advancing elites in the progressive era.[5] Their thought exhibited a marked integrative quality. They realized that the values and arrangements associated with an older *laissez faire* model no longer met the needs of an emerging corporate economy, and the European war experience after 1914 deepened their understanding of this order on a world scale. They insisted that America integrate her institutional blocs for order and stability, not alone for wartime, but for prosperity and power in the postwar world. Edward Hurley touched on this theme in a speech to the American Iron and Steel Institute in 1916: "Nowhere is cooperation among businessmen, and between them and government, more essential than in the development of our foreign trade," he explained. "The success of our European competitors is evidence enough of this."[6]

These men expected the state to provide guidance and assistance for business in creating the requisite institutional synthesis for war and for peace.[7] Take Arch Shaw, for example. Shaw lectured at the Harvard Business School on the importance of scientific principle in business enterprise, and he lectured to an even wider audience through his journal *System, The Magazine of Business*. Shaw was fascinated by the great changes that war brought to European business. It reaffirmed his belief in efficient method and applied intelligence, and he made his magazine a clearing house for information concerning the implications of war for American business. In January 1917, Shaw publicly called upon the Department of Commerce to shake off its lethargy and encourage American industry in

and *The Public Years* (New York, 1960) , ch. I; Edward H. Hurley, *The Bridge to France* (Philadelphia, 1927) , chs. 1 and 2.

[5]Robert Wiebe describes the outlook of these elites better than anyone else in *The Search For Order, 1877-1920* (New York, 1967) , esp. chs. 5, 6 and 7.

[6]*Proceedings of the American Iron and Steel Institute, 1916,* p. 194. For a more extensive statement by Hurley of this theme see his *The Awakening of Business* (Garden City, 1917) .

[7]There is a considerable contemporary literature on the virtues of business-government cooperation and the new corporate order. For one of the most intriguing statements see Charles P. Steinmetz, *America and the New Epoch* (New York, 1916) .

the kind of rationalization which war had fostered among its European competitors. Two months later the Wilson Administration asked Shaw to come to Washington to implement his scheme as chief of an independent bureau in the Council of National Defense.[8]

For Shaw as for the rest, American entry into the war in April 1917 offered an unparalleled opportunity to forward the new industrial synthesis. Owing to the war emergency, public power became available to any private group or private individual who could attach a private strategy to the public cause. Such a development was of special significance to business ideologues and dreamers who could not personally wield the power of big business in private life. Possibly during the wartime emergency they could use the power of the state to mould business and the nation to their private vision. Washington became a boomtown for organizational entrepreneurs, for men skilled in the bureaucratic technique, for men who sought alliances among the nation's leading institutions on behalf of a powerful, unified, economic system.

Once in Washington every major business advisor sought as much power as the political system would offer; and individuals and groups who obstructed this quest caught the collective scorn of these business statesmen. There were a number of prime offenders, among them businessmen antagonistic to the new corporate order, military departments which clung to older competitive instincts, politicians who objected to the gaping breach in the walls between private and public institutions, and civil servants who resented the wartime intruders. In the debate over the Food Administration, for example, many congressmen doggedly fought the kind of mandate which Herbert Hoover demanded as prospective head. At a very minimum, they preferred to entrust emergency authority to a commission rather than to Hoover alone. The Great Engineer complained later that apparently the American people had forgotten that ". . . a single

[8]Shaw outlined his proposal to the Department of Commerce in "In the Day of Prosperity," *System*, XXXI (January, 1917), 123-132. Shaw reprinted excerpts of opinion favourably disposed to his scheme in "Progress for 'A National Business Program'," *System*, XXXI (April, 1917), 444-447. "Plans for Handling War-Time Business," *System*, XXXI (May, 1917), 451-458, illustrates Shaw's use of *System* to transmit European experience to American businessmen. Shaw discusses his war experience in "Statement of Arch Shaw," Papers of Bernard M. Baruch, Princeton University.

executive head had been the basic concept of organization of our Government and our business world ever since the foundation of the Republic."[9] Personally, Hoover foresaw no danger in the absence of checks and balances in his administration.

The key descriptive words in the kind of social model these businessmen in government idealized were coordination, centralization, efficiency, and standardization. They displayed an engineering, managerial, manipulative mentality. "If I heard Coffin talking in his sleep," remarked a Washington official during the war, "I wouldn't take the trouble to go over and listen because I would know exactly what he would be saying. 'Standardize! Standardize! Standardize!' That's his motto, his slogan, his creed."[10] Moreover, the major dollar-a-year men demonstrated the same enthusiasm for substituting administrative process for political process as had their reform-minded colleagues during the progressive era.[11] Businessmen both in and out of government preferred to restrict their negotiations to a conference room rather than to open their differences to public debate.

The wartime tenure of the business synthesizers involved a continuous search for the kind of administrative centralization and coordinated public policy which would ease the way for an integrated system of private corporate planning. They were bent on creating through public power the kind of calculable environment in which their colleagues in industry would meet the demands now thrust upon them. They sought administrative centralization and concentrated power so as to secure their positions as champions and protectors of the country's industrial structure. Only insofar as they maintained control could they be sure that those hostile to or ignorant of industry's structural needs would not obstruct the proper process of integration. Obstruction from specific business groups placed them in a difficult and ambiguous position, of course, but it

<hr>

[9]Herbert Hoover, *The Ordeal of Woodrow Wilson* (New York, 1958) , p. 11.
[10]Quoted in Edwin Wildman, "Howard Coffin And The War In The Air," *Forum,* LIX (March, 1918) , 260.
[11]Samuel P. Hays offers one of the best examples of this phenomenon in the prewar years in his "The Politics of Reform in Municipal Government in the Progressive Era," *Pacific Northwest Quarterly,* LV (October, 1964) , 157-169. See also James Weinstein, "Organized Business and the City Commission and Manager Movements," *Journal of Southern History,* XXVIII (February, 1962) , 162-182.

did not alter their rationale. At some points businessmen in government believed they had to act sternly to protect their colleagues in industry from bringing disaster upon themselves.

During the course of national mobilization the business statesmen became synonymous with the very concepts of business-government cooperation and businessmen in government. The myth-making process of wartime propaganda transformed these men into symbols of the corporate structure they aimed to strengthen and protect. As a consequence, their public actions and pronouncements were calculated to win approval not just for a particular functional program — like increased aircraft production or reduced steel consumption — but for the reputation and credibility of the corporate capitalist structure itself. These men, in other words, played for stakes far greater than the businessmen sent to Washington to lobby with them or the narrower specialists in their own organizations. They had to balance the short-run demands of interest-conscious groups with their estimation of the long-run interests and needs of the corporate economy as a whole, and the reputation of business leadership in it.[12]

These dollar-a-year men had to avoid public identification with special interests or with a clearly pro-business position. Confidence in their neutrality was a prerequisite for their credibility with the Wilson Administration, with Congress, with military leaders, and with the public at large. Their ability to shape public policy so as to fashion a stable, corporate capitalist system depended directly on how well they maintained the faith of key leadership groups in major public institutions. Public restraint and caution was an essential feature of their private strategy for power. They had far more freedom to act behind the scenes out of public view. Here, private conscience and institutional realities were the chief constraints. Here, behind the scenes, the administrators took their greatest risks.

[12]For one example of the myth-making function of wartime propaganda see Robert D. Cuff, "Bernard Baruch: Symbol and Myth in Industrial Mobilization," *Business History Review*, XLIII (Summer, 1969), 115-133. My conception of the ideology of the business synthesizers leans heavily on the work of William Appleman Williams and on James Weinstein's recent book, *The Corporate Ideal in the Liberal State* (Boston, 1968).

The truly remarkable fact, however, is that businessmen in government managed to have it both ways. By a subtle combination of public caution and private daring they were able to serve both the short-run needs of specific interests and the long-run reputation of the business system and its corporate leadership. This is the great debt which the business system of the 1920s owed the dollar-a-year men of the Great War.

No single issue can illustrate all of the general comments made thus far about the business synthesizers of World War I, but the War Industries Board's experience with the antitrust problem helps to bring some of them into sharper focus. It illuminates the kinds of values which were important to men like Baruch and Eugene Meyer, Jr., Baruch's assistant at times during the war; it offers a practical example of their search for institutional coordination, as well as the kinds of obstacles they encountered; and it reveals very well how they succeeded in combining covert assistance to private groups with a renunciation of business pressure to launch a public campaign against traditional values and practices.

Almost every preparedness tactic which Bernard Baruch pursued from the summer of 1916 until he resigned from the WIB chairmanship in November 1918 ran contrary to the antitrust tradition. Throughout his wartime career Baruch strove to create an institutional and legal environment conducive to corporate planning. Especially was this the case in his early war work as head of the government's Committee on Raw Materials. He asked various big businessmen to establish volunteer committees among themselves and to design privately the distribution, price and production schedules for each major industry, nothing less than the cartelization of the American economy. Baruch readily admitted that his directives and suggestions contravened antitrust laws, but he argued that under such emergency conditions such laws no longer held. In the meantime he lobbied the Wilson Administration for an opinion "that such act or actions, when done for the benefit and in the interests of the Government, are not violations of that Act, and do not place these individuals . . . on those committees subject to penalty."[13]

[13]Raw Materials Committee to Chester C. Bolton, May 23, 1917, Records of the War Industries Board, File 21A-A4, Box 877, Federal Records Center, Suitland, Md.; hereafter cited as RG61.

John Ryan, president of the Anaconda Copper Company and Baruch's contact with that industry, presented the Raw Materials Commissioner with a typical problem in the summer of 1917. Several large producers had formed a cartel for buying in bulk and the Ordnance Department had asked it to make some purchases. In response to this request Ryan wrote Baruch as follows: "The members of the Sub-Committee on Copper do not feel that they should direct the making of a contract by one selling agency for the full amount of copper required by the Ordnance Department, or any other Department of our Government or any of the Allies, but it would undoubtedly facilitate matters and save an endless amount of work and confusion if this could be done." Ryan wanted relief from possible legal challenges for a procedure which he had every intention of pursuing, hoping Baruch would take all responsibility. "As the Sub-Committee on Copper is composed of men who are representing some of the largest producers in the country, they naturally want to be directed to consolidate this business rather than to consolidate it voluntarily, which might be considered open to question as a legal right and might be misconstrued."[14]

According to Ryan, Army and Navy officials had already indicated their approval and only awaited sanction from the proper civilian bodies. In effect, both Ryan and the military officials wanted someone else to assume all the political risks. However, Baruch's office had no intention of being used in this way, especially by the military services. Eugene Meyer, Jr., told Ryan that while no doubt existed about the superiority of the arrangements contemplated by the selling company, Baruch would not sanction them. If the military departments favoured the arrangements, he said, let them give the orders.[15]

Baruch had already endeavoured to breach the formal antitrust barrier but had had no success by July when Ryan made his inquiry. The issue was growing more embarrassing for Baruch, however, as his business clientele cried for action.[16] Editorial writers in the business press delighted in pointing out the inconsistency

[14]Ryan to Baruch, July 2, 1917, RG61, File 21A-A4, Box 463.
[15]Meyer, Jr., to Ryan, July 3, 1917, *ibid*.
[16]Walter S. Gifford to Attorney General Gregory, June 4, 1917, Records of the Council of National Defense, File 2-48, Box 86, Federal Records Center, Suitland, Md.; hereafter cited as RG62.

of the government's position and its refusal to accept the reality of its own system of supply. They needled the Administration constantly to promise openly an end to all prosecutions. Why not recognize forthrightly that the everyday operations of the cooperative committees contravened antitrust laws and admit the anomaly of the whole enterprise? The war proved the efficiency of bigness and cooperation in industry and this fact ought to be officially admitted.[17] "It has scarcely been realized how events have nullified the Sherman Law, and abrogated important parts of the Interstate Commerce Act," observed the *Wall Street Journal*. "Events, in fact, have shown the way to wise legislation, and it is surely not too much to hope that we have statesmen in Washington able to appreciate their significance."[18]

Baruch wanted to be one of those statesmen. He engaged Joseph Cotton, a prominent corporation lawyer, to do some "devilling" in Washington, as Cotton put it, and the lawyer talked with Justice Department officials in April, but without success.[19] Attorney General Gregory was in no mood to make life easier for the Administration's business advisors and their friends. The Justice Department had by no means been uniformly hostile to American big business in the pre-war years. Still, it irked Justice to see those specific interests which it had pursued use the emergency to enhance their positions. They were thus reluctant to close their eyes to antitrust violations throughout the war. Moreover, no regular federal department or agency took kindly to the idea of being pushed aside by obstreperous emergency boards like the WIB. In any case, argued Gregory, the whole question was not merely a legal one: it was "a question of national policy" and up to the President to decide.[20] It was probably in the summer of 1917 that Wilson decided to respond to Gregory's invitation, and it is clear from the

[17]See sample editorials from the *New York Times*, April 10, June 23, and June 28, 1917; and from *Iron Age*: "Antagonisms Lost in the War Crisis," 99 (February 22, 1917), 489, and "Federal Regulation of Steel," 101 (January 3, 1918), 98-99.

[18]*Wall Street Journal*, August 30, 1917. The *Journal* was particularly aggressive in calling upon Washington to face the implications of its industrial policy. See editorials of August 3, 7, 10, 13, 1917, September 28, 1917, and October 22, 1917.

[19]Cotton to John W. Davis, April 9, 1917, Joseph P. Cotton to Baruch, April 9, 1917, both in RG61, File 21A-A4, Box 784.

[20]Gregory to Gifford, June 6, 1917, RG62, File 2-A8, Box 86.

outcome that he found business arguments persuasive in this as in so many areas of his wartime industrial policy.

> "I had a conference with the President to see what he wanted done," Gregory later explained. "He remarked that if we attempted at that moment to vindicate the law, we would disorganize industry. We both agreed that we should let up on these people so that they would have no excuse for not contributing to their full capacities in the prosecution of the war."[21]

This conversation related specifically to the problem of antitrust suits then pending against the United States Steel Company and International Harvester, but its implications were of course far-reaching and indicative of the drift of official policy.

A much greater breakthrough in antitrust policy occurred in early August. Herbert Hoover had written Wilson that month inquiring about his powers under the Food Control Act. Specifically, he wanted to know if he had the right to enter agreements with industries to pool output and fix prices which would violate the Sherman Law if done by the trades themselves. Gregory replied in the affirmative ". . . because *governmental action* with respect to prices or methods of distribution is obviously not within the mischief at which the Sherman Law was aimed." According to Gregory the antitrust laws rested on the natural laws of trade which when given free rein prevented control of the market by private producers. But in times of chaos, like periods of war, these natural laws could no longer be depended upon to regulate the market. Then ". . . the only choice is between artificial control imposed by private interests and the artificial control imposed by public agencies. In these circumstances, therefore, such governmental action, so far from running counter to the purpose of the Sherman Law, is directly in line with it."[22] Such was the reasoning by which Gregory was forced to adjust to the economics of war. This pronouncement

[21]"Memorandum of Conversations With Former Attorney General Gregory At Houston, Texas, March 14 and 15, 1927," in the Papers of Ray Stannard Baker, Manuscript Division, Library of Congress. Also see Gregory to Baker, August 29, 1931, *ibid*.

[22]Gregory to Woodrow Wilson, August 2, 1917, RG61, File 2D-A1, Box 203. Also see Department of Justice, *Annual Report of the Attorney General of the United States for the Year 1918* (Washington, 1918), p. 61.

received no great publicity, yet it was really an extraordinary document in the wartime acceleration of combination and consolidation throughout American industry.

Surprisingly enough the WIB executive remained uneasy with it, and proved much more cautious than they need have been. The Board's legal advisors contributed most to a lingering unease. Concerned with the letter as well as the spirit of the law, the WIB's legal staff could not fully relax while the antitrust law remained on the statute books, and the jaundiced eye the Justice Department cast on business-government good fellowship augmented their concern. But the central difficulty from the lawyers' point of view was the anomalous legal position of the WIB. Unlike the Food Administration, which had been created by Congressional statute, the WIB was the product of administrative evolution and lacked a clear-cut, solid, legal base. It was not absolutely certain that the WIB could enter into collusive agreements with its clientele with the same impunity that the Attorney General's opinion offered Hoover's Food Administration. Both in hindsight and in the light of the WIB's actual practice such a question seems very much beside the point, but it consumed hours of debate among top WIB officials.[23]

Throughout the war, WIB leaders wondered whether or not they should launch a campaign to get Congress to abrogate the antitrust laws once and for all, or whether they should request legislation specifically to exempt them as Gregory's opinion had exempted the Food Administration. Discussion became especially intense during the summer of 1918 as a growing number of industries began to construct pooling agreements in response to coal and transportation shortages in the east coast areas. Albert C. Ritchie, the Board's major legal advisor, personally believed that such agreements among competitors would not violate the law if the government were a party to them, but he wanted a favourable word from Gregory just to make sure. Baruch wrote Gregory in June 1918 that ". . . if such a pooling agreement is authorized and would not violate the Sherman Law, I still think it should not actually be made, unless I am advised by you, as the official who enforces the Sherman Law,

[23]Baruch's chief legal aid, Albert Ritchie, expressed his doubts in Ritchie to Baruch, August 19, 1918, RG61, File 1-A5, Box 41.

that the same will not violate the law."[24] Gregory was unsympathetic, twitting the Board for lack of information and suggesting rather peevishly that it could at least follow the form of regular executive departments in seeking opinions.[25]

The WIB withdrew at this point, deciding it was safer to remain without an open endorsement than to receive a negative opinion from Gregory. Only congressional legislation would guarantee the Board's legal right to enter such agreements unchallenged, but Ritchie raised a number of objections against actually lobbying for it. First, no assurance existed that Congress would pass such a law. Second, the European administrative experience had by no means proved that a system of government-sponsored regulation was superior to voluntary combinations. And finally, "As a practical matter, industries are able to work out the situation better than might be expected." Ritchie knew that industry made "more or less similar arrangements" and the Attorney General had not prosecuted, so why bring the issue to the public's attention and chance the likelihood of a bitter debate and ultimate defeat? Better to leave the situation alone and let industries combine at will and assume that wartime conditions would afford immunity.[26]

The agitation for legislation did not stop, but Ritchie's arguments convinced Baruch and he never broached either Wilson or Congress on the matter. As in so many policy areas, the Board practised privately and informally what it refused to proclaim publicly and formally. It wanted the advantages of industrial cooperation without having to assume legal responsibility for them. At the same time it felt a certain moral responsibility to stem legal challenges against its clientele.

Most officials acted as if the Attorney General's pronouncement *vis-à-vis* the Food Administration did in fact apply also to the WIB, something which Gregory himself finally admitted to be the case in his 1918 report.[27] "Mr. Legge said that the Pulp and Paper Division should make this price directly with the mills without going to the price fixing committee," read the minutes of one meet-

[24]Baruch to Gregory, June 18, 1918, *ibid*. See also H.P. Ingels to Ritchie, June 11, 1918, and "Pooling Agreement" (n.d.) , both in *ibid*.
[25]Gregory to Baruch, June 20, 1918, *ibid*.
[26]Ritchie to Baruch, August 19, 1918, *ibid*.
[27]*Annual Report . . . 1918,* p. 61.

ing of the Pulp and Paper Division, "and that he had no fear of prosecution under the Anti-Trust Law, as agreements made through the Government were not subject to prosecution."[28] Pope Yeatman of the Non-Ferrous Metal Section encouraged agreements between producers and smelters in the zinc industry despite his inability to get an official opinion on the procedure from the Attorney General's office. And the zinc industry was appreciative of Yeatman's support. "By suggesting this," wrote one member of the industry, "you have made clear to your many friends that your conference plan is a real panacea for industrial difficulties. I bow to your good judgement."[29]

Defending such private agreements and the right to initiate them proved a delicate problem, especially when other government executive departments objected. The Board's executive, however, stood behind its staff and its business constituency, doing what it could to refute, modify or rationalize charges of monopoly, price fixing or unfair trade practices.

Consider the WIB's intervention on behalf of the cement industry, for example. In early spring the Attorney General's Department instituted an investigation at the request of government agencies and other dealers and concluded that combination among cement producers had stifled competition and raised prices. The Department was about to file suit when the WIB formally announced that an independent investigation it had conducted showed that the price rise had resulted simply from the wartime advance in the cost of labour and other materials. As G. Carroll Todd, Assistant to the Attorney General, observed, "Obviously a proceeding by this Department charging that cement manufacturers have combined to suppress price competition and thereby bring about unduly high prices would be seriously if not fatally embarrassed by an outstanding determination by another branch of the Government that competition in the cement industry has not been suppressed and that prices are no more than reasonable."[30]

---

[28]Minutes of Meeting of Section Heads, Pulp and Paper Division, Week—October 26, 1918, to November 2, 1918, RG61, File 1-C2, Box 86.

[29]Victor Rakowsky to Yeatman, April 26, 1918, RG61, File 21A-A4, Box 1962; Yeatman to G. Carroll Todd (Assistant Attorney General), April 24, 1918, and G. Carroll Todd to Yeatman, April 27, 1918, both in *ibid.*; and Yeatman to Brookings, May 14, 1918, RG61, File 21A-A4, Box 1640.

[30]Todd to Eugene Meyer, Jr., February 13, 1918, RG61, File 21A-A4, Box 316.

The WIB stuck to its guns. It refused even to consider the charge of conspiracy in restraint of trade within the industry. "I have made no finding upon the subject of competition," wrote Baruch; "it is not my function to do so."[31] Eugene Meyer, Jr., explained the economic causes behind the general price rise to the Department, emphasizing particular conditions in the cement case.[32] Moreover, the WIB officially informed the Justice Department that in any price question it "uses a very broad business judgement in a great emergency without regarding too strictly Federal Trade Commission reports or other cost data."[33]

The Justice Department wanted the Board at least to reopen the case and reconsider its findings. If they were indeed correct then proceedings would naturally be halted. Until the matter was resolved among the government departments themselves, of course, Justice was paralyzed, as the WIB well knew. The WIB simply refused the challenge and let the matter drop. But in order to avoid liability for obstructing Department procedures, Baruch informed Gregory's Assistant that he could not see any reason why the Department could not take whatever action it wished.[34]

Feeling ran high within the Department to accept the WIB challenge. "I do not know how an appeal is taken from the price-fixing of the War Industries Board, but it certainly looks as if some effort should be made to overturn this curious result," one Justice attorney informed Todd. "If we have many more investigations where the Department of Justice reaches one conclusion, which is overruled without a hearing by some subordinate board or bureau, the whole morale of a Department investigation will be lost."[35] The only place to appeal was to the President himself. But the question never went that far. Todd believed that a suit against the industry "would probably be a waste of time and money."[36] Gregory agreed.

Gregory could do little else under the circumstances. Wilson could never have been expected to regard the issue as pressing, and he had

[31]Baruch to Todd, March 14, 1918, *ibid.*
[32]Meyer, Jr., to Todd, *ibid.*
[33]H. P. Ingels to Todd, March 4, 1918, RG61, File 1-A2, Box 29.
[34]Todd to Baruch, March 7, 1918, and Baruch to Todd, March 14, 1918, and Todd to Baruch, March 16, 1918, all in RG61, File 21A-A4, Box 316.
[35]Mark Hyman to Todd, May 17, 1918, General Records of the Department of Justice, File #60-10-0, National Archives, Washington, D.C.
[36]Todd to Mark Hyman, May 18, 1918, *ibid.*

already indicated his thinking in the matter of antitrust in any case. And for Justice to have challenged the WIB publicly would have chanced a political blow-up dangerous to the Administration's entire mobilization program. The WIB had Justice over a barrel and wanted to keep it that way. To be able to achieve such successes gave it considerable popularity among various business groups. Co-operation with the WIB offered a political environment which favoured corporate consolidation and a protective shield against embarrassing public investigations.

The greatest test to Baruch's leadership on the antitrust issue came with the end of the war. Enormous pressure was brought to bear on the WIB to end antitrust laws once and for all, to clear the road for economic consolidation in post-war America.[37] It was the kind of thinking which had resulted in the Webb-Pomerene Act and would soon spawn the Edge Act — the one to permit commercial combination for international trade, the other to permit financial consolidation for expanding capital overseas.[38] A victory on the domestic scene could extend further the corporate vision for American economic power and trade expansion. Quite wisely, however, Baruch refused to depart from his general wartime strategy of doing what he could behind the scenes while steering clear of any public, political interventions which might undermine his reputation and the reputation of the concepts he and the WIB now symbolized.[39] Baruch had never been adverse to intervening on behalf of corporate groups in the federal decision-making process, but he had stayed away from public campaigns. The chief difference in November 1918 was that Baruch's room for private manoeuvering had suddenly narrowed. With the billows of patriotic rhetoric clearing away, a curious public could now see more clearly the kind of covert activity at which Baruch had been so adept in the past. Moreover, Baruch realized far better than many of the specialists and interest groups around him that no longer would the

[37]Robert F. Himmelberg describes the pressures on Baruch both from business specialists within the WIB and from business lobbies outside it in "The War Industries Board and the Anti-trust Question in November, 1918," *Journal of American History*, LII (June, 1965), pp. 59-74. I differ somewhat with Himmelberg on the motives and implications of Baruch's response to this issue.

[38]Carl Parrini deals with these acts and the motives behind them in *Heir to Empire, United States Economic Diplomacy, 1916-1923* (Pittsburgh, 1969).

[39]Himmelberg, "Antitrust Question."

public tolerate the inroads which he and other synthesizers had made in traditional institutional relationships, as between business and government, or in traditional values like antitrust, under the press of wartime crisis. Rather than expose publicly the extent to which some business groups had indeed found their uses for the state, Baruch disbanded his agency as fast as discretion would allow and quit Washington for the glories of Versailles.[40]

One of the central goals of the business synthesizers throughout the war had been to prove what private corporate leadership could do in conjunction with a friendly state. What European countries might achieve through extensive state controls, so the argument ran, America would surpass by a process of private-public cooperation administered by businessmen in government. To suggest that a state-based officialdom may have proved equally necessary for the outcome raised some question about the viability and legitimacy of private corporate leadership in the post-war world. What was the lesson of the war for America in peacetime: greater state intervention, or greater freedom for private cooperation, or both? In the early weeks after the Armistice business leaders like Baruch wondered whether businessmen could really afford to sanction an enlargement of the state in peacetime when businessmen would no longer be in government to supervise the expansion. Might that not lead to politically imposed controls rather than to the kinds of bargained compromises permitted under friendly business-government cooperation? The business synthesizers realized very well that the total absence of state administration could harm a corporate economy in peacetime, but they concluded that a powerful public bureaucracy dominated by politicians offered a far greater menace.[41]

[40]Baruch indicated his fear of public inquiries to representatives of the steel industry on November 13, 1918. See "Special Meeting With Committee Representing The American Iron and Steel Institute . . ." in Baruch Papers. "You don't forget this now;" he said, "we talk about the government doing something when this war is over; there is going to be a critical examination of what has been done. Don't forget gentlemen, we have all got politics in front of us." On November 27, 1918, two days before he resigned, Baruch recommended that President Wilson terminate the WIB as of January 1, 1919. Baruch to Wilson, November 27, 1918, Papers of Woodrow Wilson, Manuscript Division, Library of Congress.

[41]The following comment by Edward Hurley illustrates the embarrassment he and others felt over just how far they had strayed from private to state

One of the central tasks for business synthesizers in the 1920s was to redefine the relationships between business and government in an emerging corporate system so as to obtain the coordination and continuous management of wartime without the coercive power of an enlarged state bureaucracy. That such a goal was indeed possible lay at the heart of Herbert Hoover's search for the capitalist utopia, while the very ineffectiveness of his response to the depression after 1929 convinced many business leaders that indeed it was only a utopia after all.[42] By 1932, business groups were asking for, and political leaders were ready to accept, the kind of state intervention in peacetime which Baruch, for one, had refused to sponsor in November 1919. But by then, the ideology of a minority of progressive business synthesizers, expanded and deepened by a world war and depression, had become the conventional wisdom of New Deal liberalism.

---

capitalism during the war. They were anxious not to give radicals any support for arguments on behalf of state controls in peacetime. "I have been a steadfast opponent of government ownership; it means inefficiency and waste, as a rule. It so happened that the Emergency Fleet Corporation, although a government agency, was organized and managed as if it were a private enterprise. We therefore had the mechanism of private enterprise, and yet governmental control. For this reason it became feasible to assume direct charge of yard-building and ship-building, for war purposes only." Edward Hurley, *The Bridge to France*, p. 77.

[42]For the best analysis of Hoover's quest for utopia in the 1920s see Barry Karl, "Presidential Planning and Social Science Research: Mr. Hoover's Experts," in Donald Fleming and Bernard Bailyn (eds.) , *Perspectives in American History* (Cambridge, 1969) , III, 347-409. See also Ellis W. Hawley, "Herbert Hoover and the Expansion of the Commerce Department: The Anti-Bureaucrat as Bureaucratic Empire-Builder," unpublished ms.

A Canadian Businessman and War:
The Case of Joseph Flavelle

Michael Bliss

Joseph Wesley Flavelle, a prominent Toronto businessman and financier, was appointed Chairman of the Imperial Munitions Board, the Canadian purchasing agency for the British Ministry of Munitions, in November 1915. For the next three years Flavelle was the virtual czar of Canadian industrial mobilization, exercising absolute supervision of war material contracts amounting to roughly $1.25 billion. Though he was technically an employee of the British government, Flavelle was the most important business figure involved in the Canadian war effort during World War I, with the possible exception of Sir Thomas White, the Minister of Finance. It is not known whether Flavelle served as an American-style "dollar-a-year-man"; he did receive compensation beyond the reach of any American, however, when he became Sir Joseph Flavelle, Baronet, in 1917.

This paper is an examination of the influence of Flavelle's wartime experience on his concepts of institutional organization and business-government relations. The essay is also in part an exercise in comparative history, for recent American writing about business-government relations has been used as a source of guidelines to begin the analysis of a Canadian businessman's response to war (at the time of writing this is a virtually unmapped area of Canadian history). American historians have shown, for example, how a number of businessmen who participated in government during World War I became enamoured with the possibilities of postwar industrial cooperation and centralization, under either private or public auspices, to rationalize American economic life. For many of the American dollar-a-year-men war was a catalytic agent in developing their notions of what has been variously called 'welfare capitalism', 'corporate liberalism', 'political capitalism', or 'the vision of a business commonwealth'. The core of the vision was a new corporate order in which organization and associational cooperation would replace the unrestrained competitive individualism of nineteenth century capitalism. In the 1920s and 1930s many former wartime administrators were politically active trying to put these ideas into effect.[1]

To what extent did the same processes operate in Canada? Did Canadian war administrators also develop a vision of state-sanctioned institutional coordination? Did they too hope to apply wartime techniques for different ends in peacetime? Was the business-government relationship that developed in war seen as a precursor of a new kind of consolidated or rationalized Canadian capitalism? Was Joseph Flavelle a made-in-Canada replica of the early twentieth century American business-bureaucrat?

I

Parallels between Flavelle and the 'progressive' American businessmen in government should hold. Flavelle's prewar reputation was based upon his administrative and managerial ability — ability that had been demonstrated in the private sphere in what has been

[1]A good summary of recent American work as well as a challenge to Canadians to explore these problems is Robert Cuff, 'Organizing for War: Canada and the United States During World War I', Canadian Historical Association, *Historical Papers, 1969,* pp. 140-56. American historiography on the subject includes Gabriel Kolko, *The Triumph of Conservatism* (New York, 1963) ; James Weinstein, *The Corporate Ideal In the Liberate State* (Boston, 1968) ; Robert M. Wiebe, *The Search for Order* (New York, 1967) ; Samuel Haber, *Efficiency and Uplift* (Chicago, 1964) ; William E. Leuchtenberg, *The Perils of Prosperity, 1914-1932* (Chicago, 1958) , and 'The New Deal and the Analogue of War', in John Braeman *et al*, eds., *Change and Continuity in Twentieth Century America* (Columbus, Ohio, 1964) ; Ellis W. Hawley, *The New Deal and the Problem of Monopoly* (Princeton, 1966) .

I would like to thank Professor Cuff for reading an earlier version of this paper and steering me away from a number of egregious errors in interpretation. Those that remain are entirely my own. Professor R. Craig Brown of the University of Toronto generously allowed me to use the notes on Flavelle he has compiled in research for the biography of Sir Robert Borden.

called a "well-nigh flawless" entrepreneurial performance as general manager and president of the William Davies meat packing company,[2] and in public service with his contribution to the reorganizations of the University of Toronto and the Toronto General Hospital into modern institutions. Moreover, Flavelle was well known to be a 'progressive' businessman who had influenced Conservative leader Robert Borden to come out for a nationally-owned transcontinental railway system in 1904 and whose newspaper, the Toronto *News,* spearheaded Canadian movements for honest, efficient, dynamic government rising above the party politics of self-interest.

In wartime the Imperial Munitions Board under Flavelle's direction was an almost perfect demonstration of what could be achieved when a government organization set out to stimulate capitalism into maximum efficiency and production. In addition to the impetus given private enterprise by the IMB, the seven 'National Factories' that Flavelle established for the production of special goods ranging from nitro-cellulose to aeroplanes were a dramatic innovation in Canadian economic life that seemed to demonstrate the possibilities of a creative government role in industrial development.[3] Combined with his prewar record these experiences suggest that Flavelle should have come out of the war as an enthusiast of the idea of an alliance between government and capitalism in Canada to promote the reorganization of economic life in the interest of national efficiency.

In fact from the end of the war until his death in 1939 Flavelle held attitudes towards the role of government in society and industrial organization that are generally thought to be characteristic of a reactionary free-enterpriser. Even before the war ended Flavelle believed that most of the plans being put forward for a new postwar society involved the state doing for the individual what the individual had to perform for himself.[4] Two days after the armistice he

[2]A. J. E. Child, "The Predecessor Companies of Canada Packers Limited, A Study of Entrepreneurial Achievement and Entrepreneurial Failure" (unpublished M.A. thesis, University of Toronto, 1960) , p. 258. Child notes that Cyrus Eaton told him that Flavelle was one of the six most capable businessmen he had known.

[3]David Carnegie, *The History of Munitions Supply in Canada, 1914-1918* (London, 1925) .

[4]Douglas Library, Queen's University, Sir Joseph Flavelle Papers, Flavelle to

was announcing privately that reconstruction could not be worked out by government, but had to be largely a function of business leadership.[5] He went back to public service for a time in the early 1920s as Chairman of the Grand Trunk Railway, presiding over its metamorphosis from private to public ownership; but he accepted the job only to make the best of a bad thing, and he refused Prime Minister Meighen's pleas that he become permanent head of the Canadian National Railways, one of his reasons being that he did not believe in government ownership.[6] By 1920 he was opposing not only the minimum wage laws, but all attempts to correct social problems by legislation or by economic group organization to achieve political favours. Writing to Sir John Willison in that year he agreed with "the increasing weight of opinion that the effort to correct inequalities and injustices by legislative enactments, or bureaucratic control, is a dangerous proceeding. It seems to be demonstrated that emergency measures necessary for the war are not applicable to peace times. As indicated by you, we will more safely travel the old road whereby 'the best and greatest of mankind have reared [sic] in patience and tribulation and sweat and sacrifice'."[7]

Flavelle's rare public speeches in the 1920s were homilies to the virtues of "patience, courage, and self-reliance," combined with warnings that political action would fail to improve national life in Canada.[8] In the 1930s he explicitly rejected the idea that "a correction of systems will set us going on the right track."[9] Although he still hoped for "authoritative" political leadership in Canada, by 1933 Flavelle wanted both dominion and provinces to introduce five years of "skeleton Governments" whose first duty would be to stop spending.[10] Bennett's 'New Deal' of 1935 represented the

---

W. R. Rundle, April 3, 1918. Hereafter the Queen's collection will be signified as FQ; the collection of Flavelle Papers in the Public Archives of Canada, Ottawa, mostly dealing with the IMB, will be signified as FO.

[5]FQ, Flavelle to Sir Thomas White, Nov. 13, 1918.

[6]FQ, Flavelle to Sir John Willison, April 30, 1921; PAC, J. W. Dafoe Papers, Flavelle to Dafoe, Sept. 7, 1921; Arthur Meighen Papers, Flavelle to Meighen, March 30, Sept. 15, 1921.

[7]FQ, Flavelle to Willison, May 11, 1921; to Rev. J. W. MacMillan, Nov. 23, 1921; to William Flavelle, April 19, 1922; to D. Carnegie, Dec. 27, 1922.

[8]FQ, Case 57, Winnipeg Board of Trade, March 10, 1924; clipping from Halifax *Herald*, April 29, 1925.

[9]FQ, Flavelle to Rev. A. J. Johnston, Nov. 23, 1933.

[10]FQ, Flavelle to E. R. Peacock, March 29, 1933.

zenith of state-organized welfare capitalism in Canada; Flavelle, a life-long Conservative, hoped that Mackenzie King would win the 1935 election.[11] In these years when so many former wartime administrators in the United States looked back longingly on wartime methods as models of how governments should mobilize society for industrial recovery, Flavelle's remembrance of war was absolutely different: "The fact that I believe that the collective effort in Government and the machinations of politicians gave us the appalling tragedy of the Great War, . . . does not lead me to have faith in the collective efforts under political guidance now being introduced into business and marketing."[12] The former progressive who had achieved so much in public service now believed that government had been the least effective of all the organized institutions of human society.[13]

Had something 'gone wrong' with Joseph Flavelle in his old age? Had the fires of his progressivism burned out in the war? Did his war experience cause a radical discontinuity in his beliefs about governments and organizations in society? The answer to all of these questions is no. To show this requires closer examination of what will turn out to be Flavelle's quite consistent premises about business, cooperation through organizations, and the role of government in economic life. The war did have a catalytic effect on Flavelle's thought, but because he entered it with values different from those of the American business-bureaucrats he also drew quite different conclusions from his experience of war.

II

To understand Flavelle it is vital to realize that although he was a superb administrator he seemed remarkably unconcerned with organizational structures. He spoke of the Imperial Munitions Board, for example, as being run with a "minimum of form," and he warned subordinates of the dangers of "over-organization," claiming that it did not matter "if our work is not as orderly as it might be" so long as the work was accomplished effectively.[14] When

[11]FQ, Flavelle to Sir Robert Kindersley, June 7, 1935.
[12]FQ, Flavelle to Dr. R. Roberts, April 21, 1934.
[13]FQ, Flavelle to R. J. Cromie, July 19, 1935.
[14]FO, Flavelle to W. L. Hichens, Dec. 7, 1918; to Col. W. E. Edwards, Aug. 22, 1917.

asked to comment on a memorandum outlining the organizational structure of the Canadian Trade Commission Flavelle thought he could say little of value, because "I have so long worked without a pre-considered plan that I hardly know what to do with one when it is presented apart from the man or men who will operate it." A few years later he would make almost exactly the same comment on the problem of organizing the nationalized railway system.[15]

The last phrase of that quoted remark — "apart from the man or men who will operate it" — is the key to Flavelle's notion of administration. For him organization was little more than finding competent, hard-working individuals, giving them autonomy in their jobs, and then coordinating their efforts.[16] None of his comments about the success of the IMB referred to its structure; all centred around the hard work, efficiency, service, and devotion of his staff. Indeed, throughout his life, when Flavelle commented on how to get things done he always used the idiom of individualism — terms like 'energy', 'grip', 'vision', 'vigour', 'earnestness', 'service', and 'application'.

A critical aspect of Flavelle's organizations — both the Davies Company and the IMB — was the centralization of power in his own hands (and he criticized both American and English wartime bureaucracy for excessive decentralization). But this was simply Flavelle's way of giving himself the power to act as the linch-pin of all his operations; in other words to give free play to his own noted capacity for efficient hard work. He seemed to think that the cement of his organizations had nothing to do with formal structure, but rested informally on the qualities of his own leadership, the sense of fellowship and teamwork he was able to inspire in his subordinates, and the common devotion of all members of his teams to individual excellence in the service of their cause. He constantly spoke of organizations in metaphors of teamwork, fellowship, and family spirit.[17]

As an administrator Flavelle did not concern himself with *ways* of handling personnel, *methods* of supervising technical operations,

[15]FO, Flavelle to H. M. Jones, March 3, 1919; Meighen Papers, Flavelle to George Buskard, Aug. 16, 1921.
[16]Child, *op. cit.* pp. 49-52; FO, Flavelle to R. H. Brand, Dec. 29, 1916.
[17]For a revealing exchange with an employee see FQ, Case 44, R. N. Watt to Flavelle, May 22, 1912, and reply.

or the *process* of decision-making. He made his organizations work intuitively. He claimed that he had adopted his simple business principles in the 1890s and never departed from them.[18] In this sense, despite his reputation as one of the supreme organizers in early twentieth century Canada, Flavelle did not share the concern for the problems of administration and management that character-ized many 'progressives' in business and government during the period. He was an individualist who succeeded so well that he was mistaken for a master of the art of management.[19]

In his attitudes to the problems of industry-wide organization and rationalization Flavelle was particularly divorced from one of the dominant themes of American business progressivism. Most of the impulse to industrial rationalization in North America came from crises of surplus capacity and ruinous competition. Flavelle never experienced these situations in his business life. Before the war the Davies Company was packing bacon for export to what seemed to be an infinitely elastic British market. Flavelle ran the firm so efficiently that no one could challenge his position in that market. When competitors seemed about to become bothersome Flavelle rejected all ideas of cooperation through associational activities in favour of a policy of 'aggression', by which he meant harder work, expanded operations, and lower costs.[20] Nothing irked him more than to be charged with having participated in price-fixing agree-ments. These fundamentally unenterprising flights from compe-tition (which were, however, the essence of what North American businessmen meant by 'rationalization') ran counter to his deepest business principles.[21] Similarly, nothing baffled him more

[18]FO, Flavelle to Brand, Sept. 26, 1917; FQ, Flavelle to Newton MacTavish, June 12, 1933.

[19]Flavelle did, of course, manage highly complex organizations and devoted long hours to establishing the kinds of structures he wanted as means to the greater end of securing hard work and service. In the sense that he did handle complicated organizational problems all the while that he preached the rhetoric of individualism, Flavelle might be seen as a transitional figure between the old individualistic entrepreneur and the new organization man.

[20]See the Flavelle memorandum quoted in Child, pp. 36-40.

[21]FQ, Flavelle to J. G. Rutherford, July 29, 1909. Flavelle opposed the Com-bines Investigation Act of 1910, not because he defended combines, but because he thought the machinery set up offered too many opportunities for irrespon-sible agitators to attack innocent, responsible firms like his own. See PAC, R. L. Borden Papers, Flavelle to Borden, Feb. 21, 1910; also the revealing letter which cannot now be located that is reprinted in R. C. Brown and Margaret

about the farmers who raised hogs for the Davies Company than their continued attempts to form organizations to agitate on their behalf when it was obvious to Flavelle that the whole answer to the farm problem was more hogs, better hogs, and harder-working farmers.[22]

The IMB's aim in World War I was to maximize Canadian munitions production, not to facilitate the consolidation of over-expanded industries. The IMB does not seem to have worked through trade associations or industrial organizations in the way that American mobilization bodies like the War Industries Board did. Consequently there was no possibility of business interests using the IMB as a cover for stabilization activities that would otherwise run afoul of antitrust legislation. In fact the IMB was set up precisely because of the profiteering, price-fixing, and inefficiencies that had characterized the Canadian Shell Committee — a quasi-public manufacturers' cartel that handled British munitions contracts in Canada in 1914-5. Despite some confusion about its legal status, despite its heavy reliance on administrators drawn from private industry, the IMB was always a government purchasing organization imbued with its Chairman's sense of integrity in the public service. With one exception, discussed below, its operations do not seem to have been characterized by a confusion of public and private interests.[23]

The one kind of government aid to industry that the IMB practised and that Flavelle always favoured was the use of vigorous state action to maximize production when private enterprise proved disinterested or incompetent. In the early 1900s Flavelle was taken with a vision of Canadian economic development so grandiose that its execution required dynamic government leadership, notably in transcontinental railway policy. When the Laurier Liberals proposed a bold transcontinental railway scheme in 1903

Prang, eds., *Canadian Historical Documents, Confederation to 1949* (Toronto, 1966), pp. 133-4.

[22]FQ, Flavelle to Hon. J. S. Duff, June 18, 1910 ('An Open Letter to the Honorable the Minister of Agriculture for Ontario, by Mr. J. W. Flavelle'): "The farmers of this and other provinces have been diverted from enterprise and have been encouraged to look for returns through agitation, . . . the farmer, like every one else in the community, can, on the last analysis, secure results only from his own effort, supported by intelligence, sound sense, and industry."

[23]Carnegie, *The History of Munitions Supply in Canada.*

Flavelle worried that the Conservative party might, through re-
flex action, back itself into the same negative, timid approach to
nation building that had characterized the Liberals during
the construction of the CPR in the 1880s. His encouragement of
Borden's policy of government ownership of transcontinental
railways was not predicated on any belief in the merits of nation-
alization *per se,* but rather on a determination that Canadian
Conservatives must present "an alternative plan not one whit
smaller than the one presented by the Government".[24] Similarly
the IMB's National Factories in World War I were Flavelle's
pragmatic response to private industry's inability to produce certain
kinds of war materials; unlike certain of C. D. Howe's Crown
Corporations in World War II, Flavelle's National Factories were
all closed down and their assets sold immediately after the war.
Flavelle never favoured public ownership in an area where private
enterprise was operating or could operate efficiently, opposing, for
example, the establishment of publicly-owned hydro in Ontario.
Because, however, he recognized that industry required aid and
inspiration if it was to pursue aggressive export policies and mount
large scale industrial research programs after the war, he did
call for government support of these activities in the closing days
of the war, and for several years in the interwar period served as
Chairman of the Ontario Research Foundation, a joint venture of
the Ontario government and the Canadian Manufacturers'
Association to raise funds for industrial research.[25] These programs
all reflected Flavelle's concept of government having a promo-
tional but not a regulatory role in economic life.

Flavelle's view of government and politics, like his approach to
business, was framed entirely in terms of individuals and their abilities. He had a true progressive's hatred of political parties, patronage,
brokerage politics, corruption, and above all the failure of politicians to offer vigorous national leadership. To his mind, though, it
was the last failure that determined everything else that was wrong
with government. If only a political leader would instill in government the same qualities of personal force, integrity, highmindedness,

[24]FQ, Flavelle to A. E. Kemp, Aug. 7, 1903; to Willison, April 8, 25, 1903; to
Borden, Aug. 16, 19, 24, 1903, May 31, 1904.
[25]FO, Flavelle to Carnegie, Oct. 31, 1918; to Rundle, Jan. 3, 1919; *Canadian
Annual Review,* 1927-8, p. 373.

courage, and dedication that Flavelle considered to be the hallmarks of success in private organizations, all other problems of government — like those of private organizations — could be worked out without difficulty.[26] In many ways his was the simple progressive faith that substituting good men for bad was all that had to be done to reform government. And possibly if government could be reformed by the right kind of leadership it could then assist private business with its immense task of national economic development. In Robert Borden Flavelle felt for a time that he had found his reforming leader.

Borden's conduct of Canadian affairs from 1911 to 1920 dashed Flavelle's hope for a new era of dynamic political leadership. Borden had barely been Prime Minister a year before Flavelle was beginning to criticize his caution and lack of imagination.[27] The most constant theme in his wartime correspondence was impatience with the quality of political leadership that was being exercised at Ottawa. By 1917 he felt that only Borden's retirement could pave the way for a creative national government. The formation of the Union Government and the introduction of conscription were too little too late to change Flavelle's belief that Canada required leaders who had "a prophet's vision".[28] Without such leadership politics and government continued to be a struggle of selfish men for pelf and prestige.

That, too, was a view Flavelle had had confirmed by his wartime experience. Even though he was the agent of another government and worked in organizations deliberately designed to minimize the influence of politicians, Flavelle found that partisan politics in general and the specific demands of Canadian politicians for patronage favours from the IMB made public service in Ottawa almost unbearable for a man of his highmindedness. Worse still, in 1917 Flavelle found himself faced with the ultimate horror that can befall a businessman in public service in wartime: he became the centre of a sensational profiteering inquiry into the earnings of the William Davies

[26]FQ, Flavelle to Willison, Nov. 11, 1913; to Borden, Nov. 23, 1909.
[27]FQ, Flavelle to W. N. Grigg, Oct. 31, 1912; to J. W. Wheeler-Bennett, April 21, 1913; to Willison, April 26, 1913.
[28]FQ, Flavelle to Willison, Jan. 24, 1917; to Willison, March 17, 1916, Jan. 9, March 2, 1917; to W. A. Cameron, Sept. 14, 1917; to E. C. Fox, July 31, 1918; FO, Flavelle to Borden, Sept. 20, 1915; to Brand, Dec. 29, 1916, Feb. 13, March 19, Aug. 24, 1917; to F. Perry, Aug. 24, 1917.

Company — with which he had not broken his connections, thinking that there could be no conflict of interest because the firm had no dealings with the IMB. Vilified in Parliament and the press ('Joseph the Provider' now became 'Old Black Joe'), though ultimately acquitted of any deliberate wrongdoing, Flavelle was so utterly convinced of his complete innocence that he could only believe the charges were the inventions of malicious and incompetent political hacks.[29] He was doubly disillusioned with the machiavellianism of politicians when Borden failed to leap to his defence with proper vigour. By the end of the war their personal relationship was far from happy.[30]

To be fair to Borden, it is clear that Flavelle's conception of what could be achieved in politics was both utopian and naive. His model of political leadership was identical with his model of business leadership. He wanted a politician who could run Canada the way he ran the William Davies Company and the IMB. This contradiction between what could be achieved in private industry and the limi-

[29]The Davies Company was accused of profiteering on meat sold in Canada and to Great Britain. There were also charges in the press that Flavelle had used his position with the IMB in the interests of the Davies Company and in other ways for his personal profit. It emerged that the Davies Company had made very high profits on very heavy turnover, but at a low profit margin. Flavelle had never misused his influence as a public servant. Believing as he did that profits were a legitimate reward for efficient service, Flavelle saw nothing wrong with his company making money during the war; he was, on the contrary, proud of its service. Nevertheless, he was on record as having told a meeting of Canadian businessmen that "your profits ought to go to the Hell to which they belong." He said this, however, in the context of lecturing businessmen on their habit of putting profit before service. The fact that the Davies Company's service was all that could have been expected would have been Flavelle's reason for not consigning away its profits. For the rest of his life and for many years after his death Flavelle's public reputation was tarnished by the affair.

For details of the controversy see *Canadian Annual Review*, 1917, pp. 444-450; also *Report of the Commissioners Appointed to Investigate The Business of William Davies Co., Ltd. and Matthews-Blackwell, Ltd.* (Ottawa, 1917) . Flavelle's correspondence with his general manager during the crisis is in FQ, Case 44; for Flavelle's reactions and his charges of political motives see FQ, Flavelle to A. F. Sheed, Oct. 10, 1917; FO, Flavelle to Sir Charles Gordon, July 19, 1917; to Brand, Sept. 26, 1917.

[30]FO, Flavelle to Carnegie, Nov. 29, 1918: "In all the matter in question I have thought no one acted towards me personally as badly as Sir Robert, and for many months past I knew that if I were asked to do after-war work by Sir Robert, or his Cabinet, I would refuse, . . ." See also the account of their falling-out in Augustus Bridle, *The Masques of Ottawa* (Toronto, 1921) , p. 183.

tations of political action was at the root of Flavelle's disillusionment with Borden and his postwar distrust of government.

By 1921 Flavelle had decided that "democracy had conditions inherent in government which necessarily produced inefficiency in business administration."[31] There was something about government — either the kind of man it attracted or what it did to men — that made it impossible for the vigorous leader in private life to function in public life.[32] He now felt that his own leadership style, transposed into public administration, would mean "impossible idealism" that would embarrass governments he served.[33] There was no longer any hope, then, of establishing a businesslike government to play a serious leadership role in national economic development. Flavelle never found, probably never seriously looked for, another Borden.[34] In the postwar years he believed that the greatest leadership capacity necessarily rested in the private sector.

The capstone of Flavelle's disillusionment with the possible consequences of active government was his belief after the war that Canadian society had fragmented into a collection of organized interest groups each trying to capture government for its own end. In most cases the end was to have government do what the members of the interest groups should be doing for themselves as individuals. In the postwar years Flavelle believed that all national economic problems could be solved by increased production to make up for the wastage of war. For him the aim was exactly the same as it had been before and after the war — maximize production. The methods he favoured were exactly the same as he had always favoured: hard, dedicated, unselfish work by every individual. The organizational model he thought would achieve this was exactly the model Flavelle had always used: decentralized structures cemented by the devotion and fellowship that come from inspired leadership.

[31]Dafoe Papers, Flavelle to Dafoe, Sept. 7, 1921.
[32]FO, Flavelle to Sir Charles Gordon, March 26, 1918; FQ, Flavelle to Rundle, March 28, 1918. There is some partially contradictory evidence suggesting Flavelle had grown more aware and tolerant of the limitations a democracy imposes on politicians. See FQ, Flavelle to Rundle, Nov. 4, 1918; to Rev. Peter Addison, Nov. 19, 1918. Also the letter referred to in note 31.
[33]Meighen Papers, Flavelle to Meighen, March 30, 1921.
[34]For a time in 1919 he seems to have thought Sir Thomas White might rally the business forces of the country. See FQ, Flavelle to Sir Charles Gordon, Dec. 17, 1917.

Instead of following Flavelle's models, though, the Canadian people were thinking only of rights rather than duties, only of luxury and affluence instead of thrift and self-denial. Canadians, especially farmers, were organizing to evade the duty of hard work and to throw their burdens on a central authority that never could do more than coordinate and supplement the work of individuals, and in the case of governments could not do that very well. A society that was characterized by the restless struggle of organized groups had lost its cement of national consciousness and purpose. But without this cement, this fellowship or family spirit, a nation could no more function as an economic or social organization than could any private organization.[35] In a similar vein Flavelle would come to believe in the 1930s that the Great War had shattered the bonds of brotherhood and fellowship that had held the nations of the world, what he called the "human family," together in an effective economic order.[36]

In a curious way Flavelle did not want an equivalent of war in the 1920s and 1930s. When he referred in his public speeches to the 'service' to their country of the young men who had given their lives in the war, Flavelle was challenging Canadians to recapture the spirit of dedication, sacrifice, and commitment that had underlain Canada's war effort. These qualities had characterized both the men at the front and the team Flavelle had put together in the IMB. Nothing about the war so impressed Flavelle as the willingness of men to undergo hardship and serve selflessly for the sake of a great

[35]FQ, Flavelle to Carnegie, Oct. 14, 1922: "In a somewhat confused way, I wonder what all this organization means. The machine and machinery representing church organization is better than ever it has been, but so many of our churches are empty, or nearly so. An ever increasing body of people grow careless concerning worship. Many of the better classes using the golf links, or weekend automobile trips, and tens of thousands of workpeople and their families spending the Sunday picnicing, or out of doors in their Ford or other cheap cars. Back of it all, is the restless desire of each group or class to compel the community to give an increasing share of what is going to them, and to their class. Men are talking a great deal about their rights, and little about their duties. They are claiming for economic and social justice, and forgetting the deep and greater sense of justice in responsibility to the State and to their fellows. I do not know what it all means." See also FO, Flavelle to Lloyd Harris, Jan. 22, 1919, with copies to Rundle, Willison, H. H. Fudger, and Edward Gurney; Flavelle to Carnegie, Feb. 16, 1920; to Edward Fitzgerald, Nov. 1, 1919; FQ, Flavelle to Carnegie, April 22, 1921.
[36]FQ, Flavelle to R. J. Cromie, July 19, 1935.

cause.[37] If that willingness could only be recaptured in postwar Canada, he felt, then most social and economic problems would disappear. The equivalent of war, then, that Flavelle searched for afterwards was not the organizational equivalent, but the moral equivalent. Labour unions, agricultural organizations, trade associations, indeed any kind of formal collective action was to this supreme individualist the wrong kind of cooperation. He believed that "co-operation, at bottom, is not a system, but a spirit."[38] That spirit, which Flavelle had upheld all his life, was best demonstrated to him in wartime.

Joseph Flavelle was too good a businessman ever to find it necessary to participate in the search for stability and security through organization that characterized much of North American capitalism in the first half of the twentieth century. He had based his business life on premises of individualism, hard work, and complete free enterprise.[39] He was a self-made man who had worked so well within the system of *laissez-faire* private enterprise that it was still his model when other North American businessmen were abandoning it and turning to government to help reorganize the system. Before the war he hoped the qualities that worked for him in business could be transposed to government and society in general. During the war he introduced these qualities into the mobilization of the Canadian munitions industry through the IMB. After the war, he still felt that government and society should adopt his values, and was disappointed that they did not. Insofar as the problems of the 1920s involved inequalities in the distribution of wealth and those of the 1930s centred on excessive productive capacity, a man like Flavelle who wanted people to work harder and produce more was now an anachronism.

[37]See note 8; also FQ, Case 54, Address to the Canadian Club, Toronto, Dec. 18, 1916.

[38]FQ, Flavelle to J. W. Tyson, April 30, 1934.

[39]The question of the sources of Flavelle's premises raises the issue of the role that his Methodism played in his life. I have chosen to avoid discussing Flavelle's religious beliefs in this essay because (i) the interpretation that derives his principles from his business career seems internally consistent; (ii) the relationship of his Methodism and his business principles may well be a chicken-and-egg problem. It is true, however, that Flavelle's view of the war and its effects on individuals exactly reflects orthodox Methodist thought until about 1918.

Generalizations based on a single case are very tentative. Nonetheless one may suggest that the general characteristics of Flavelle's reaction to the war and to postwar problems were not untypical of Canadian businessmen. Certainly his colleagues in the IMB seemed to reflect his attitudes. So did other observers like Sir John Willison, often a bellwether of conservative Canadian opinion. For the most part Canadian businessmen before World War I had not shared the American concern that government would have to play a role in the reorganization and rationalization of the competitive system. Some, like Flavelle, found competitive economic life quite to their taste, and only looked to government for further assistance to expansive private enterprise. Their concern was aid to development, not assistance to consolidation. Other Canadian businessmen, notably bankers, steelmen, farm implement manufacturers, and textile men, had consolidated their industries and enjoyed the security of oligopoly by 1914. But the structure of the Canadian economy had permitted them to achieve this without direct government assistance. For quite different reasons than those that motivated Flavelle, these businessmen were like him in finding less need than American industrialists to use the powers of government for the purpose of economic reorganization. The Canadian business community as a whole, therefore, was much less likely to favour any permanent change in government functions based on wartime precedents. In addition, the most significant use of public authority to aid private enterprise that had taken place during the war — the rescue operation performed on the semi-bankrupt railroads — had only created an expensive public enterprise that posed an enduring threat to the nation's largest private company. Even Flavelle came to regret that the government had ever pulled the railway investors' chestnuts out of the fire. All told, then, Canadian businessmen had been doing quite well under the old system, thank you, and a return to prewar industrial normality — with government aid only for development purposes — seemed highly desirable.

The hostile atmosphere of the 1920s made such a return seem especially desirable. The postwar surge of Western agrarianism, combined with deep public resentment at wartime profits, made it impossible for Canadian businessmen to believe that governments were likely to use their powers in ways always friendly to business. In the United States, by contrast, the widespread acceptance of the goals of welfare capitalism made it likely that the Republican administrations of Harding, Coolidge, and Hoover would use the powers of government only in ways acceptable to business. For this reason American businessmen could conceive of positive government action (say, to sanction and enforce schemes of industrial 'self-government') rather more optimistically than their Canadian counterparts. In the United States it was less necessary or desirable to return to the situation of 1914 when the Progressive attack on business had been at its height, more possible to advance from it.

(Ironically, in the immediate postwar era the most cited instance of profiteering in Canada was the William Davies Company's wartime earnings. Innocently, naively, Joseph Flavelle had done as much or more than any other Canadian businessman to bring his class and its values into disrepute in the postwar world.)

Moreover, the basic issue of business-government relations in Canada during the first third of the twentieth century was radically different from central problems in the United States. The main control in restraint of trade that Canadian business leaders wanted government to maintain before, during, and after the war was the protective tariff. The tariff was the crux of Canadian political capitalism long after it had ceased to be a major issue in the United States. Tariff problems stood largely independent of industrial mobilization in wartime. Thus what happened in the war was in some ways quite irrelevant to the central concern of Canadian businessmen in their relationship to government. The business-government alliance of 1879 was still far more important than anything that had been worked out in 1914-18.[40]

Approaching the problem from quite another perspective, it is difficult to resist the somewhat chauvinistic conclusion that the Great War was in some ways a more profound experience for Canadians than it was for Americans. Canada was at war three times as long as the United States. Canadians suffered proportionately ten times the casualties inflicted on Americans. Getting through World War I in

[40]Flavelle himself was always a staunch National Policy supporter, but was less obsessed with tariff problems than the average Canadian industrialist. Tariffs were not very important to either the meat-packing industry or to retailing — which was Flavelle's major postwar interest as president of Simpson's.

Canada required at least as much moral fortitude as it did organizational excellence. And perhaps Canadians who had gone through the war remembered the spirit of wartime as much or more than they did the techniques of mobilization.[41] Certainly for Joseph Flavelle the dominant impression of being at war was not the opening up of a brave new world of institutional coordination. Above all he was impressed with what he called "the refining influences of suffering" that took place in wartime.[42]

Finally and most tentatively, one is struck by the realization that Joseph Flavelle's values, especially as shaped by his war experience, were much closer to those that some American intellectuals developed in the post-Civil War period than to the values of the American business-bureaucrats of the 1920s and 1930s.[43] Does this only mean that Joseph Flavelle was an anachronism? Or, as has been suggested, was Flavelle an apparent anachronism partly because of differences in the Canadian and American economies? In addition to that, and enlarging on the suggestion that World War I was different for Canadians than it was for Americans, may it not be possible that for some purposes the more exact analogue of the Canadian experience in World War I is not the simultaneous American experience, but rather the earlier American agony of the Civil War?[44]

The study of comparative history, even of societies as similar as Canada and the United States, involves a baffling number of variables. The easy parallels one expected to find between Canadian and American businessmen and their war experiences are not there. If nothing else, the case of Joseph Flavelle and his American counterparts shows that we are dealing with men holding different values, operating in differently structured economies at different stages of development, and, perhaps, experiencing different wars.

[41]This might help to explain why Canadian historiography emphasizes the effects of the War on national spirit or Canada's lack of it, and has largely ignored the prosaic details of organization for war.

[42]FQ, Flavelle to Willison, May 29, 1916.

[43]George M. Frederickson, *The Inner Civil War* (New York, 1965), ch.'s 11-14.

[44]Other hints of Canadian parallels to the Civil War can be found in the problem of unity, mobilization of recruits, and certain reconstruction plans such as the determination to settle soldiers on the land. It may also be useful to examine C. D. Howe's work in W.W. II in comparison with the American businessmen in government in World War I. There are more parallels to be found here than in the case of Flavelle.

The American Military and the Melting Pot in World War I

Bruce White

American military history has in the past seemed barren ground
to students of social history. They have left the field to historians
primarily interested in strategy, technology, or political relationships, to sociologists such as Morris Janowitz, and to Civil War buffs
and others who write "bugles in the afternoon" histories of warfare. There are probably two reasons for this. First, the American
military during most of the history of the United States has seemed
weak and isolated from the mainstream of American life. Second,
since army officers are admitted social conservatives who do not consider the army a proper agency to initiate social reforms, it has appeared that any study of military social thought would be dull
reading indeed, and perhaps the shortest book ever written.

Nonetheless, the army's experiences with ethnic and racial minorities constitute an important and neglected aspect of American social
history. Immigrants, blacks, and Indians who served in the army
during peacetime were affected in various ways,[1] and during major

[1]The army, for example, had a recruitment problem during most of the nineteenth century; this spelled opportunity for thousands of immigrants who were
unable to find employment. In the army they learned American customs and the
English language, or at least the army versions of both. For many of them the
army meant mobility, for the immigrants were recruited in eastern seaboard
cities and transported to the frontier, where many of them settled. The recruitment problem also led to the formation of four black regiments following the
Civil War, which meant economic, if not physical security, for a number of
Negroes. Both immigrants and blacks benefited from the army post educational
system established after the Civil War.

wars the attention of the nation has been focused on military activities and thus on ethnic and racial minorities in the army. The opportunity thus existed for creating a more favourable public image of minorities and for stimulating a sense of identity among members of minority groups themselves.[2]

The Civil War is a good example of a conflict which benefited the immigrant. As Maldwyn Jones has shown, nativism declined because of "the realization that, in the new situation brought about by the war, immigrants were not a menace to the existing order but one of its stoutest props." Moreover, military service in national units stimulated a sense of identity among immigrant nationalities. "The many thousands who fought for the Union," Jones concludes, "did so upon terms of equality with the native population, and thus lost the sense of inferiority which had dogged them since their coming to America."[3] The potential for social change was even greater during the First World War, although the handicaps to be overcome were also more considerable. The immigrant was on the defensive because of the adverse reaction to the "new immigration" from Southern and Eastern Europe, because of the fact that certain nationalities could be identified as the enemy or possibly in sympathy with him, and because of the growing fear of "bolshevism." In such a situation ethnic groups needed, even more than during the Civil War, the opportunity to display their commitment to America by forming national units.

The army's relationships with the American Indian were, of course, less peaceful ones. Since the War Department controlled Indian affairs, until the creation of the Department of the Interior in 1849, and almost regained control during the 1870s, army officers exercised control over Indian reservations and prisoners for considerable periods of time, and frequently served as Indian agents on the reservations. Their collective record showed the army was not the proper agency to effect the acculturation of the Indian, but it was a considerably better one than civilian agents compiled during the same time. In addition, a number of Indian scouts served with the army, and during the 1890s the army experimented with Indian regiments.

[2]As Glenn Gray has eloquently pointed out, the crisis of combat itself forges personal bonds "among people of unlike desire and temperament, links that are utilitarian and narrow but no less passionate because of their accidental and general character." J. Glenn Gray, *The Warriors: Reflections on Men in Battle* (New York, 1967), p. 27. As the quotation implies, however, the importance of such links after the end of the war diminishes rapidly, as many veterans have discovered upon attending reunions with wartime comrades.

[3]Maldwyn Allen Jones, *American Immigration* (Chicago, 1960), p. 175.

In this situation military policy was to prove on the whole detrimental to immigrant needs. Since the 1890s the army had been hostile to the enlistment of immigrants,[4] but military attitudes began to change as the European situation deteriorated. Army officers began to campaign for their panacea of preparedness through universal military training. This coincided with the increasingly popular Americanization movement in the United States, and the army was quick to see the possibilities this movement offered in furthering the cause of universal training; the army could provide the needed alembic for the Americanization of the immigrant. Unleashing their verbal armouries against the traditional educational institutions of the home, family, church, and school, military men charged that these agencies had left the immigrants concentrated in urban ghettos, speaking only their native tongues and clinging to their former customs. Obviously, concluded General Leonard Wood, the high priest of preparedness, some institution should remove them from this physical and mental environment and force them to make outside contacts so that they might "speak American and think American."[5] It took very little imagination to guess which institution Wood believed could best do the job.

Ironically, what had been a rationale for universal military training turned into unpleasant reality after the declaration of war on April 6th, 1917 and the subsequent Selective Service Act, which provided for the registration for military service of all men between the ages of 21 and 30, inclusive. The problems created by the massive influx into the army of non-English-speaking aliens and illiterate native Americans were all too real. The widely publicized statistic that 24.9 per cent of those drafted were unable to read and understand a newspaper or write letters home was too high, but it revealed the extent of the problem. Convinced that in the army everyone must be treated alike, many officers and NCO's were highly frustrated when it became apparent that those who could not understand simple military commands in English would have to be treated differently. An officer at Camp Meade may have been exag-

[4]In 1894 Congress enacted legislation prohibiting enlistment of non-citizens (except American Indians) who could not speak, read, and write English. Although the impetus for this was primarily civilian, the army increasingly supported the motive behind the act. U.S., *Statutes at Large*, XXVIII, pp. 215-216.

[5]Leonard Wood, "Heat Up the Melting Pot," *Independent*, July 3, 1916, p. 15.

gerating when he claimed that the first time he called roll not a single man recognized his own name, but that when he sneezed ten men stepped forward; his point was made, though, about the lack of communication.[6] The potential for misunderstandings was great, and often an alien's lack of compliance was misinterpreted as stupidity or surliness. At one camp a recruit reportedly had his jaw broken and some teeth knocked out by a sergeant who became enraged when the private could not spell his own name. In another instance a Polish recruit was court-martialled for answering a question in Polish, and a Russian spent six weeks in the guardhouse for evading the draft before it was learned he had been arrested before receiving his draft notice. Not being able to speak English, he could not communicate this fact.[7]

Naturally, those who could not understand commands in English could not be sent into battle, at least in integrated units. Such men, as well as those considered security risks, the physically handicapped, and others who were simply not wanted for one reason or another, usually ended up in depot brigades in the South, where they were put to work at menial tasks such as kitchen and police duty. The army's ultimate response to this potentially dangerous situation was the establishment in May 1918 of development battalions, which were to be set up in each National Army, National Guard, and Regular Army divisional camp. The battalions were to be filled with those considered unfit for general service, and the officers of these battalions were to decide which of them were capable of being trained for some duty, to train these, and to discharge all others. The order specifically stated that all soldiers with an insufficient knowledge of English were to be transferred to these units.[8]

As a result of preliminary experiments with instruction in English in the battalions, the War Department issued a circular in July 1918 directing the establishment of schools to teach English. Classes were to be normally for four months, with instruction from two to three hours daily, preferably in small groups and segregated accord-

[6]Edith Terry Bremer, "Our International Communities and the War," National Conference of Social Work, *Proceedings,* 1918, p. 445.

[7]Edward Alexander Powell, *The Army Behind the Army* (New York, 1919), p. 372.

[8]General Order No. 45, War Department, Adjutant General's Office, May 9, 1918.

ing to progress. A designated officer was to be in charge of each school, attendance was to be compulsory, and the Y.M.C.A. was to furnish instructors, books and other supplies.[9] The Y.M.C.A. system of instruction for foreign-born adults, developed by Peter Roberts and featuring oral instructions and carefully structured lessons dealing with everyday experiences, was adapted for military use. The curriculum was subsequently broadened to include French, American history and government, citizenship, and geography.

Most instruction in the schools continued to be given by army officers and enlisted men, although the educational secretaries of the Y.M.C.A. supervised the work, conducted normal school courses for instructors, and did some of the teaching themselves. Volunteers from nearby communities also were recruited as instructors. As early as February 1918, almost 25,000 illiterates and non-English-speaking soldiers were receiving instruction, and by the end of the war, despite a variety of problems including personnel and unit transfers and a chronic shortage of textbooks, equipment and supplies, 107 development battalions were in operation.

The development battalions might well have been a vehicle for creating a favourable public image of ethnic groups and might even have been a force toward cultural pluralism had they resulted in the creation of large ethnic units. It must have occurred to military men that a thorough knowledge of English was not so vital for the rank and file had this been done. The War Department did, in fact, draw up a memorandum recommending that the battalions be subdivided into companies by nationality and that the officers and non-commissioned officers of each company be of the same nationality as their men, or at least familiar with that ethnic group.[10] In one of the two earliest experiments with development battalions, at Camp Gordon, Georgia, Major Bernard Lentz of the Operations Division of the General Staff divided the battalion into two companies, a Slavic one under Polish and Russian-speaking officers, and an Italian one under officers of that nationality. He not only initiated intensive instruction in English, but also instituted a broad in-

[9]"Instruction in English of Soldiers Who Have Not Sufficient Knowledge of That Language," July, 1918, National Archives, Record Group 165, Records of the War Department General Staff, Office of the Chief of Staff (hereinafter cited as NA, RG 165, OCS), file 7519.
[10]Powell, *The Army Behind the Army*, p. 378.

doctrination and training program and special activities and religious services. More sensitive than most army officers to ethnic needs and problems, he even instructed the cooks to prepare racially and religiously acceptable food.

The Camp Gordon plan was highly successful, and ethnic segregation, as well as the other aspects of Lentz's program, was begun at other camps. The potential inherent in this concept was not realized, however. This was partly due to the exigencies of the situation and partly because of the opposition of high-ranking officers who argued that aliens could better learn English when integrated into units of English-speaking soldiers. In addition, they concluded, the time and expense involved in transportation to the new units and the training of them could be saved.[11] Undoubtedly, many officers also worried about the potential for enemy propaganda.

The major reason, however, for the lack of more enthusiasm for the creation of national units from the development battalions was that the focus throughout the war was on the enlistment of "foreign legions." The War Department announced in March 1918 that it opposed such organizations. "It is not the policy of the United States Army," wrote Brigadier General Henry Jervey to Isaac Kushner, "to encourage or permit the formation of distinctive brigades, regiments, battalions or other organizations composed exclusively or primarily of the members of any race, creed or political or social group. This policy will be adhered to whether the proposed recruit unit is intended for service within the American Army, or with the armies of our Allies."[12]

If the War Department was really serious about Americanization, then this alone might explain its stand. But the circumstances surrounding the announcement suggest there were other motivations. First, the War Department had been resisting without much success the recruitment of aliens in the United States not subject to the American draft for service in Allied armies. Second, Isaac Kushner was one of three civilians who had sent a telegram to President Wilson advocating recruitment of American Socialists into a "Red Guard" to fight in Russia against the Germans. The War Depart-

[11]"Memorandum for the Chief of Staff," Oct. 16, 1918, and "Memorandum for the Adjutant General of the Army," Oct. 24, 1918, NA, RG 165, OCS, file 7519.

[12]Henry Jervey to Isaac Kushner, March 13, 1918, *ibid.*, file 10050.

ment viewed this proposal with less than unbounded enthusiasm.[13]
Third, the army had been urged by H. A. Garfield, United States
Fuel Administrator, and by representatives of the coal industry, to
resist attempts by Polish workmen to organize an army because they
were needed in the mining districts.[14]

During the following two months the controversy over "foreign
legions" continued to centre on the question of Polish volunteers,
and although other armies now had the authority for enlistment of
Poles in the United States, their enlistment as a national unit in the
American army was still opposed by the War Department. This was
partly because of the resolute opposition of General Pershing to
ethnic units and the expressed opinion of the War Plans Division that if this request were granted "a precedent would be set
which, if followed in other cases, would tend toward inefficiency by
greatly complicating the military machine."[15]

A dramatic reversal, however, was about to take place. President
Wilson and Marshal Foch were favourable to the formation of such
units; the advantages of utilizing the services of many Poles, Yugo-
slavs, Czechoslovaks, and Ruthenians who were eager to fight in the
American army but could not because they were technically enemy
aliens were obvious. The potential dangers in ignoring them were
also clear. The moral effect "of large, powerful, nationalistic units,"
wrote Brigadier General Lytle Brown, Director of the War Plans
Division, "fighting for the freedom of their compatriots will be of
inestimable value."[16] The lack of commitment of the army to
Americanization was revealed when a staff report concluded that "It
may rightly be claimed that such segregation of races into regiments,
etc., does not make American citizens and possibly this is true, but
we are not in this war to make more American citizens, we are in
to win the war. . . . "[17]

As a result of the War Department's change of attitude, a Slavic
Legion was authorized by Congress in July 1918. Arrangements were
made for local draft boards to act as recruiting agencies for the

[13]"Memorandum for the Chief of Staff," Jan. 10, 1918, *ibid.*, file 10073; *ibid.*,
March 13, 1918, file 10050.
[14]"Memorandum for the Chief of Staff," Jan. 10, 1918, *ibid.*
[15]"Memorandum for the Chief of Staff," May 22, 1918, *ibid.*, file 10762.
[16]"Memorandum for the Chief of Staff," July 6, 1918, *ibid.*
[17]"Memorandum for the Chief of Staff," May 17, 1918, *ibid.*, file 10050.

Legion, but the war ended before the plan could be carried out. Nonetheless, the immigrant was to loom large in army plans for the future, for the success of the development battalions set military minds to thinking. By the beginning of 1919 a movement was under way to continue the concept in the peacetime army as part of a broader program of educational and vocational training, the so-called "university in khaki" concept. The objective was, as usual, universal military training, and once again army officers argued that since civilian Americanization agencies had failed to do their job the army must step in.

Taking advantage of wartime emergency powers, recruiting officers began the enlistment of illiterates and non-English-speaking aliens and citizens for a period of three years. Recruiting was actively pursued by means of posters in foreign-speaking localities, advertisements in the foreign language press and other means, but confined to members of the white race. Aliens were required to declare their intention of becoming citizens before they could enlist. Immediately following induction, illiterates and non-English-speaking recruits were sent to the Recruit Educational Center at Camp Upton, New York, where they were taught English and instructed in the duties of a good soldier and citizen. At the end of their three-year term of service aliens would receive their final naturalization papers and be sent forth into the world to spread the army's version of what it meant to be a good citizen.

The army was successful in obtaining authorization in June 1920 for the peacetime enlistment of non-English-speaking citizens and aliens and five additional Recruit Educational Centers were established to supplement the original center. A course entitled *Army Lessons in English* had already been prepared, designed not only to teach English but also to inculcate citizenship and to influence the civilian community as well. The first project was a letter home by the end of the first two weeks, to be followed by others. Suggestions were made as to content and, of course, these were more than suggestions since they were almost the only English words the recruit knew. The results must have been disturbing to some civilians. In the first lesson, for example, one of the assigned sentences was "We want to learn to use a gun, a book and a pencil."[18] Suggestions for

[18] *Army Lessons in English* (Camp Upton, New York: Recruit Educational Center, 1920), Book I, p. 14.

44

letters included encouragement for others to enlist, for improved sanitation methods, and warnings of the dangers of bolshevism. The more advanced English lessons concentrated on stories of immigrants who had been successful, on native American and foreign heroes, and on vignettes of military life with a moral. One of the stories, entitled "The American Way," included the following:

> 'You did!' shouted José, madly. 'Don't tell me I did,' yelled Rudolf. And as José seized a knife from the mess table, Rudolf picked up a chair and swung it at the wrathful José's head.
> With a leap, Sergeant Hart sprang between the two men. 'Stop that!' he ordered. 'Drop that knife and put down that chair. We will not stand for any European methods of settling arguments around here.'[19]

In a visit to Camp Upton, Willis Fletcher Johnson also found that recruits were being taught the army version of economics:

> He was, I believe, an Italian. He listened with rapt attention to a discussion of the high cost of living and strikes, and what not else, dawning appreciation kindling in his face till at last it blazed forth in words:
> 'I see! I see! I get two dollar a day. Not enough. So I strike, get four dollars; twice as well off as before. Pretty soon fellow in shop across the street, he strikes, too. He get four dollars. Some other fellows strike; all get more wages. So many strikes, so little work done, things get scarce, prices go up. Pretty soon when I go to buy things, my four dollars not buy as much as two did. Strike no good!'[20]

To promote enlistment, a detachment from Camp Upton representing fourteen nationalities toured fifteen major cities east of the Mississippi River. The group demonstrated the "cadence system" of drill, in which an officer gave orders and the soldiers being drilled repeated them in unison and executed the movement on their own commands. The system was developed by Bernard Lentz, who believed it would synchronize "oral, verbal, and motor impressions." The detachment was especially well received by industrial firms; Henry Ford was so impressed he made movies of the occasion and distributed them to theatres across the country. In the following

[19]*Ibid.*, Book VI, pp. 6-7. The "American Way" turned out to be with boxing gloves.
[20]Willis Fletcher Johnson, "Students at Camp Upton," *North American Review*, CXI (Jan., 1920), p. 49.

summer Lentz formed five smaller units which joined the Radcliffe Chautauqua circuit, thus spreading the army's message to dozens of smaller cities and towns. Their repertoire included drills, sitting-up exercises, singing, and dramatic entertainment, and they now called themselves the "Americans-All Detachments," after a war-time poster showing a list of names representing various nationalities.

Despite all this publicity, and in spite of the authorization of peacetime enlistment of non-English-speaking aliens, the experiment was short-lived. The familiar problem was Congress, whose niggardly appropriation forced the army to suspend recruiting in 1921 and to close all Recruit Education Centers. The experiment, which had looked so promising in the rosy sunset of victory, died in the cold financial dawn of peace.

As in the case of the immigrant, military prejudices against the black man increased during the 1890s, and by the first decade of the twentieth century equal justice for the Negro in the army was no longer possible. The black infantry and cavalry regiments continued to exist, but in 1907 a committee of the General Staff concluded that Negroes lacked the requisite intelligence to become artillerymen,[21] and several years later the Judge Advocate General ruled that their enlistment in the Coast Artillery was not legal because Congress had only designated that infantry and cavalry regiments could be formed. The implication was that they could not serve in any other branches.[22] General Leonard Wood was successful in excluding Negroes from the Plattsburg training camp, commenting that he didn't even want anyone in the country "with whom our descendants cannot intermarry without producing a breed of mongrels; they must at least be white."[23]

Thus by the declaration of war in 1917 military policy toward blacks was one of discrimination and segregation. Before 1917 the latter policy was acquiesced in by blacks in the United States. The National Association for the Advancement of Colored People, for example, petitioned Congress in 1916 to create four more black regiments.[24] After the United States entered the war, however, there

[21]Richard C. Brown, "Social Attitudes of American Generals, 1898-1940" (unpublished Ph.D. dissertation, University of Wisconsin, 1951), pp. 182-183.

[22]*Army and Navy Journal,* Sept. 27, 1913, pp. 103-104.

[23]Wood to Theodore Roosevelt, March 5, 1915, quoted in Brown, "Social Attitudes of American Generals," p. 186.

[24]*Army and Navy Journal,* April 1, 1916, p. 996.

was less unanimity about accepting segregated black units. W.E.B. DuBois of the N.A.A.C.P. was severely criticized for his call to "close ranks" and put aside domestic grievances until the end of the war, and Joel E. Spingarn, also of the N.A.A.C.P., was equally attacked, especially by the Negro press, for his advocacy of a segregated military training camp for black officers and his circular letter urging Negroes to sign up for it.[25]

Spingarn's critics argued that such a camp would be a tacit approval of racial segregation. Spingarn, however, had by far the sounder argument, pointing out that the black man needed, above all, the opportunity to demonstrate his potential for leadership.[26] He was right, at least so far as the military was concerned; since the Civil War the greatest barrier of prejudice Negroes had had to surmount had been the difficulty of entering the ranks of commissioned officers. The black man had had few opportunities to demonstrate his competence to lead other men, and few stereotypes about him were more firmly entrenched than the belief that he was innately incapable of doing so. Spingarn also correctly pointed out that the army had displayed great reluctance to train Negro officers at all, arguing that all fourteen of its camps were too full to accommodate a single black officer candidate.[27] Under increasing pressure, the War Department did allow some blacks to enter officer training, but not as many as Spingarn was able to have admitted at the Negro training camp at Des Moines, Iowa. Furthermore, although Spingarn did not give much credence to this argument, it was certainly true that black officers and officer candidates integrated into white units would not get a fair chance. It would be a relatively easy matter to pass them over for promotions, to give them the most menial of assignments, and to discriminate against them in a hundred other ways.

Some of Spingarn's critics argued that there were enough NCO's in the already existing black regiments who could be commissioned, but he replied that most of them lacked the literary skills to function in the higher officer grades, or even in many cases as lieutenants.

[25]"Military Training Camp for Colored Men: An Open Letter from Dr. J. E. Spingarn," Feb. 15, 1917, Spingarn papers, Howard University.
[26]*Ibid.* See also Spingarn to Mary White Ovington, April 11, 1917, Spingarn Papers.
[27]George William Cook to Spingarn, May 14, 1917, *ibid.;* "Military Training Camp for Colored Officers: Dr. J. E. Spingarn explains his Reasons in a Nutshell," March 8, 1917, *ibid.*

This was subsequently borne out at Fort Des Moines; many of the candidates from the Negro regiments (250 out of 1,250) were reportedly "scarcely literate."[28] There were many shortcomings in the carrying out of the plan, to be sure. The instruction at Fort Des Moines was generally poor, with instructors in some cases reading from army manuals without comment. Des Moines graduates were somewhat prepared for infantry assignments, but were woefully unprepared for assignments in other branches, and subsequent officer training was haphazard and marked by race prejudice at every step. These were failures of operation, however, not of concept, and the failures in subsequent officer training merely underscored Spingarn's objections to integrated training.

The demand for black officers in other branches than infantry was occasioned by the decision to form a Negro division. There was never any question about the use of black soldiers in the war, but there was a justified fear that most blacks would be used only in labour organizations. Spingarn and Robert Russa Moton, Booker T. Washington's successor at Tuskegee Institute, began agitating for the creation of a black combat division, and the War Department was increasingly receptive to the idea when it became apparent how many Negroes would be enlisted and how many combat divisions would be needed.

The crucial question for the army was not whether such a division or divisions would be created, but who would be the officers. It was now inevitable that blacks would serve as company grade officers, but army officers were generally repulsed at the thought of having a black man as a superior officer. The immediate problem was Charles Young, a black West Point graduate, the popular choice of Negroes to command the division because of his almost unique position as a black officer. The army got rid of him, to the chagrin and anger of Negroes, by declaring him medically unfit. In January 1918, it also made clear that blacks were to be confined, so far as possible, to the company grades. Negroes, explained the Assistant Chief of Staff, were not entitled to any proportion of officers as a matter of right; it was a matter of efficiency only. "The best officers," he concluded, "are to be found among candidates possessing the

[28]Howard H. Long, "The Negro Soldier in the Army of the United States," *The Journal of Negro Education*, XII (Summer, 1943) , p. 310.

greatest mentality, natural intelligence, initiative and qualities of leadership. These qualities exist among white candidates to a greater extent than elsewhere."[29] This was to be official War Department policy for the remainder of the war and, more than any other War Department action, it crippled the Negro's chances to prove his leadership potential. A great many of the white officers in the resulting 92nd Division and the black regiments which were supposed to constitute the 93rd Division were openly antagonistic toward both the black officers and enlisted men in these units. Many of them seized every opportunity to discredit black officers and to have them replaced, often successfully, and openely criticized the performance of the enlisted men. The Chief of Staff of the 92nd Division, Colonel Allen J. Greer, ridiculed the fighting abilities of the men of his own division and tried to have the division's black officers reassigned. Even the division commander, Major General Charles C. Ballou, was convinced that the Negro lacked initiative and the capacity for leadership.

Friction between black and white officers was primarily responsible for the incident in which two battalions of the 368th Infantry Regiment of the 92nd Division crumbled and were routed in France, and this incident did more than anything else to perpetuate the stereotype that the black man was an adequate soldier only under white leadership.[30] Again, the concept of segregation was not to blame; it was the most effective road toward overcoming race prejudice and convincing the American public that the Negro had undeveloped potential. It was the way in which the policy was carried out that was at fault. If the 92nd Division had been entirely officered by well-trained Negroes, and had it been well-equipped, the rout of a portion of the 368th Infantry would never have occurred. Since the record of the division was otherwise good, and that of the other regiments brigaded with the French ranged from good to excellent, it would have been considerably harder for officers and civilians, black as well as white, to perpetuate the time-honoured stereotypes.

[29]Memorandum for the Chief of Staff from General Henry Jervey, Assistant Chief of Staff," July 13, 1918, quoted in Brown, "Social Attitudes of American Generals," p. 196.

[30]Edward M. Coffman, *The War to End all Wars: The American Military Experience in World War I* (New York, 1968), pp. 314-320.

Not surprisingly, army officers were overwhelmingly critical of the performance of black officers during the war and determined that they be eliminated from the post-war army.[31] The wartime experience had, however, benefited the black man by releasing a powerful force not planned or desired by whites. The First World War, as the editor of the *Southwestern Christian Advocate* commented, had "lifted the Negro problem out of the provincialism of America into the cosmopolitanism of the civilized world."[32] Returning black veterans would no longer acquiesce in the pre-war patterns. Thousands of blacks who had moved north during the war, lured by wartime employment opportunities, would ultimately no longer be willing to accept a subordinate position in American society. They would force America to awake to the fact that discrimination was a national, rather than a regional, problem.

The army's experiences with ethnic and racial minorities during World War I reveal that the military was unable to make good on its often stated promise of equal treatment. Military men have had little tolerance for differing backgrounds and customs; their relationships with minority groups have been marked by constant attempts to apply the time-honoured army rules and regulations, to fit all

---

[31]A good example was the comment of Major Fred R. Brown, who had served in the 92nd Division during the war. "History has repeatedly proven," he wrote to the Assistant Commandant of the General Staff College in April, 1920, "that normally the negro, as a race, is and has always been lacking in bravery, grit, and leadership, as well as some other qualities which are necessary in an officer." No amount of training could overcome this. During the war, he charged, all Negro officers had displayed "inertia, lack of dependability, and lack of appreciation of the responsibility resting upon officers . . . ." They were completely devoid of courage or initiative. Fred R. Brown to Assistant Commandant, General Staff College, April 5, 1920, Office of the Chief of Military History, Records of the Historical Section, Army War College, file 3272.

In comparison, no such hostility existed toward the American Indian. After the army experiment with Indian regiments failed during the 1890s, mainly because of the army's inflexibility, the War Department was convinced that the Indian should be integrated as completely as possible into white units. Thus during the World War I period there were few Indian units. It was a mistake from the Indian's standpoint, for whites needed to be constantly reminded that the Indian was a part of society, with potentiality and personality, and the Indian needed to develop his own leadership and a sense of racial pride in order to stimulate the confidence of others. His basic problem was the continuing apathy of whites.

[32]"After the War: A Symposium," *The Southern Workman,* XLVIII (March, 1919) , pp. 138-139.

comers into a common mould. It is essentially an Anglo-Saxon mould, which is not surprising in view of the upper-middle class, Anglo-Saxon, Protestant background of most army officers.[33] But the army does implicitly promise that prejudice has no place within its ranks, and it does not always fulfill this promise. In its relationships with the immigrant during World War I and in other periods, nativism has been an undercurrent which occasionally rises to the surface. Army policy toward the black soldier has to a greater degree been determined by racial prejudice.

When the common mould does operate as intended, minorities are not necessarily aided. During World War I strict segregation, rather than integration, and unequal, rather than equal, treatment would have most benefited immigrants and blacks. The military was not, of course, taking the needs of minorities into account in determining its policies, but the decisions it made affected minority groups, especially during wartime. The relationship can best be described as tangential. The army has been concerned with problems of professionalism and functionalism; ethnic and racial minorities have been concerned with identity, mobility, acculturation, and integration. During the nineteenth century this tangent aided minority groups; during World War I it hindered them.

[33]C. Wright Mills, *The Power Elite* (New York, 1959), p. 180; Morris Janowitz, *The Professional Soldier: A Social and Political Portrait* (New York, 1964), pp. 82-100; Brown, "Social Attitudes of American Generals," pp. 1-16.

The Woman's Peace Party and the First World War

Jill Conway

The story of the attempts of women's groups to mediate between
the warring powers during 1914-18 has elements of high comedy. The
comedy is historically significant because the inflated goals of the
women's peace movement led its supporters unerringly if uncon-
sciously into a situation which put to a test the entire ideology upon
which arguments for the liberation of women had been based in the
United States. Women's organizations responded to the war on the
assumption that women could have a separate political reaction to
international conflict, a reaction unique to their sex. Women's
groups of all political leanings were in theory pacifist in 1914. This
was because the central assumption of all participants in the movement for women's rights was that women were free from aggressive
instincts, a freedom which made them men's moral superiors at all
times. Woman as the nurturer of life could have no warlike emotions, and should she receive her political rights it followed that
society would be cleansed of conflict and nation states would no
longer go to war.

Powerful forces in nineteenth century culture had encouraged
acceptance of such beliefs, however naive they may seem today.
Victorian literature and social thought were obsessed by the image of
the passive nurturing woman, an image in marked contrast to the
domineering and politically astute Queen who gave her name to the
era. This stereotype managed to ignore the harsh realities of the life

of working class women and the cultural attitudes which permitted their ruthless sexual exploitation. So strong was the tendency to idealize and etherealise the "angel in the house" that historians of the period have concluded that the cult of the morally "pure" woman was a substitute for religious faith for anxious Victorians troubled by uncertainty.

Similarly in the United States a strong belief in the moral powers of the nurturing female existed in the nineteenth century. These powers constituted an important source of moral uplift for American society as it became more highly competitive and suffused with commercial values.[1] In Northern fiction the idealised woman, secluded within her domestic world, untouched by the sordid realities of business life, was an important source of reassurance that some areas of American life were free from business values. In the South the chaste, ethereal white woman was a necessary guarantee of social stability for a society which could not examine the truth of miscegenation and could not rid itself of sexual guilt. Southern whites were obliged to idealise white women and to celebrate their "purity" as a compensation for the fact that white men of all social backgrounds felt free to indulge themselves sexually with black slave women. The more Southern society departed from the traditional ideal of a monogamous society, the more it became necessary to celebrate the virtues of white women secluded within an idealised family. The fact that white men frequently did not acknowledge the bastards which were the offspring of inter-racial unions produced a guilt which compelled Southerners to eulogise the virtues of family life and to cherish purity in white women.

Given the symbolic function of the stereotype of white women for American culture, it is not surprising that feminists as well as their opponents accepted the idea of the passive and morally pure female personality. Feminists argued for the extension of political rights to women not on grounds of liberal principle, but on grounds that their special qualities should be given an extended sphere, that is on grounds of expediency. They hoped to see women's special virtues given expression in public life, thereby inevitably affecting and elevating public affairs. This argument from

[1]For the best treatment of this question see William R. Taylor, *Cavalier and Yankee: The Old South and American National Character* (New York, 1961).

expediency proved a hollow one because the movement to extend women's rights was discredited when the granting of the franchise failed to alter appreciably the moral and political tone of American society.[2]

It has been customary to berate American feminists for the poverty of their ideology and the weakness of their arguments for extending women's rights, and in particular for their failure to see through the stereotype of women so central to nineteenth century culture.[3] No series of events illustrates with greater clarity the controlling power of that stereotype than the history of the women's movement during the First World War. At the same time no single episode illustrates so vividly the disastrous consequences of basing an ideological position upon a cultural image so profoundly at odds with reality.

In 1914 women's groups such as the General Federation of Women's Clubs or the National Consumers' League rested their opposition to war on grounds articulated by Jane Addams in her *Newer Ideals of Peace* of 1907. This work extended a popular series of Chautauqua lectures delivered in 1902 and subsequently published in a variety of periodicals.[4] Jane Addams's theme was that modern industrial society was subject to violent class conflict. She hoped that it would prove possible to educate capital and labour, both of which she saw as equally militant, on the virtues of pacifism. She had no solution to the conflict itself because she was blind to the power realities of capitalism. She blamed much of the militance of capital and labour on the American worship of frontier violence. However, she was quick to point out that there was one group in American society which had not been encouraged to value aggression and conquest. American women had been trained to conform to non-military values and to achieve what sense of worth they might have as human beings through non-violent action. Working from this assertion, she then took up the larger question of whether American culture would be able to develop anti-heroic values which would set it apart from Western Europe where the values of courage and honour were derived from an aristocratic and military ruling class.

[2]The best study of feminist ideology is William L. O'Neill's *Everyone Was Brave: The Rise and Fall of Feminism in America* (Chicago, 1969).
[3]*Ibid.*, p. 64.
[4]Jane Addams, *Newer Ideals of Peace* (New York, 1907).

Her answer, of course, was the traditional feminist one, that American culture could develop into one appropriate for a peaceable, commercial democracy only when it celebrated the feminine, nurturing powers and rejected the masculine ideas of aggression and conquest.

In urging the feminization of American culture she was obliged to confront the question which so agitated both Theodore Roosevelt and William James: what would be the peaceable equivalent of the soldier's self-sacrifice in wartime? Her answer is revealing, for although she preached non-violence her image of the moral equivalent of war involved conquest. She thought the non-military hero would be the efficient engineer who was at work curbing the forces of nature and bringing the benefits of industrial technology to Latin America, Africa and Asia. This anticipation of the ideas of the Peace Corps and the New Frontier, which saw a virtue in strenuous effort and contained a thinly veiled urge for conquest, is not surprising from one of the leading figures of the Progressive era. What is perhaps more startling is that Jane Addams also tried to imagine what would be the secular equivalent of the Christian martyr for American culture. She expected martyrdom for those who tried to overcome the evils of class and race oppression in the United States, and in her own private fantasies she hoped for martyrdom while playing her role as mediator between capital and labour in some great industrial conflict. Her search for martyrdom was, however, not to be rewarded in the attempt to reconcile opposing sides in industrial conflict; instead she achieved it in her attempt to play the role of mediator on the international scene and to bring about a peaceful settlement of the First World War.

Her desire for martyrdom can be documented from her letters and from notes made while she was working on the first version of *Newer Ideals of Peace*.[5] She was thus psychologically prepared for some enormous moral effort undertaken in the face of tremendous odds. However, given her psychological idiosyncrasies, what made one of the best read and most intelligent of America's women leaders believe that in the power of organized women there was a force which could silence the guns of August? The answer is

[5]See Jane Addams to Mary R. Smith, Lake Placid, New York, Aug. [?] 1904, Jane Addams Correspondence, Jane Addams Papers, Swarthmore College Peace Collection (hereafter referred to as J. A. Papers, S.C.P.C.).

that like all Progressives she put her faith in science. There was much to encourage feminine pretensions to peacemaking in the current interpretation of the evolutionary significance of sex-differences.

The most important work in English on sex-differences was Patrick Geddes and J. Arthur Thomson's *The Evolution of Sex*.[6] The work was published in an American edition in 1890, and in 1900 its sales were boosted by the personal appearance of Patrick Geddes on an American lecture tour. In his travels across the country Geddes stayed at all the major settlement houses. At the Henry Street Settlement and at Hull-House he stayed long enough to deliver a series of lectures on biology and the moral and political significance of sex-differences. Working from the growing body of knowledge about cell metabolism which was available in the 1880s, Geddes concluded that sex-differences had arisen from differing capacities to expend or conserve energy developed in the simplest single-celled organism. Male cells dissipated energy, female cells conserved energy and thus could nurture new life. This view of the nature of sex-differences was outmoded within a decade because of the development of genetics and the discovery of the endocrine glands. However, Geddes's ideas were the only ones lucidly expressed and easily understood to the layman, and they became the received scientific wisdom on both sides of the Atlantic. In fact his work was cited by every major writer on pacifism and on sex roles between 1900 and 1914. The social and political implications of his ideas were of enormous range. By far the most striking was the assumption that the innate male tendency to aggression and dissipation of energy could only be balanced by the inherent female tendency to conserve energy and nurture life. This meant that women were biologically predestined to be peacemakers while it was man's destiny to make war. In contrast, women's concern with nourishing and protecting life was not culturally acquired but part of the whole

[6]Patrick Geddes and J. Arthur Thomson, *The Evolution of Sex* (London, 1889) . References in this paper are to the New York edition of 1890. Patrick Geddes (1854-1932) , later Sir Patrick, was best known for his career as a town planner and urban theorist. The standard biographies are Philip Boardman, *Patrick Geddes: Maker of the Future* (Chapel Hill, 1944) and Philip Mairet, *Pioneer of Sociology: The Life and Letters of Patrick Geddes* (London, 1957) . See also Jill Conway, "Stereotypes of Femininity in a Theory of Sexual Evolution," *Victorian Studies*, XIV (Sept., 1970) , 45-62.

evolutionary design from the smallest organisms to man.[7] Hence it could be relied on to be stronger than feelings aroused by nationalism or by military propaganda, because these emotions were induced by cultural factors.

It was with this apparently firm scientific backing that leading feminists moved confidently to take up the task of mediating between the belligerent powers on the outbreak of World War I. On the eve of the war there had been an international women's suffrage conference held in Budapest which set up a planning committee for a further meeting of the International Suffrage Alliance to be held in 1915. When the outbreak of the war prevented the meeting it was decided to replace it with an International Congress of Women to be held at the Hague where women's groups could meet to discuss plans for ending the war. The American delegation to this congress was by far the strongest. It was backed by a national organization, the Woman's Peace Party, formed in January 1915 with the participation of the major women's organizations of the United States. By April 1915, when the American delegation set out for the Hague, nothing had happened to shake the conviction of its members that women were innately opposed to war and incapable of chauvinistic male nationalism. Jane Addams, as head of the Woman's Peace Party and leader of its delegation to the Hague, had telegraphed President Wilson, requesting an interview before her departure so that she could speak there with authority on the views of the American government. Wilson replied with customary ambiguity, explaining in a handwritten letter that he could not meet her publicly, but assuring her that he would welcome a report from her on her return from the Hague. When the *Noordam* sailed for the Hague it carried forty female peace delegates as passengers, plus one male, the reporter Louis Lochner. Jane Addams was accompanied by her personal friend and physician, Dr. Alice Hamilton. Herself an internationally respected authority on industrial medicine, Alice Hamilton travelled as a delegate but kept an appropriate scientific detachment in the daily letters which she wrote home to Hull-House and to representatives of various women's groups. The *Noordam,* she recorded, resounded to resolutions, votes of confidence, and the endless buzz of earnest talk. "It

[7]Geddes and Thomson, *Evolution of Sex,* p. 250.

is like a perpetual meeting of the Woman's City Club, or the Federation of Settlements," she wrote after one particularly demanding day of resolutions. These discussions took place in absolute ignorance of the course of the war because the captain of the *Noordam* refused to pass on the daily news to his forty middle-aged lady peace delegates for fear they would come to blows in disagreements about strategy.[8]

Once arrived at the Hague, Jane Addams placed before the Congress a proposal for continuous mediation between the belligerent powers by a group of experts who would represent the neutral governments without committing them to any specified plan of action. The committee would thus serve as a channel of communication between the warring governments and would provide the groundwork for any belligerent wishing to explore possible peace settlements. This plan, though presented as the work of the American delegation, was actually the work of a Canadian, Julia Grace Wales, then an instructor at the University of Wisconsin. The Congress immediately approved the scheme and appointed two delegations of women to visit the governments of belligerent and neutral powers to gain support for the idea of a neutral commission. In each country visited the delegates were to interview the head of the government and the foreign minister to explain the method of mediation proposed and to offer the services of the International Congress of Women to carry it out. Jane Addams was asked to head the delegation of women to visit the belligerent governments, and to the utter astonishment of her travelling companion, Alice Hamilton, she accepted. "The whole experience has been tremendous," Jane Addams wrote home to Hull-House. "I don't think I have lost my head. There is just one chance in ten thousand."[9] Of course she had lost her head. There was not one chance in a million of a women's mission or any other making peace in May of 1915. The Central Powers had made gains far too encouraging for any thought of negotiation, while peacemaking at this stage of the war was politically impossible for the Allied Powers. The very day that Jane

[8]Alice Hamilton to Mary R. Smith, *Noordam*, Apr. 2, 1915, J. A. Papers, S.C.P.C.

[9]Jane Addams to Mary R. Smith, The Hague, May 9, 1915, J. A. Papers, S.C.P.C.

Addams set out brought the news of the sinking of the *Lusitania* and the beginning of the train of events that was to bring the United States overtly into the struggle.

Alice Hamilton, the ubiquitous correspondent, accompanied Jane Addams on her visits to the various belligerent powers. "I have no responsibility myself," she wrote. "I just trail along as lady's maid."[10] She did notice that in most belligerent countries the women seemed every bit as belligerent as the men. "The very best of them" in Germany, she noted, "accepted the *Lusitania* incident without questioning." She and Jane Addams had been particularly horrified by meeting one of their old German feminist friends who had declared a family holiday on hearing the news of the sinking of the *Lusitania* and had taken her children off to the country for a picnic to celebrate.[11]

So far as heads of state and foreign ministers were concerned the standard response to the mission was polite bafflement. Delcassé dismissed Miss Addams with an abruptness which she thought amounted to rudeness. Grey and Asquith were polite. In Berlin she was treated very formally by Bethman Hollweg and Von Jagow. In Vienna she was treated with considerable curiosity because there was some incredulity in government circles about the nature of a female peace delegation. In Budapest there was support for the idea of a neutral commission, but this was one of the few positive responses Jane Addams received. In June the indefatigable pair were in Switzerland discussing the mediation scheme with the Swiss government and making plans to visit Italy which had just become a belligerent. Their reception by Salandra and Sonnino was barely civil since the two Italian men could not comprehend the motives of their American lady visitors nor take their mission seriously. Once in Rome there was nothing for it but to visit the Pope, an audience which two profoundly anti-Catholic women expected to be something of an ordeal. The two committee women set off briskly, identically gowned in their customary black dresses and trailing unaccustomed veils of black Spanish lace reluctantly acquired for the occasion. They expected nothing from

[10]Alice Hamilton to Louise de Koven Bowen, Amsterdam, May 16, 1915, J. A. Papers, S.C.P.C.
[11]Alice Hamilton, *Exploring the Dangerous Trades* (Boston, 1943) , p. 172.

Benedict XV and spent their time on the journey to the Vatican worrying about the troublesome Protestant question of whether to kiss rings. Once arrived they found the first head of state was enthusiastic in his belief that a women's organization could be of great importance in advancing the cause of peace. When the awful moment came to end the audience and the two women began to back awkwardly from the pontiff's presence, to their astonishment the most extreme representative of male dominance shook them each briskly by the hand, gave each a pat on the shoulder and ushered them solicitously from the room.[12]

After Rome they set out for the United States. They arrived in New York on Independence Day to find a message from President Wilson waiting at the Henry Street Settlement summoning Jane Addams to the White House. She spent over two hours with him recounting her travels and offering suggestions for new attempts at meditation. She believed her mission had been a success. The fact that she had been received by the governments of all the countries she had visited made to her mind a strong case for urging Wilson to launch a public attempt at peace negotiations. Wilson listened to her attentively, and she left him confident that she had strengthened his resolve to seek the role of mediator.

Nothing indicates so clearly her failure to comprehend the growth of sentiment for the Allied cause during her absence than her speech to a large audience at Carnegie Hall some days after her arrival in New York. The subject of her speech was the Hague Conference and her own efforts as a negotiator. In passing she made some reference to the British custom of issuing a daily tot of rum to troops in the trenches. This custom, she said, indicated that the horrors of trench warfare and bayonet charges were so great that even naturally aggressive males could only be nerved for them by regular doses of alcohol. She expected her audience to respond with revulsion to the idea of soldiers becoming brutes after their tin pannikin of the demon rum. Instead she was attacked in the press the following day for suggesting that British soldiers lacked courage. Within days she was the subject of a national press date, the recipient of hundreds of abusive and threatening letters, and the object of mounting public criticism. The moment of her martyr-

[12]*Ibid.*, pp. 174-75.

dom seemed dangerously close over the ensuing summer as a series of threats were made upon her life.

The public response to Jane Addams's supposedly anti-British position was sufficiently extreme to affect the finances of Hull-House and to persuade its head to stay out of the public eye until the beginning of the campaign for Wilson's re-election, when she urged the Woman's Peace Party to give him their full support as a "peace" candidate. When the blow of Wilson's war message fell she had been prepared for it by his demeanour when meeting with the representatives of American peace societies in February 1917. However, she was not prepared for the divisions which immediately began to appear in the Woman's Peace Party. Its membership of some 25,000 women split into three warring factions after a convention in Philadelphia which established conclusively that females can harbour war-like feelings. The only motion upon which all the delegates could agree was that "those of opposed opinions should be loyal to the highest they know, and let each understand that the other may be equally patriotic." Some state branches of the Woman's Peace Party decided to accept the war as justified. A radical group from the New York City branch continued to oppose the war. Others found acceptable war-work which they managed to reconcile with their opposition to American participation in the conflict.[14] Jane Addams decided that women's nurturing role was consistent with working for Herbert Hoover's Food Administration. Through her appearances as an itinerant lecturer for the Food Administration she was able to encourage women's groups to be concerned with the world's food problems instead of leaving them to listen to destructive war propaganda. The alternative to this form of public speaking, she discovered, was silence. Magazines which had begged her for articles now returned her manuscripts. Organizations which had once sought her as a speaker no longer wanted to be associated with a woman who was held to have questioned the rightness of the Allied cause.

In her travels about the country she found no hint that members of the General Federation of Women's Clubs were moved by any

[13]Jane Addams, *The Second Twenty Years at Hull-House* (New York, 1930), pp. 132-33.

[14]Addams, *Second Twenty Years*, pp. 144-46. See also Jane Addams, *Peace and Bread in Time of War* (New York, 1922).

but the most militant nationalist feelings. Many feminists expected that the war would provide employment opportunities for women as it had in England where one quarter of the labour force was in military service. As it turned out, however, this was a mistaken expectation because the American labour force was never significantly affected by the war effort. For a brief period women were employed in heavy industry, but by the end of 1919 they had been replaced by men. Had the war continued another six months there might have been significant changes in employment patterns. As it was, the war years remained years in which middle class women enjoyed raising money for war bonds and conserving food for the Food Administration, while the position of working women remained unchanged.

If the militant nationalism of most middle class American women had not disabused pacifist leaders like Jane Addams concerning women's innate gentleness, the storm which broke over her internationalism immediately after the Armistice must have been a cruel blow. On November 13 a group of German women sent a telegram to Jane Addams urging her to use her influence with the American government to persuade it to ship supplies of food to civilians in blockaded Europe.[15] The telegram was not delivered but its contents were released to the press. The adverse publicity which followed showed that Jane Addams had not been successful in persuading America's clubwomen to be nurturing to their defeated enemies. Former peaceworkers, undaunted by the break-up of the Woman's Peace Party, immediately seized upon the blockade and the refusal to feed civilians as evidence that the male leaders of the Allied Powers could not be trusted to bring about a just peace. A Congress of the newly formed Women's International League for Peace and Freedom was accordingly called to meet in Zürich at the same time as the masculine delegations from the great powers were assembling in Paris. The Congress would show a doubting world that women could draw up a "better," "wiser," and "more liberal" European settlement than male diplomats.[16] This would not have been difficult to do; but there was no more agreement about peace in Zürich than there was at Versailles.

[15]Telegram to Jane Addams, Nov. 13, 1918, J. A. Papers, S.C.P.C.
[16]Madelaine Doty to Jane Addams, Chicago, Dec. 1, 1918, J. A. Papers, S.C.P.C.

Alice Hamilton went along with Jane Addams as usual. She wrote home to Hull-House that ". . . I do long for you to be here to see J.A. in all her glory, happier I am sure, than she has been in five whole years. It is the opening morning of the Congress. The big room is full of the subdued babel of many tongues, up on the platform, which is charmingly decorated, is the lady, surrounded by seven selected women of the different countries, and in a few minutes she will make her opening address."[17] The opening session proved to be a splendid occasion for international amity, but the subsequent sessions bogged down on the question of war guilt, something which the German delegation stubbornly refused to acknowledge. At the conclusion of the conference nothing had been achieved except a statement of some general principles. These were that the political settlement of Europe could not be achieved along nationalistic lines; that the economic rehabilitation of devastated areas was of greater importance than a political settlement; that poltical stability and order were functions of economic security; and that no system of political guarantees alone could secure a stable Europe.[18] It is ironic that while the women of the Women's International League for Peace and Freedom were reaching these conclusions in Zürich, the most trenchant male critic of the Peace of Versailles was engaged in setting out identical views while working with the British delegation at Versailles. This was John Maynard Keynes whose *Economic Consequences of the Peace*,[19] published some six months later, demonstrated definitively that women were not alone in perceiving the follies of Versailles. As the history of the Women's International League for Peace and Freedom was to demonstrate over the next decade, there was no necessary correlation between strict feminism and support for the League's stated goals of economic rehabilitation and political stability for Europe. Indeed, as its secretary was to complain in 1921, it was becoming hard to drum up membership. Economic radicals who understood the necessity for economic reconstruction in Europe seemed to want to work with men. Conservatives interested in political stability also seemed curiously willing to work with men. For extreme feminists

[17]Alice Hamilton to Mary R. Smith, Zürich, May 12, 1919, J. A. Papers, S.C.P.C.
[18]Addams, *Peace and Bread*, pp. 173-77.
[19]John Maynard Keynes, *The Economic Consequences of the Peace* (London, 1919) .

interested only in securing women equal rights with men, the League's position on the special qualities and concerns of women was an embarrassment.[20]

The embarrassment of the League's position on the special qualities of women became acute as the decade of the twenties progressed. Developments in genetics and endocrinology indicated that the Patrick Geddes view of the political significance of a supposed female temperament was nonsense. In popular psychology the most striking new wave of thought was that of the behaviourists which revealed that instincts once thought to be the bedrock of personality could be manipulated. Thus the whole variety of speculation about biologically determined temperaments which Patrick Geddes represented became unfashionable. Besides this change in the climate of scientific opinion there was also the unquestionable historical fact that women had been as aggressively inclined as men under conditions of wartime propaganda which made displays of hostile feelings legitimate and not "unfeminine." Thus there was no longer an historical or scientific basis for a special women's peace movement. Indeed women in the United States had shown themselves only too willing during World War I to display the qualities of aggression normally attributed to the dominant male society.

It was this recognition which made an empty victory of the suffrage because there seemed no valid basis upon which women as political beings could be distinguished from men. It was for this reason that once active feminist organizations like the National Consumers' League began to lose strength in the 1920s and the League of Women Voters never found a decisive political role to play. In this sense American women's organizations did not return to normalcy during the twenties. The norm in American culture in the nineteenth century was the acceptance of women as a special moral group in society. The Progressive era had seen this perception of women stated with characteristic moral zeal. After World War I the idea of the female half of society as a potential source of reform for America vanished completely. So far as the women's movement was concerned, the decade of the twenties saw not a return to old ways of looking at the place of women in American society, but the

[20]Emily G. Balch to Jane Addams, Geneva, Jan. 8, 1921, J. A. Papers S.C.P.C.

disintegration of a stereotype of women which had been important for more than a century. In the history of the women's peace movement during World War I we see more or less in capsule form the whole complex of intellectual and social forces which worked together to bring about this change.

The Protesting Voices:
War Poetry in Left-Wing and
Pro-German Periodicals, 1914-1920

James A. Hart

Scholars have paid considerable attention to American fiction and British poetry of the First World War; American war poetry has received scant notice. One reason is clear: the number of war poems published by major American poets, even by those who lived in Europe during hostilities, is not large; nor do the works play a crucial role in the development of any of them, excepting perhaps Ezra Pound. Furthermore, a sampling of various magazines shows that it is unlikely that an unknown major war poet is waiting to be discovered by an assiduous researcher. *McClure's,* the *Atlantic, Seven Arts,* and the slim *American Field Service Bulletin,* for example, are on the whole disappointing.[1] Too often the verse is derivative and second-hand in thought as well as form. Whether writing in an armchair or an ambulance unit near the trenches, authors appear incapable of recognizing the distortions created by propaganda or national prejudices, or of asking themselves whether a war on so vast a scale did not require a poetry outside the models afforded by the English Romantic poets, the *Rubaiyat,* A. E. Housman, or Kipling.

Since much of the British poetry which still arouses interest is anti-war or at least neutral toward the struggle, the periodicals

---

[1]*Poetry* (Chicago) is an exception to these generalized strictures, for though it did not publish a vast amount of good war poems, it included more than any other periodical.

which were opposed to national wars in general or American intervention in particular may seem the most likely to offer vivid poems attacking war, works that might bear comparison with Owen's or Sassoon's.[2] Such works would be more attuned to the disillusioned, even cynical mood of many present-day readers than effusions of patriotism.

One of the best-known magazines that refused to follow the sympathies of the majority was the pro-German magazine, the *Fatherland*. Unlike the left-wing magazines, which were dedicated to social and political revolution, or at least to fundamental changes in the United States, the *Fatherland* concentrated upon expounding the cause of the Central Powers. Naturally, fiction, poetry, editorials, and illustrations extolled and explained Germany's cause.

To establish the image of Germany as a law-abiding nation ruled by a Kaiser noted for his sincere desire for peace, George S. Viereck, the editor, published his poem, "William II, Prince of Peace," within a few days of Germany's invasion of neutral Belgium. Viereck argued that the Kaiser was forced to unsheath his unstained blade in order to maintain the freedom of the Teutonic race in the face of British financial domination, French murders, and Russian pogroms. The German people, he declared, would withstand the attacks and achieve a holy peace:

> Against the fell Barbarian horde
> Thy people stand, a living wall;
> Now fight for God's peace with thy sword,
> For if thou fail, a world shall fall![3]

The numerous pro-German articles by American and foreign writers came to a climax with the printing of "To the Civilized World," a declaration signed by many professors in Germany that now seems grimly humorous in its assumptions:

[2]The following magazines were studied in the preparation of this paper: the pro-German *The Fatherland* (1914-1920), the anarchist *Mother Earth* (1914-1917), the *International Socialist Review* (1914-1917), *Masses* (1914-1917), *Liberator* (1918-1919), *Class Struggle* (1917-1919), *Intercollegiate Socialist* (1914-1919), and the liberal *New Republic* (1914-1920). Only the *Fatherland* and the *Masses,* along with its successor, the *Liberator,* will be discussed in detail.

[3]I (Aug. 10, 1914), 3.

It is not true that our troops treated Louvain brutally. Furious inhabitants having treacherously fallen upon them in their quarters, our troops with aching hearts, were obliged to fire a part of the town as punishment. The greatest part of Louvain has been preserved.[4]

At the end of 1914, one contributor declared that war poetry written by Germans compared favourably with that of English writers. English war poets were full of boastful pride and hatred; the Germans, on the contrary, were controlled by self-discipline: "We have lived too much for the joys of the day and the pomp of the outer world; now the hour of need and of sadness has come upon us . . .. The whole meaning of life is to do one's duty."[5]

Several Americans published pieces in the *Fatherland* in 1914 and 1915 which show their confidence in Germany's right or in her ability to emerge victorious in spite of being surrounded by a ring of foes. William P. Trent, a professor at Columbia University, was moved to admiration of her valour and self-respect. He was not surprised by these qualities, since he maintained that in peace as in war she was a "wisely ordered state." She had a right, he declared, to hold what she had won by "toil and science, thrift and art."[6]

In "Die Wacht am Rhein," Ludwig Lewisohn, a German-born novelist, professor, and art critic, justified Germany's actions by saying that she was fighting not only for her own land, but also for the safety of Europe.[7] This viewpoint is not surprising; others believed in the superiority of the white races, especially the Anglo-Saxon or Teutonic, and in the need to defend these races against the dangers that threatened from the East. Viereck's poetic appeal to the Americans to remember their kinship with the Germans was a mild expression of this idea.[8] Reasoning along similar lines, Pauline Carrington Bouve thought it almost incredible that England and France should ally themselves with Japan to destroy a sister nation fighting the barbaric Slavs.[9] In his desire to explain how England and France could ally with the Slavs against their kinsmen, C. Edwin Hutchings ventured this opinion: "Old England, forced to play a part, / Goes grimly, with a sullen heart," and "Mercurial

[4] I (Nov. 11, 1914), 4.
[5] "The War and German Poetry," I (Dec. 30, 1914), 28.
[6] "Germany — 1915," II (Mar. 24, 1915), 6.
[7] II (June 9, 1915), 10.
[8] "The German-American to His Adopted Country," I (Aug. 17, 1914), 10.
[9] "Kiaouchau," I (Oct. 7, 1914), 15.

France," forgetting her racial kinship, "Joins hands with Tartars to regain / Small worthless Alsace and Loraine."[10] Others declined to attack the Allied nations and instead praised the Germans for their generous valour in battle. Pro-German poems without animosity were few, however, in comparison with the multitude which vehemently and sarcastically attacked the Allies. Many were protests against the distortion of Germany's conduct in war and of her military fortunes. Such were following closely the purpose of the *Fatherland,* and manifested the belief that most of the American press treated Germany unfairly, making her appear a villain close to defeat.

William Ellery Leonard, an American scholar and poet, had a sense of justice and candour that compelled him to express a hatred of American "hypocrisy and cant" (the words are the *Fatherland's*). He believed that there was a harsh contradiction between what America did and what she said. She spoke of moral laws, but sold munitions. If she could not admit the brilliance of Germany's military campaigns, she ought to admit openly the paramountcy of the profit motive in determining her attitudes.[11]

With a lighter touch that is uncommon in the war verse of the time, Groesbeck Walsh commented on (and exaggerated) the way in which some New York afternoon newspapers falsified the Battle of Jutland, May 31, 1916, into a great naval victory for the British:

> They sank the Yorck, the Von der Tann,
>   The Kaiser and the Roon,
> The Moltke passed at two o'clock —
>   The Seydlitz just as soon;
> The "extra" got the rest of them
>   At five that afternoon.

Such a report, Walsh maintained, was worth ten thousand men to the Allies.[12]

[10]"To the Fatherland," I (Dec. 9, 1914), 13.
[11]"America — 1915," III (Aug. 25, 1915), 48.
[12]"The Battle of Jutland," V (Jan. 31, 1917), 420. Although Walsh's main point, that some American journalists were quick to accept British interpretations of events, has some truth, it is interesting to note that several of the New York dailies, including the New York *Times,* took care to report each side's version of Jutland; and their editorial judgment, that Germany may have

A necessary corollary of the defence of Germany was the need to attack the motives and behaviour of the Allies. Since it was difficult for the supporters of the Central Powers to make effective propaganda out of the attacks on Belgium or Serbia (no matter how blameworthy the small countries may have been), these countries were treated infrequently. Nor was France an easy target, since many Americans saw her as a twentieth-century Joan of Arc. Instead, attention was concentrated upon Russia and England.

The former was attacked not only as an oppressive autocracy, but also — and this theme occurred often — as the chief representative along with Japan of the Eastern threat to Western Europe's racial purity, in particular to the unique quality and supremacy of the Teutonic race. James C. Hickey's attack on Russia in his mocking "Freedom's New Champion" was therefore astute. Here he exploited a weak spot in Allied propaganda, since many found it difficult to see the Allied side as wholly devoted to the cause of democracy so long as the Tsarist regime controlled Russia.[13]

But the main and most bitter condemnation was reserved for England, who was reviled as a traitor to her sister race, a fomentor of troubles on the continent, a vulture sucking Europe's blood, and a profit-obsessed nation making sure that other nations, including the United States, fed her and fought her battles. The preponderance of such attacks as compared with those on other Allied countries is very marked. Since there were many Americans who, if they did not hate England, at least mistrusted her, the *Fatherland* was able at first to obtain numerous pro-German articles and poems. C. R. Dasher and John L. Stoddard emphasized the continued subjection of the American economy to British influence; F. Winthrop, remembering the racial kinship of England and Germany, called her "The Judas of the Race," a country "corrupt and sapped with jealousy and guile"; and Mrs. Upton Sinclair poured forth vituperation:

---

inflicted more losses but Britain retained control of the seas, has been supported by later historians, e.g., Theodore Ropp, *War in the Modern World*, rev. ed. (New York, 1962), pp. 234-35; and Cyril Falls, *The Great War* (1959; rpt. New York, 1961), pp. 209-219.

[13]I (Feb. 3, 1915), 12. For a fuller treatment of this subject, see Leonid I. Strakhovsky, *American Opinion About Russia, 1917-1920* (Toronto, 1961).

> Oh, heart of England, rotting to the core! —
> That offers up your sons for sordid Gain!
> Oh, beardless youths and dotards, — hapless spawn
> Of England's lust for Power and wide Domain![14]

Realizing that the more militant Irish-Americans shared the German-Americans' belief that there was an Eastern, Anglophile conspiracy to denigrate the Central Powers,[15] the editor soon published several anti-British pieces by Irish sympathizers. And the propaganda potential of England's severe reaction to insurrection was too great for him and other pro-Germans to ignore. Thus when Padraic Henry Pearse, a minor Irish poet, and two of his comrades were executed for their part in the Easter Rebellion, Louis Untermeyer seized the occasion to castigate England.[16]

Viereck appealed in his prose and poetry for a determined and just effort by the United States to bring peace. Since the country was obviously going to play an important role in deciding the success or failure of the Allied cause, it was natural that he should devote a good deal of attention to the key figure: Woodrow Wilson. When the President appeared to be allowing more and more help to be sent to Germany's foes, Viereck derided him ("Woodrow Wilson is nothing if not theatrical"); yet when in mid-1916 Wilson seemed to have a change of heart, he applauded. His praise reached a height in the January 31, 1917 issue, where Wilson was acclaimed for his "Declaration of Peace."[17] Even after the President had decided on war, Viereck was still partial toward him because of his public statements that animus should not be shown toward the German people as a whole, only toward the warmongers.

It was also at this time, the first half of 1917, that changes were made in the *Fatherland* which suggest that Viereck was trying to enlist more support from his fellow countrymen by stressing the

[14]Dasher, "The Last Review," VI (May 23, 1917), 260: Stoddard, "Divided," III (Dec. 8, 1915), 314; Winthrop, "The Judas of the Race," I (Nov. 11, 1914), 11; Sinclair, "Challenge," II (Feb. 24, 1915), 13.

[15]This belief is discussed by Henry F. May, *The End of American Innocence* (New York, 1959), p. 367.

[16]"To England," IV (July 12, 1916), 356.

[17]"Let's Have Peace," IV (Apr. 26, 1916), 179; "The New Woodrow Wilson," IV (June 7, 1916), 282-83; "Mr. Wilson's Sermon on the Mount," (Jan. 31, 1917), 419.

American nature of the magazine. The title was first changed to *The New World: The American Weekly,* then to *Viereck's The American Weekly.* It was clear that Viereck was losing subscribers. In order to convince readers after the declaration of war that it was not a treasonable publication, Viereck published numerous zealously patriotic pieces. With the country at war, he was compelled to cease defending the Central Powers. Faced with a changed political situation and a rapidly dwindling income from subscriptions, Viereck declared that he would follow the decision of his fatherland, the United States. He did not, on the other hand, feel bound to cease his attacks on America's allies. As a result, the assailing of Great Britain in verse and prose continued. Yet because of the lack of contributors and, perhaps, because of the restrictiveness of the magazine's outlook, its contents became increasingly poor as the war went on. Nonetheless, if at times the reader of today loses patience with the stridency and defiant tone of the *Fatherland's* poetry, he should remember that its writers must have felt on the defensive in view of the greater amount and effectiveness of Allied propaganda, of the difficulty in justifying the attack on Belgium, and of the preponderance of sympathy for the Allies among educated Americans, especially along the eastern seaboard. The *Fatherland* had from the beginning no easy or popular task.

The reader sees again and again in the *Fatherland* a poignant problem that Hermann Hagedorn has since portrayed in his autobiographical *The Hyphenated Family,*[18] the need of German-Americans to reconcile the cherishing of their ancestral land with a duty to their new home. The adequate expression of this problem would have challenged the resources of a skilful and thoughtful prose writer or poet; but little good verse on this topic appeared in the magazine. Traditional metres and unoriginal imagery did not convey the anguish that many German-Americans must have felt at seeing Germany reviled, rightly or wrongly, by so many Americans.

Because they were designed to defend or further the beliefs of a minority increasingly surrounded by a hostile world, most poems were tendentious, some savagely so. Forced to counteract the dominant Allied propaganda in the United States, the affinity which

---

[18]New York, 1916. The book tells of a family that "tried to live in two countries at once" — and failed.

many Americans felt for France and England, and those German actions, such as the invasion of Belgium and the burning of Louvain, which no explanation or apology could render acceptable to the overwhelming number of Americans, the pro-German poets became violent and abusive. Unconvincing poetry resulted. Often, an aggressively querulous tone spoils the verse either as propaganda or poetry. Thus, for tracking the course of pro-German sentiment, the *Fatherland* is invaluable, but as a source of good war verse, it is negligible. The left-wing magazines are a somewhat richer quarry.

For bitter descriptions of national wars as a means whereby capitalists, whether a Krupp or a king, continue their economic and political exploitation of the workers, the uncompromisingly anarchist *Mother Earth* is a rich source. In its pages the romantic clichés of the battlefield were employed in favour of only one war that "of all the peoples against their despots and exploiters — the Social Revolution."[19] A refusal to accept the justifications offered for the First World War may also be seen in the *International Socialist Review,* the monthly voice of the revolutionary socialists.[20] Because their continued opposition to recruitment after the passage of the Selective Service Act was regarded as subversive, both the *ISR* and *Mother Earth* were forced to cease publication in late 1917 by the Post Office's indirect censorship or legal action against the editors.

The most worthwhile left-wing periodical from the literary and artistic point of view, however, is the *Masses*. Its socialist policy was frequently and uncompromisingly stated after Max Eastman took over the editorship in 1912:

This magazine is Owned and Published Co-operatively by its Editors. It has no Dividends to Pay, and nobody is trying to make Money out of it. A Revolutionary and not a Reform Magazine; a Magazine with a Sense of Humor and no Respect for the Respectable; Frank; Arrogant; Impertinent; Searching for the True Causes; a Magazine Directed against Rigidity and Dogma wherever it is found; Printing what is too Naked or True for a Money-Making Press; a Magazine whose final

[19]"The Promoters of the War Mania," XII (Mar., 1917) , 5-6.
[20]For the terminology and description of the different types of American socialism I have relied upon Donald D. Egbert and Stow Persons, eds., *Socialism and American Life* (Princeton, 1952) , I, 3-20.

Policy is to do as it Pleases and Conciliate Nobody — not even its Readers — A Free Magazine.[21]

When dealing with the *Masses,* one is soon aware that here is a radical magazine of greater artistic and literary worth than *Mother Earth* or the *ISR.*

Until 1916, when several of the artists resigned on account of a dispute concerning the scope of the chief editor's powers, its numerous drawings, including biting cartoons and graceful nudes, made it one of the best illustrated magazines in America. Its drawings as much as, or perhaps more than, its prose and verse, support Max Eastman's assertion that it was a pioneer in realism in American periodicals.[22] Eastman has good-humouredly suggested that the drawings were the important part of the periodical, so that all he had to do was fill the remaining space with revolutionary matter;[23] but the extensiveness and good quality of much of the writing show that his statement should not be taken too seriously. Moreover, much of the verse and prose, reflecting perhaps his literary and aesthetic interests, was irrelevant to the political aims of the magazine. Yet, whatever the range of socialist beliefs held by the contributors to the *Masses,* the magazine was designed as a vehicle by which radical artists and writers could appeal both to their fellow intellectuals and to the working classes. But despite its title or intention, it is doubtful that it had a large proletarian audience; it was too highbrow for this.[24]

It is not unusual, of course, to see a magazine fail to realize its aims or to discover a contradiction of a political kind within it. In the *ISR,* for example, advertisements designed to lure would-be petty capitalists made strange companions for tirades against capitalism in the adjacent columns. But the *Masses* showed obvious signs of trying to work according to two very different philosophies of literature. Art and letters were manifestly important in their own right to some contributors, whereas others saw them only as tools to be used in spreading political dogma: talented drawings of female nudes faced caricatures, sometimes monotonously bloated, of

[21]Reprinted on the inside of many front covers.
[22]*Enjoyment of Living* (New York, 1948) , p. 549.
[23]*Journalism Versus Art* (New York, 1916) , p. 9.
[24]*Ayer's Guide* gives an estimated circulation of 17,000 for 1917.

capitalists, religious leaders, and patriots; a reflective poem about nature was sandwiched between attacks on the sanity of the American government; and sweet, if unoriginal, love lyrics stood next to polemical verse on the criminality of war lords. This catholicity may only show, it is true, a contrast of the topics treated rather than a contradiction of policy. But it is more probable that, no matter how zealous the *Masses* was in spreading the gospel of socialism, its editors and some of the contributors did not want socialist propaganda to drive out artistic works uncommitted to a political creed.

Before the United States forsook neutrality, many contributors of verse to the *Masses* paralleled those to *Mother Earth* and the *ISR*, for they too condemned all who encouraged men to enlist and tried to push the country into war. Louis Untermeyer ridiculed the armchair patriot who, knowing nothing of the misery of the soldiers and civilians in the war zones, prattled of war:

> What was your singing for,
> With its two-penny craving for gore;
> With its blatant and shoddy glamor
> False to the core?
> Evil enough is the poisonous clamor —
> Why should *you* yammer
> Of war?[25]

Several poets said that the war was not only engineered by the corrupt, but also corrupted its victims, the ordinary soldiers, because in order to be effective fighting men, they had to fill themselves with hatred. In "Death Masks," a mother replied to comforters speaking platitudes by protesting that her gentle and dutiful son had been turned into a murderous being dominated by hate and anger; and Fuller Miller condemned the First World War, not because it was the bloodiest in history, but because it harmed the souls of men.[26] As in other left-wing periodicals, this and other manifestations of opposition were often based on the identification of the capitalists with the warmongers. War was but

[25]"To a War Poet," VI (Jan., 1915) , 3.
[26]Gertrude Hopkins, VI (Nov., 1914) , 20; Miller, "This Is the Sun," VIII (May, 1916) , 5.

a part of the capitalistic struggle for profits; ordinary men were cannon fodder.

Contributors told the workers who had enlisted or been conscripted to consider why they were fighting. If the ordinary soldiers, especially the Negroes in the American army, or the Jews in the German, would ask themselves whether their sacrifice was worthwhile, they would then deny the rulers who had exploited their gullibility.

Occasionally, poets were annoyed by the inability of workers to see the conflict as a capitalist conspiracy. The annoyance became sharp if the workers came from a country which could be plausibly accused of imperialism. Thus Witter Bynner, closely paralleling earlier prose comments by John Reed, condemned British volunteers as subservient fools or, even worse, unmanly cowards, because they fought for their king:

> If only Britishers were men
> How quickly they would sing
> Their anthem to a call like that
> And end — "God damn the King!"[27]

The more charitable Clement Wood suggested that workers volunteered to escape the drudgery of civilian life.[28] Freda Kirchwey spoke of another means of escape for poorly paid drudges — alcohol; but to her, to drink in order to forget Europe's misery was not necessarily commendable.[29] Workers should study the battles and be ready to fight for the overthrow of the capitalist hegemony. The Russian Revolution, in particular, gave poets a chance to proclaim that the time to fight had arrived.

The right of the Allied cause and the validity of the reasons advanced for American intervention were sceptically treated. In August, 1915 — a time when the sinking of ships with Americans on board was arousing an outcry in America — an anonymous poet satirized a featherbrained passenger travelling, most likely, to Europe:

[27]"Gentleman, the King!" VI (Apr., 1915), 11.
[28]"A Breath of Life," VI (Nov., 1914), 6.
[29]Freda Kirchwey, "To a Soap-box Orator," VI (Feb., 1915), 8.

O the pleasantest sort of trip is on the ammunition ship,
The danger zone I consider my own by right of citizenship.
And if I should chance to die I love to think that I
Another *casus belli* to my country would supply.[30]

Other writers attacked the smug neutrality of the United States.
The Preparedness campaign brought forth several strong anti-militarist editorials and poems. Sarah N. Cleghorn opposed Preparedness because it would increase, she believed, the danger of war and waste money that should go to the American poor.[31] It was inevitable that conscription in peace or war would be strongly attacked in cartoons and poems. Slogans and catchwords that encouraged the war effort were derided. The capitalists, instead of making a world safe for democracy, were making a "safe for democracy . . . / To keep until the war's safely past."[32] Willard Wattles expressed his belief that old patriotic phrases were freely used to fool the young into giving their lives, while the old statesmen dwelt in comfortable and profitable safety.[33] Words like "honour," "glory," and the pious phrases of modern religion seemed of little use, for was it not apparent, asked some writers and cartoonists sarcastically, that Christ in all His omnipotence and catholicity was on both sides at once?
Opposing the ringing rhetoric that extolled the glory of death on the battlefield, Edmond McKenna sardonically addressed the spirits of pre-war suicides, telling them a soldier's death was but a form of self-destruction which was insincerely honoured:

Poets had sung you,
Calling your dying heroic.
Civilization — poor huzzy — had wept for you
Out of her Million Eyes —[34]

The sacrifice of one's life was clearly in vain if only a few hundred meaningless yards were gained. Carl Sandburg, who contributed

[30]"Song of the American Neutral," VI (Aug., 1915) , 8.
[31]"And Thou, Too, America," VIII (May, 1916) , 8.
[32]Elizabeth Wadell, "Making a Safe," IX (Aug., 1917) , 42.
[33]"Young Lads First," IX (Sept., 1917) , 6.
[34]"To the Suicides," VI (Feb., 1915) , 10.

numerous war poems to left-wing magazines, declared that it could be no comfort that such an advance allowed a laughing fair-haired youth at home to move a few coloured buttons on a large outdoor map as an advertising stunt.[35]

The poets in the *Masses* repeatedly stressed the misery of modern warfare. This viewpoint was not, of course, to be found only among the American radicals. The prolonged campaigns and too-eloquent lists of casualties made British and American poets who were not socialists write of the horror and futility of the battlefields. But to the socialists, the agony and appalling waste of human life fitted into their anti-capitalistic campaigns so well that they eagerly seized the chance to join economic and political doctrines to the undeniably glamourless and cruel aspects of war. This tactic was used by N. H. Matson when he described how a weak, syphilitic clerk could, in a way that mocked Nietzsche's concept of the superman, kill a thousand strong men by "turning a crank."[36] Mary W. Slater's description of a battle-scarred hill as "gaunt earth torn down with festering trenches," and Louis Untermeyer's un-romantic picture of the "blundering fight through the sleet / Waist-high in the water-filled trenches" were similar to John Reed's prose accounts.[37]

Nor were the sufferings of the civilians neglected. Untermeyer expressed horror at the ravishing of women "in a gust / Of horrible, hasty lust" and at the conceiving of children in a "frenzied and cancerous hate."[38] Yet in a desire to attack the militarism of a nation or group, a writer would sometimes deal harshly with soldiers and civilians. Charles W. Wood, eager to ridicule England's "League for the Marrying of Broken Heroes," effectively but cruelly parodied sentimental clichés and attitudes:

> Put your wooden arms around me,
>   Hold me in a cork embrace.
> Let me kiss that northeast section
>   Where you used to keep your face.

[35]"Buttons," *ibid.*
[36]"Appeal," IX (Nov., 1916) , 19.
[37]Slater, "When Spring Came up the April Hill," IX (July, 1917) , 51; Untermeyer, "To a War Poet," VI (Jan., 1915) , 3.
[38]*Ibid.*

78

You are mine and mine forever,
   Darling patriotic boob:
And my lips they long to press the
   End of that new silver tube.
Get yourself all tied together,
   Fly to me by parcel post.
Whom the Lord hath put asunder
   I would join — at least, almost.[39]

A few poets in the *Masses* saw the horrors and dangers of modern warfare as suitable material for the exercise of their skill in writing limericks and other light verse. "A Militant Nursery" by Howard Brubaker is an example:

Four and twenty sailors went to kill a whale,
The darn thing was a submarine, and now they're all in jail.[40]

Apparently frivolous verse may have resulted from a desire to puncture pompous patriotism and righteousness.

Often no particular nation was condemned by those who contrasted the world of nature with that which was man-made. When contemplating the peacefulness of the countryside before battle, Edmond McKenna was stirred to protest against the absence of men who would sing a "healing song of peace in keeping with nature's tranquility."[41] Some poets stated that man's destructive powers blasted the countryside and almost stopped the cycle of the seasons; more often, however, writers wondered at nature's ability to overcome the devastating effects of man's artillery so quickly that gentle breezes ruffled fields of cornflowers and red poppies, where a little earlier a bloody engagement had occurred. Amid the shriek of shells and blowing to pieces of soldiers, "all serene, unmoving beauty / The Spring [would] come."[42] No U.S. government official could object to such a generalized, "non-political" poem, but since the *Masses* printed works more clearly discouraging recruitment, the

[39]"Modern Love Letters," VIII (July, 1916) , 24.
[40]VIII (Oct.-Nov., 1915) , 9.
[41]"Prelude," VI (Oct., 1914) , 7.
[42]Paul S. Mowrer, "Tricolor," VII (Dec., 1915) , 8; Anne Arnold, "Spring," IX (Sept., 1917) , 43.

magazine, by a combination of Post Office "censorship" and a neat legal manoeuvre, was forced to cease publication. Its direct successor was the *Liberator*.

There were few attacks in the *Liberator* on the right of the United States to participate in the European struggle.[43] As Woodrow Wilson's ideals began to attract the less extreme socialists, and the Russian Revolution followed its course, poems and articles began to appear which spoke without sarcasm or cold political calculation of the benefits that could come from the European battlefields. It is true that some poets in the *ISR, Mother Earth,* and the early war issues of the *Masses,* had predicted that benefits could come from the fighting, but for them these were to emerge from the wholesale melting of the social structure in the holocaust and war-induced scarcity of labour. Some almost welcomed the "involuntary martyrdom" of the proletariat because it would hasten the millenium.

In the *Liberator,* on the other hand, writers for a time saw the fighting as a way to freedom for all. But the support given to Woodrow Wilson did not last. By the end of 1918, Eastman was unable to maintain his confidence in a man whose liberalism, he alleged, had mesmerized his hearers and whose "business internationalism" was hindering the making of a just peace. Instead of reading about a Negro fighting without rancour, one finds Mary Burrill bitterly asking why a black soldier gave his life in the cause of a freedom he himself never possessed.[44]

In 1919 the diplomatic machinations of the peace makers, the terms of the treaty itself, and Allied interference in Russia caused the *Liberator* to be a mixture of hope and disillusionment. Thus whereas Oliver T. Dargan showed a woman weaning her lover from "the strange dark Thing/That he has seen," and John Macy asked that his companion not live "in the gardens of the dead," Evelyn Gutman, anticipating the conclusion held by many people today, said that the end of the war brought nothing for which the world could be grateful:

[43]This policy may have resulted from fear of "censorship by indirection," i.e., by the withholding of mailing privileges. This subject is discussed by James R. Mock, *Censorship 1917* (Princeton, 1941).

[44]Eastman, "Editorial," I (Dec., 1918), 6; Burrill, "To a Black Soldier Fallen in the War," *ibid.,* p. 11.

> Thank God! There's nothing left to harm
> And all we loved is bruised and cut;
> A crippled world lays down her arms.
> Thank God! For what?[45]

What conclusions then can be reached about the war verse in the left-wing and pro-German magazines? First, there is a surprising amount of it. Editors must, presumably, have looked upon the verse either as good literature — and this is often doubtful — or effective propaganda. Compared to some of the European left-wing editors, the Americans displayed an amazing faith in poetry's efficacy.[46] A second conclusion is that in all the publications treated in this paper, there was, even in the *Masses,* little verse opposing the editors' politics. From the literary point of view, some of the verse shows an interesting use of free verse and brutal diction and a desire to thrust poetry into the centre of even unpleasant human activity. The energy generated in outraged protesters finds expression in versified vituperation or bitter denunciation that still lives. More often, however, as in tens of thousands of war poems written in the United States between 1914 and 1920, the verse is doggerel, the imagery stale, the stanzaic patterns worn-out or unsuitable. Above all, the desire either to vent one's protest or to convert by propaganda overrides any thoughtful concern with literary art. The result is bad literature and unconvincing propaganda.

Why is this so? Why is it the cartoons in the *Masses* are effective as propaganda and perhaps art, whereas the poems on the same subject are more often a failure? A comparison of the cartoon "Conscription" by Henry J. Glintenkamp showing young nudes bound to a piece of artillery, with Robert Hillyer's "To Congress Concerning the Bill for Universal Military Service" will suggest the reasons:

> Ignorant tyrants, reckless and uncouth,
> Mad with the fury that foretells your end,
> Soldiers and lawmakers and fools, attend
> For once the unfamiliar voice of truth.

[45]Dargan, "Home," II (June, 1919), 26; Macy, "Victory," II (Aug., 1919), 10; Gutman, "My Neighbor Says," II (Sept., 1919), 25.

[46]There is much less, for instance, in the *Socialist Review* (London), *Die Neue Zeit* (Stuttgart), *Der Kampf* (Vienna), or *Sozialistische Monatshefte* (Berlin).

You force a sword into the hand of Youth,
Foredooming him to battle, you pretend
That weapons and that threats of war defend
The cause of peace, — as Europe shows, forsooth!

Beware, the loud injustice of your plan
Sets vibrant the long-silent tocsin bell,
And consecrated treason walks abroad,
Betraying nations for the cause of Man, —
When nations with their strife go down to hell
Mankind as one shall see the face of God.[47]

Although in the cartoon the nudes are perhaps too plump, the arrangement of them, particularly the central nude, awkward, and the crushing of Democracy's body beneath the wheels indistinctly delineated, there is an aesthetic arrangement of the parts. The exploitation that conscription entails is simply and succinctly conveyed. That, after all, is what a political cartoon does, though whether a cartoon like this converts many viewers is debatable.

Hillyer's poem, on the other hand, seems a decided failure.[48] When translated in words, the brutal simplicity of the cartoonist's viewpoint appears shallow and opinionated. Furthermore, a cartoonist at least begins with the concrete, the particular, leaving the viewer to make the generalization, whereas Hillyer, like many authors of lower stature, has presented a curiously unsatisfying abstraction when he speaks of forcing "a sword into the hands of Youth." With a still-living and relevant Goya-tradition to guide him, Glintenkamp has used his medium appropriately; Hillyer has chosen a form, the sonnet, that on the one hand has restricted him (the need for a rhyme seems to have led to the bathetic "forsooth!") and on the other has not prevented him from concluding with a religious reference that is out of keeping with most of the poem. His sonnet is too strident and too sweeping. Here is political and social protest that, like much other verse of the time, has a message, an attitude,

[47]Hillyer, *Masses,* IX (Apr., 1917), 14; the cartoon is reproduced in *Echoes of Revolt: the Masses, 1911-1917,* ed. William L. O'Neill (Chicago, 1966), p. 288.

[48]Hillyer's "Thermopylae and Golgotha," on the other hand, is a successful indictment of international peace-politicking. Reprinted in William S. Braithwaite, ed., *Anthology of Magazine Verse for 1919* (Boston, 1919), p. 183.

82

with which many of us today may agree, but it is clothed in an ill-chosen garment.

French Canada and War, 1868-1917:
The Military Background to
the Conscription Crisis of 1917

Desmond Morton

A few days after war broke out in 1914, George Perley, the acting Canadian High Commissioner in London, received a suggestion through the Colonial Secretary. Why not raise a "Royal Montcalm" regiment in Canada "to associate the name of Montcalm & the Province of Quebec specifically with an Empire War"?[1] Transmitting the notion to the Prime Minister in Ottawa, Perley added no endorsation: " . . . personally doubt wisdom of doing anything to accentuate different races as all are Canadian."[2]

At the outset of the war, Perley seemed to be right. There was remarkable unity in Canada in the face of news from Europe, and popular excitement was reported to be even greater in Montreal and Quebec than in Toronto. The French Canadian press was almost as unanimous as the English-speaking papers in supporting the war effort. From the beginning Sir Wilfrid Laurier, leader of the Opposition and French Canada's leading politician, declared a truce in party conflict.[3] Even Henri Bourassa, who had barely escaped intern-

[1]Austen Chamberlain to Lewis Harcourt, August 6, 1914, P.A.C., Perley Papers, vol. I, f. 12.
[2]Perley to Borden, August 8, 1914, *ibid*.
[3]O. D. Skelton, *The Life and Letters of Sir Wilfrid Laurier* (Toronto, 1921), II, 425. On other French Canadian reactions, see Mason Wade, *The French Canadians* (Toronto, 1968, rev. ed.), II, 643; Elizabeth Armstrong, *The Crisis of Quebec, 1914-1918* (New York, 1937), pp. 61-77.

ment in Germany, was not immune from the early mood of solidarity.[4]

That solidarity between French- and English-speaking Canadians soon disintegrated. By 1917 the gulf could no longer be bridged. Fundamental differences in history and outlook, old grievances and some new ones, such as Ontario's attempt to eliminate French-language schools, helped to divide Canadians on linguistic and cultural grounds.[5] After their initial hesitation, Bourassa and other nationalist leaders threw themselves into a fearless and tireless campaign against the war effort, but their participation was more catalyst than cause. If war is one of those shared experiences which transform a people into a nation, Canada indeed became a country of two nations.[6]

Against this tide of feeling, the Borden government proved largely ineffective. Bourassa and other opponents of the war effort were, after all, only amplifying arguments which had helped win Conservative seats in Quebec in 1911. Uninspired and often ill-advised in dealing with French Canada,[7] the Borden government had full control over only one area which might have influenced public attitudes: military policy and administration. It would be absurd to argue that brilliant management of this aspect of the war could have overcome the resistance of Quebec; it is reasonable to suggest that it might have helped. It is therefore worth considering why the Canadian military system operated as it did and to understand the consequences. Military policy was by no means the most important factor in producing the conscription crisis of 1917, but it played a signifi-

[4]Henri Bourassa, *Le Devoir et la Guerre* (Montreal, 1916) pp. 16-20.
[5]In addition to Armstrong, *Crisis*, see Robert Rumilly, *Histoire de la Province de Québec* (Montreal, n.d.), vols. XIX-XXI; André Siegfried, *Canada: puissance internationale* (Paris 1936); and the more interesting reply, Jacques Michel, *La Participation des Canadiens Français à la grande guerre* (Montreal, 1938). On the Ontario school dispute, see Margaret Prang, "Clerics, Politicians and the Bilingual Schools Issue in Ontario, 1910-1917", *Canadian Historical Review*, XLI (December, 1960).
[6]See, for example, the comments of C.P. Stacey, "Nationality: The Canadian Experience," *Canadian Historical Association Report, 1967*, 12.
[7]Rumilly's comment deserves repetition: "Or les Anglo-Canadiens restaient sur cette conception simpliste du Canada Français: un peuple ignorant, arriéré, soumis en toutes choses à son clergé, l'unique et facile moyen de faire marcher les Canadiens-français est d'obtenir le concours du clergé, lui-même tres hiérarchisé. C'est auprès des évêques qu'il faut agir." (Québec, vol. XIX, p. 58.)

cant part. It is also an aspect of the problem which has been the least explored and the worst understood.[8]

Few of the problems of French Canadian recruiting or service at the time of the First World War were new. The formation of French-speaking units, senior appointments for French Canadians, the language of command and instruction, even the development of special symbols and traditions which might command the loyalty of French Canadians — all of these had been recurrent preoccupations of military policy in Canada since before Confederation. Unfortunately, although the Militia as a whole had never been more efficient or healthy than in 1914, these particular problems were further than ever from a satisfactory solution.[9]

To Sir George Etienne Cartier, the Dominion's first Minister of Militia, this would have been a grave disappointment. When he introduced his first Militia Bill in 1868, he emphasized that the new institution would be an essential part of the new Canadian nationality: "Aucun peuple ne saurait prétendre au titre de nation s'il n'a chez lui un élément militaire des moyens de défense." His introductory speech took five hours because he took the exceptional step of repeating much of it in French.[10]

Cartier's militia was not really new. From the former United Province he inherited a British-model military force with English as the language of command. However, both structure and staff respected bilingualism. The Deputy Adjutant-General for Lower Canada was invariably French-speaking. When a volunteer militia was authorized in 1856, the first unit was a French-speaking field artillery battery from Quebec, and thereafter corps were either French- or English-speaking.[11] If orders had to be given in English, explanations could be offered in French. None of this was altered by Confederation. Two of the three new military districts in Quebec were

[8]A work in this area which proves to be only a worthy follower of Benjamin Sulte, the prolific 19th century French Canadian historian, is Charles-Marie Boissonault, *Histoire Politico-Militaire des Canadiens-Français (1763-1945)* (Trois-Rivières, 1969).

[9]The problem is dealt with more fully in Desmond Morton, "French Canada and the Canadian Militia," *Histoire Sociale/Social History,* III (April, 1969).

[10]Joseph Tassé, *Discours de Sir Georges Cartier, Baronnet, accompagnés de notices* (Montreal, 1893), p. 566.

[11]Province of Canada, *Report on the State of the Militia of the Province,* 1857, para. 39.

designed to include virtually all the French-speaking units and to provide vacancies for French-speaking staff officers. French-speaking instructors were employed for militia training courses and in 1872, when a tiny permanent force was created to replace the departed British garrison, the French fact was borne in mind. Most of the officers and half of the other ranks in the artillery battery organized at Quebec were French Canadian. In 1883, when the permanent force was expanded, one of the three new infantry schools was designed for the French-speaking militia. Moreover, in Sir John A. Macdonald's cabinets, the militia portfolio was normally held by a French Canadian minister while the Militia Department's deputy minister was a French Canadian until after the Second World War.

Cultural considerations were not forgotten when the militia went on active service. One of the two militia battalions in the Red River Expedition of 1870 was officered by French Canadians and recruited in Quebec, while in 1885 two French Canadian battalions were included in the force sent to the North-West to quell the Métis and Indian rebellion. In 1899 a French Canadian was included among the three senior officers of the First Contingent, and one of the eight companies was commanded by French Canadian officers — though only a small handful of French-speaking recruits actually served in the ranks.

In fact, representation in the higher appointments was no guarantee of real participation. In 1870, only 77 of the 350 men in the ranks of the Quebec Battalion were French-speaking, while one of the French Canadian battalions called out in 1885 had to recruit most of its men from the streets of Montreal.[12] Of course, it is not hard to explain French Canadian reluctance to go to the North-West or South Africa; it is less obvious why the militia should have been so weak in Quebec itself. In 1870, when three French Canadian battalions were called out to protect their homeland from Fenian invaders, only 358 of a nominal strength of 1,005 appeared.[13] In

[12]Lt. Gen. James Lindsay to Sir John Young, August 4, 1870, Canadian Forces Historical Section, mfm. W.O. 32/815/058/316; C.R. Daoust, *Cent-vingt jours de service actif: Récit historique très complet de la campagne du 65e au nord-ouest* (Montreal, 1886) , pp. 215-7. On the French Canadians on active service, see Desmond Morton, "Des Canadiens Errants: French Canadian Troops in the North-West Campaign of 1885," *Journal of Canadian Studies,* (August, 1970) .

[13]Lindsay to Young, *op. cit.*

Montreal, where there were five battalions of English-speaking militia, only one, the Carabiniers Mont-Royal, represented the French Canadian half of the population. In Quebec City there was one battalion for each language group, while in rural Quebec there were fourteen French-speaking battalions to ten English-speaking units.[14]

Both French- and English-speaking militiamen shared many of the same problems across Canada. Until the eve of the South African War, interest in the force was often limited to polite ridicule. Government defence spending was tightly limited, and rural battalions really only existed for a few days in alternate years when they were assembled in camp. City corps could train throughout the year but their efficiency and growth depended on generous contributions of cash and enthusiasm from officers and friends. Money was essential to buy smart uniforms, finance the band and provide the lively social life which attracted recruits. When money and enthusiasm were scarce, as they often were in French Canadian units, there was little else to attract new men or persuade would-be officers to go to the expense of buying uniforms or qualifying for their rank.[15]

One explanation of the tribulations of the militia which proved popular among its officers was Cartier's insistence on a volunteer basis for the force, even when sufficient suitable recruits were not forthcoming. While English-speaking officers argued that the restoration of the ballot and compulsory service were a practical necessity to help captains recruit their companies and enforce discipline, there were French-speaking advocates of compulsion who maintained that it was an inherent part of French culture and tradition. In 1867 a staff officer explained the failure of local people to enlist by reporting that they were waiting for the "French system" to be invoked.[16] Sir Etienne Taché, veteran of the War of 1812, former staff officer, and Macdonald's titular head in the Great Coalition, argued from experience that the voluntary system was "un système nouveau, impracticable dans les campagnes, étranger à nos moeurs, à nos habi-

[14]Based on *Militia List*, 1885.
[15]The problems of militia life and organization are dealt with more fully in Desmond Morton, *Ministers and Generals: Politics and the Canadian Militia, 1868-1904* (Toronto, 1970), esp. chs. II-IV.
[16]Canada Department of Militia and Defence, *Annual Report*, 1867.

tudes, à nos souvenirs, et qui a besoin d'être soumis au creuset de l'expérience avant que l'on puisse en parler avec assurance."[17]

By insisting on a volunteer militia, Cartier undoubtedly respected the wishes of civilian politicians in both English and French Canada, but his claim that the militia was a success without compulsion was only partially true. In places like Toronto, where enthusiasm for military pursuits was high, the ranks of local battalions were kept full; it was much harder where the spirit was lacking. "Several well-to-do people have told me they would willingly shoulder the musket were they obliged to do so," reported the staff officer for one of the French-speaking districts, "but their occupations would not allow them to voluntarily neglect their businesses and impair their fortunes. . . ."[18]

Since men were not to be compelled to serve in the militia, something had to be done to make it attractive. In English-speaking districts the close imitation of British military uniforms, customs and values could exercise an appeal for many, but there was little corresponding patriotic evocation from scarlet tunics or British mess etiquette in the French-speaking counties of Quebec. One distinct attempt was made to capitalize on an authentic French Canadian military achievement, the recruiting and despatch of more than five hundred young men between 1868 and 1870 to serve in the ranks of the Papal Zouaves. Although this particular display of ultramontanism had been criticized by Quebec *Rouges* and denounced by Ontario Protestants, the service of the Zouaves constituted as legitimate a part of Canadian military tradition as the artificially inseminated customs of British line regiments. Unfortunately, neither Canadian nor British officials saw it that way. When an attempt was made to commemorate the Zouaves by organizing a new French Canadian militia battalion, wearing a similar, Algerian-style uniform, it was frustrated by a combination of British military objections and Sir John A. Macdonald's renowned capacity for a politically judicious delay. As British Commander-in-Chief, the Duke of

[17]"Un vétéran de 1812" (Sir E-P. Taché) , *Quelques reflexions sur l'organisation des volontaires et de la milice de cette province* (Quebec, 1863) , p. 5. See also Benjamin Sulte, *Histoire de la milice Canadienne-Française, 1769-1897* (Montreal, n.d.) , p. 65.

[18]*Militia Report,* 1871, appendices, p. 27.

Cambridge noted that he could not allow any of Her Majesty's forces to be arrayed in foreign fancy dress.[19] Doubtless the decision struck the Duke as trivial but it ended the one significant attempt to adapt the Canadian militia to its bicultural setting. Lieutenant Colonel Gustave d'Odet d'Orsonnens, a militia staff officer who had helped organize both the original Zouave contingents and the proposed regiment, made the point:

> Les canadiens-français n'ont pas tous oublié qu'ils portent l'uniforme du vainqueur, non pas que je veuille dire que notre dévouement à la cause anglaise en souffre, point du tout; mais sous le point de vue de la valeur du soldat, je prétends qu'un canadien-français avec un uniforme de zouave sur les épaules, est un homme fanatisé par la gloire; l'orgeuil, autant que l'honneur national, le fera tuer deux fois plutôt que de le voir reculer.[20]

In the absence of military traditions, real or synthetic, or of any external threat which they could have recognized, French Canadians could still find some reasons for joining the militia. Throughout the Dominion there were modest political advantages in being a militia officer. There was prestige, prominence and a chance to distribute small favours. In the formative years of the force, many militia colonels represented their county in Parliament or Provincial Legislatures. In the long period of depression in Quebec, humbler citizens could welcome a chance to spend a few weeks in camp, even at the meagre wage of fifty cents a day. To the indignation of the commandant of the military school at St-Jean, militia commanding officers used vacancies in the school as political patronage, sending illiterates, ne'er-do-wells and other social misfits for a winter's lodging at public expense.

All across Canada political considerations impregnated militia administration. In 1891, when the Minister of Militia secured the nomination in the remote lower-St. Lawrence riding of Rimouski, the site of the district militia camp went down river with him.[21]

[19]On the Zouaves, see Leopold Lamontagne, "Habits gris et chemises rouges," *Canadian Historical Association Report, 1950,* and "The Ninth Crusade," *Canadian Historical Review,* XXXII (September, 1951). Morton, "French Canada and the Militia", pp. 37-8.

[20]Gustave d'Orsonnens, *Considérations sur l'organisation militaire de la Confederation Canadienne* (Montréal, 1874), p. 50.

[21]Canada, House of Commons, *Debates,* September 25, 1891, p. 6182; April 8, 1892, p. 1178.

A legitimate concern for maintaining racial balance in militia appointments sometimes meant purely political selection. In 1869 Antoine de Lotbinière Harwood (who later acknowledged "I never was a military man before") was persuaded to resign his seat in the Quebec Legislature to become a lieutenant colonel and Deputy Adjutant General for the French-speaking militia in the Montreal area.[22] It was notorious that he never did learn drill. Although such abuses occurred throughout post-Confederation militia administration, French Canada offered few of the pressures for efficiency which came from militia enthusiasts in English Canada. Instead of securing the French Canadian position in the force as a matter of deliberate policy, it existed as a result of highly informal, *ad hoc* political arrangements.

In large part, that was why the serious reform of the militia, which began with the appointment of Major General I. J. C. Herbert in 1890, eventually proved so devastating to the French Canadian role in the militia. Despite French Canadian ministers and senior officers, despite linguistic enclaves, a British model had persisted. By statute, the General Officer Commanding was British. So were the training, the administration and the official set of values. These values, of course, explicitly repudiated the kind of political arrangements which overlooked limitations of knowledge or efficiency for the sake of representation and partisan satisfaction. There was nothing in the British model which intentionally excluded French Canadians. The British took a keen pride in producing soldiers of the Queen from every race and creed. What unified the Imperial forces was that the officers were white, spoke English and shared British values. If, like the renowned Colonel Sir Percy Girouard, they were also French Canadian, that could even be an advantage. What British officers and their Canadian disciples rarely asked themselves was how far their criteria of military efficiency were relevant to Canada.

The reforming General Herbert was a case in point. A strong Catholic with a perfect command of French, he seemed ideally suited to winning genuine French Canadian involvement in the force. He certainly tried. He attended camps in Quebec, lectured the troops in their own language, and largely won their affection. At the same

[22]A.C. de Lotbinière Harwood to Sir John A. Macdonald, June 12, 1887, Public Archives of Canada, Caron Papers, vol. 194, ff. 5775-6.

time, he routed out inefficient officers, unearthed minor peculations, and enforced discipline without regard to politics. He concentrated much of his energy on the sadly neglected permanent force, reorganizing it, insisting on more rational attitudes to discipline, and sending the better officers, including some French Canadians, to England for further training.[23] However, the scourge of Herbert's reforms seemed to fall more heavily on the French-speaking than the English-speaking units if only because there were more old, unqualified and unsuitable officers to be removed and fewer young enthusiasts to take their place. The fact that permanent force officers were now obliged to acquire a professional competence meant that they had to go to British military schools. In turn, this meant barriers against young French Canadians who might consider a military career but not if it meant divorce from their cultural and linguistic roots.

The more able and reform-minded of Herbert's successors, Major General Edward Hutton and Lord Dundonald, were also bilingual and also concerned to recognize their French-speaking subordinates. Hutton, in particular, set an officer to the task of translating the drill book into French, and issued a highly unpopular order that staff officers would henceforth have to learn French if they expected to be promoted.[24] While Hutton made a deliberate play for the support of French Canadians in his campaign to build a Canadian force to Imperial military specifications, there was little underlying sympathy. As he explained to a British colleague, he believed that Quebec would only really catch the spirit of the imperial crusade ". . . when the more energetic and professionally educated English-speaking officers should get at the French Canadians."[25]

After the South African War the progress of reform in the militia accelerated. Many Canadian officers had added wartime experience to a rising level of professional knowledge. In 1904 the Militia Act was changed to open command of the force to Canadian officers, and in 1905 Canada's assumption of responsibility for the two imperial fortresses at Halifax and Esquimalt allowed a considerable expan-

[23]O.C.C. Pelletier, *Memoires, souvenirs de famille et récits* (Quebec, 1940), pp. 275-300 describes the experience of one such French Canadian officer.

[24]Militia General Order (12), February 14, 1899.

[25]Hutton to Lt. Col. Gerald Kitson, January 7, 1899, British Museum, Hutton Papers, add. 50079.

sion of the permanent force. This meant increased responsibility for officers who had taken their profession seriously. Only two of these rising professionals were French Canadian, Colonel Oscar Pelletier and Colonel François Lessard. Even with these two officers, the effects of professionalism were apparent. While Pelletier, son of the Liberal Speaker of the Senate, retained his roots in Quebec, Lessard had virtually cut his ties with French Canada and was best known in equestrian circles in Toronto where he had spent much of his service.

One institution which contributed to military efficiency and professionalism was the Royal Military College, opened at Kingston in 1876. For the first time a military institution had been created in Canada which paid no attention to French Canadian needs. Its first commandant, a highly competent British officer, firmly refused to compromise standards for young candidates whose first language was French. One result was that of the first thousand cadets who passed through the college, only thirty-nine were French Canadian.[26] However, the RMC was only one example of how institutions and innovations which brought greater efficiency to the militia as a whole worked against French Canadian influence as well. By 1914 the Militia could look back on almost a quarter-century of continuous reform but, in many respects, the French Canadian part of the force had been left behind. In 1870 there had been fifteen French Canadian infantry battalions and sixty-four comparable English-speaking units. In 1914 there were now eighty-five English-speaking battalions and still only fifteen French. (The relative size of the two language groups had changed very little during the period from 1870 to 1914). Since 1899 a militia staff course had been training officers for senior appointments in time of war. By 1913 there were fifty-eight graduates; only seven were French-speaking. In 1912 one of the four brigadier-generals and three of the twelve full colonels in the Canadian permanent force were French Canadian — but only 27 of a total of 254 officers. It was in the middle ranks, where wartime advancement would come, that French Canadian representation was proportionately weakest. When it came to making policy and filling appointments, their absence would be felt.

[26]R.A. Preston, *Canada's R.M.C.: A History of the Royal Military College* (Toronto, 1969), p. 70.

The advent of Colonel Sam Hughes as the new Conservative Minister of Militia in 1911 altered many of the settled policies of his Liberal predecessor. Borden's choice for the militia portfolio was to have major consequences, precipitating problems which had previously been almost imperceptible. Personally, Hughes always maintained that he bore French Canadians no ill-will. After all, some of his own ancestors had been Huguenots and two of them had fought under Napoleon at Waterloo. It was characteristic of Hughes's insensitivity that he assumed that these facts would win him friends in French Canada. His past record made that improbable. In 1894, when General Herbert had delivered a speech praising the Papal Zouaves, Hughes, as an Ontario Orangeman, had demanded his dismissal.[27] Four years later he denounced the government for allowing troops to attend the funeral of Cardinal Taschereau. The new Minister had always been much more explicit in his detestation of the permanent force. As a militia officer he had repeatedly tangled with the red tape generated by the professionals, and now he could have his revenge. As many as possible of the older officers, Pelletier among them, were retired. Others, including Lessard, were posted where Hughes could watch them, and militia officers were brought in to fill the vacancies. Some of them were personal cronies of the Minister's, others owed their advancement to politics. At Quebec City Pelletier was replaced by Lieutenant Colonel J. P. Landry, former commanding officer of the 61st Regiment and son of the new Conservative Speaker in the Senate. Landry's appointment brought no peace in the Quebec militia. In June 1914, there was a minor explosion when Hughes forbade the Carabiniers Mont-Royal to march in Montreal's traditional Corpus Christi procession, finally relenting enough to permit them to parade without arms.[28] A few weeks later there was another storm when the 17th Régiment de Lévis was refused permission to provide an escort for the newly consecrated Cardinal Begin.

Both incidents demonstrated Hughes's complete incomprehension of French Canada: both also demonstrated his insistence on controlling every aspect of his department's activities according to a

[27]Canada, House of Commons, *Debates*, May 14, 1894, pp. 2733-4.
[28]*La Presse,* June 18, 1914; Public Archives of Canada, R.L. Borden Papers, o.c. 190, vol. 17, pp. 15614-19.

highly personal and impetuous whim. In peacetime Hughes could do his party little good and his country no irreparable harm. In wartime it was different.

The Minister's detestation of professionalism and his absolute confidence in himself were never more in evidence than at the moment war broke out in 1914. Some years earlier, a mobilization plan had been prepared for Canada by British and Canadian staff officers. It projected a regionally and racially balanced force based on the existing militia organization.[29] Hughes had known of the plan, taken little interest in it and, now that it was needed, scrapped it. Mobilization was organized his way, by means of hundreds of telegrams to commanding officers and personal friends. Almost as if it were a principle of life, everything was to be improvised.

In Montreal, the commanding officer of the Carabiniers was invited to meet with senior officers of two English-speaking regiments. The result was the formation of the Royal Montreal Regiment, with the Carabiniers responsible for recruiting two of the eight companies.[30] This was managed with little difficulty and the new unit soon left for the Canadian contingent's brand new staging centre, Valcartier, where Hughes was personally engaged in sorting order out of the chaos he had created. The Montreal regiment became the 14th Battalion of the First Contingent. Volunteers from other French-speaking militia units were clustered in the 12th Battalion, together with men from New Brunswick and Prince Edward Island. Of the 36,000 men who appeared at Valcartier, 1,245 claimed French origin, and just over seven hundred came from French-speaking units.[31] They were now divided, minorities in two battalions, with individuals scattered elsewhere in the contingent. Although Hughes could hardly have cared, for the first time a Canadian military force was being organized without apparent

---

[29]On the mobilization plan, see Col. A. Fortescue Duguid, *Official History of the Canadian Forces in the Great War, 1914-1919*, General Series, vol. I, *Appendices etc.* (Ottawa, 1938), appx. 11, p. 12. In 1912, Colonel Pelletier proposed one of the few changes in the plan, reducing the contingent from his district from two infantry battalions to one "with full knowledge of local conditions and sentiment."

[30]R.C. Featherstonehaugh, *The Royal Montreal Regiment* (Montreal, 1927), pp. 4-7.

[31]Duguid, *Official History, Appendices,* pp. 56-8.

thought about providing for adequate French Canadian representation. To be fair, there was no specific battalion from the Maritimes either.

By the time the First Canadian Division had finished its training and was ready to move on from England to France, its French Canadian representation was limited to a single company of the 14th Battalion, one forty-eighth of the divisional infantry. The 12th Battalion was left in England to provide reinforcements. Within weeks of entering the line, the First Division had won enormous prestige from its role in the crucial Second Battle of Ypres. From its ranks were to come most of the commanders who led the subsequent Canadian divisions and brigades and, eventually, the Canadian Corps itself. The qualifications of men who had actually won their experience in battle had usually to take precedence over those of men whose rank had been won in peacetime manoeuvres or through friendship with the Minister. The few French Canadian officers in the First Division gained advancement like the others, although the fate of most of them was to return to Quebec for the hopeless and humiliating struggle to recruit their compatriots for the front.[32]

Responsibility for the failure to provide a sufficient and distinctive French Canadian representation in the Canadian Expeditionary Force belongs to Hughes alone. There were just sufficient suitable French Canadians at Valcartier to complete a battalion. However, not realizing how much of their opportunity was now irrevocably lost, French Canadians began to organize to ensure that they would be more adequately represented in the second Canadian contingent. Arthur Mignault, a French Canadian industrialist and military enthusiast, offered $50,000 to meet the cost of raising a French Canadian battalion. A delegation of fifty-eight prominent Quebec politicians, businessmen and professionals travelled to Ottawa to lobby Sir Robert Borden. Perhaps because Hughes was absent in England, their campaign was successful. Authority was granted for the organization of a "Royal French Canadian Regiment" as the

[32]The most senior French Canadian officer in the First Contingent was Lt. Col. H.A. Panet, a permanent force officer who commanded the Royal Canadian Horse Artillery Brigade in 1914 and, by 1916, was commanding the 2nd Divisional Artillery. Another former RMC cadet, Thomas L. Tremblay, began the war as an artillery major, commanded the 22nd Battalion for a time, and ended the war as a brigadier general.

22nd Battalion of the C.E.F. Lieutenant-Colonel F. M. Gaudet, an RMC graduate who had been managing the Dominion Arsenal at Quebec, was made available as the commanding officer. On October 15, 1914, 15,000 Montrealers gathered in the Parc Sohmer to see a galaxy of politicians and publicists of all political persuasions and to hear Laurier cry: "If there are still a few drops of the blood of Dollard and his companions in the veins of the Canadians who are present at this meeting, you will enlist in a body for this cause is just as sacred as the one for which Dollard and his companions gave their lives."[33]

Bourassa scornfully denounced the meeting as an "explosion of empty and sterile chauvinism,"[34] and, in fact, the response was a little less than electric. Twelve days after the Parc Sohmer meeting, the newspapers were claiming that more than nine hundred men had enlisted in the 22nd; in fact, the regimental rolls showed only 27 officers and 575 other ranks. French Canadians were diverted from other battalions recruiting in the province and a final draft of a hundred was needed to bring the unit up to strength before it could go overseas.[35] However, on May 20, 1915, the 22nd Battalion left Halifax for England, and by September 20 it had entered the front line, the first French Canadian battalion in the Canadian Corps — and the last.

For the first time French Canadians could feel that they were represented among the fighting troops. They also felt entitled to be represented among the senior commanders. Having failed to get a major appointment in the First Contingent, Colonel J. P. Landry was given command of a brigade in the Second Division. However, shortly before the formation was transferred to France, the divisional commander, Major General Sir Sam Steele, and two of the three brigadiers, including Landry, were relieved, to be replaced by officers who had served with the First Division. It was almost inevitable. Steele and his officers were too old or inexperienced to take their men into action. However, in many French Canadian news-

[33]Skelton, *Laurier*, II, 437; Laurier-Borden, September 23, 1914, Public Archives of Canada, R.L. Borden Papers, O.C. 209, f. 21272.
[34]Rumilly, *Quebec*, XIX, 112.
[35]On recruiting the 22nd Battalion, see Duguid, *Official History, Appendices*, no. 711, pp. 344-5; Col. J-H. Chabelle, *Histoire du 22nd Bataillon Canadien Français*, tome I, *1914-1919* (Montreal, 1952), pp. 20-26.

papers Landry's removal was simply interpreted as a spiteful blow at one of their own, the son, moreover, of a man who was leading the struggle of the Franco-Ontarians against Regulation17.[36]

Having sent off two complete divisions, the Minister of Militia came to the conclusion that the easiest way to find recruits for the Canadian Expeditionary Force was to invite prominent men to accept commissions and to raise their own battalions. The North had tried a similar technique during the American Civil War, with particularly unfortunate results, and now Canada followed suit. There was little recognition of the necessity of finding replacements for casualties in battalions already in France, nor was there any firm decision on the size of the eventual Canadian contribution, a subject on which Hughes held characteristically grandiose ideas. Instead, men were simply promised that they could go to war with their own friends and neighbours, under the command of the trusted and highly popular gentlemen who addressed them from the recruiting platforms. Politicians, would-be politicians, contractors, businessmen, all blossomed forth as khaki-clad colonels. Battalions of Scotsmen and Irishmen, of sportsmen, Orangemen, Methodists and Bantams — men so short they did not reach the officially authorized minimum height of 5'2" — were all authorized.[37]

To spur on the efforts to find volunteers, recruiting leagues and committees were formed, frequently headed by clergymen, convinced as ever that they were doing the work of the Lord. In Montreal the local military commander, Major-General E. W. Wilson, sought to launch his recruiting drive under the joint sponsorship of a Catholic priest and a Protestant clergyman. He found his clergyman without difficulty, the Rev. C. A. Williams, a Methodist minister of unfashionably broad-minded views. Unfortunately, the French-speaking community did not produce a suitable priest and, as a result, Williams became an acting major and the only Director of Recruiting for the Montreal area. This was the basis for the charge, uttered with some embellishment by Rodolphe Lemieux

[36]Wade, *French Canadians,* II, 169; Landry to Borden, n.d., R.L. Borden Papers, O.C. 4141, ff. 43456 ff; Perley to Borden, June 14, 1915, Perley Papers, vol. IV, f. 89. (Regulation 17 ended public Francophone education in Ontario.)

[37]Col. G.W.L. Nicholson, *Canadian Expeditionary Force, 1914-1919* (Ottawa, 1962), pp. 212-4.

and other Liberals, that Hughes had handed over recruiting in Quebec to an Orangeman.[38]

Although the legend of Hughes and the Methodist recruiting officer was based on an unfair distortion, it was a mild offence compared with the confidence trick, realized or not, which Hughes was playing on his would-be battalion commanders and the men they recruited. It was a trick involving many influential men, not least the Prime Minister himself, who gave his name and considerable money to the task of raising an impressive Nova Scotia brigade of four complete battalions. In fact, almost none of the specially raised battalions ever reached France as a unit. By August 1916, the Canadian Corps was complete, and all of its forty-eight battalions were in France. Most of them had been sent to England early in 1915 and a few had been organized there. Meanwhile, more than two hundred battalions were being recruited in Canada in the full conviction that they would be going into action as units. They didn't. Many never even reached England. Some that did were posted to the Fifth Canadian Division, a formation kept to defend England against German invasion and to provide a dignified command for Hughes's son, Garnet. The great majority of the battalions were simply broken up, with the senior officers left to fill time and the junior officers and men shipped to France as reinforcements. By the time Hughes had been dismissed as Minister of Militia in November 1916, the damage had been done. The accumulation of disgruntled senior officers in England, discontent among the would-be recruits, and the general disorder and mismanagement of Hughes's recruiting methods were unpleasant legacies for his harried successors.[39]

All of this is necessary background to understand the sad fate of efforts to raise more French Canadian battalions to take their place beside the 22nd Battalion in France and, as many French Canadians hoped, to form a complete French Canadian brigade of four battalions. Early in 1915 authority was granted to raise additional French-speaking battalions. By the end of 1915, a 41st Battalion had

[38]On Williams, see *ibid.*, p. 221 and Borden Papers, O.C. 310.

[39]On the confusion in England, see D.M.A.R. Vince, "The Acting Overseas Sub-Militia Council and the Resignation of Sir Sam Hughes," *Canadian Historical Review*, XXXI (March, 1950). For the experience of a victim of the recruiting methods, see Leslie M. Frost, *Fighting Men* (Toronto, 1967).

been sent to England to serve as a reinforcement depot for the 22nd, and five other units were still recruiting. The most interesting was the 163rd.

Armand Lavergne had rapidly become one of the most outspoken Nationalist critics of the war. He was also a militia officer, indeed the successor of Landry in command of the 61st Régiment de Montmagny. For some reason, Hughes retained a warm affection for Lavergne and in October 1915, he invited his friend to raise a battalion. Bluntly and publicly, Lavergne refused the offer, dismissing the war as "a somewhat interesting adventure in a foreign country."[40] To general astonishment, the offer was taken up by an even more tempestuous battler in the Nationalist cause, Olivar Asselin. His reasons were complex and not totally convincing. The facts were, as his biographer has pointed out, that Asselin loved France and ached to see action.[41] Although he insisted that the actual command of his battalion, the 163rd, must go to a more seasoned officer, Asselin became a major and threw himself, with all his notable energy, into the task of finding recruits. No sooner had he collected two-thirds of his men than he discovered that another political colonel, Tancrède Pagnuelo, had been authorized to raise a battalion in the same area. A furious Asselin sped to Ottawa and extracted authority to transfer his fledgling battalion to Bermuda. As a further revenge, recruits in the rival battalion were transferred to the 163rd. Quite beside himself at his fancied injustice, the unhappy Pagnuelo virtually told his men to desert, an outburst which won him court martial and a six months prison sentence.[42]

By the summer of 1916 a total of eleven battalions had been authorized in French Canada. One was in France, two were in England, one was training in Nova Scotia, and the 163rd was in Bermuda. There was one at Quebec City, providing reinforcements for overseas, and the remaining battalions were collected at Valcartier. As military units they barely existed, undisciplined, weak in numbers, and plagued by bad officers and desertion. However, for many in French Canada this agglomeration of military ineffectives represented a fresh hope of forming a distinct French Canadian

[40]*Le Devoir*, November 2, 1915.
[41]Marcel A. Gagnon, *La vie orageuse d'Olivar Asselin* (Montreal, 1962) , p. 174.
[42]*Canadian Annual Review, 1916*, p. 353.

brigade. Such was the advice which poured in on Sir Robert Borden and his colleagues, some of it from Gustave Lanctot, a future historian and at that time an officer in the 163rd. Like those of others, Lanctot's arguments blended political and military considerations. Creating the new brigade would give French Canadians representation on the higher staff and would convince the men in the ranks that they would be properly understood. "It will thus satisfy the province at large, civilians and military men, with the result of increasing the goodwill in all spheres and of disposing better the people for the party in power who will grant this proposal."[43]

There was not much possibility. The senior officers of the Canadian Corps were unenthusiastic about upsetting their increasingly effective military machine to insert a politically inspired brigade. Nor did the government look kindly on suggestions, even from Lord Atholstan of the Montreal *Star,* that French Canadians might be recruited for the French army if they were reluctant to fight for Britain. In any event, there was sufficient difficulty in finding enough men to fill the ranks of the one battalion of French Canadians actually at the front. On September 15-18, 1916, the 22nd Battalion won great distinction and lost a third of its men in capturing Courcelette. Two weeks later another third were lost at Regina Trench. It proved enormously difficult to fill the gaps. Two of the Valcartier battalions were shipped to England as reinforcements, another was transferred to the forestry corps. In November the 163rd sailed from Bermuda for England and, after only a month's reprieve, it, too, was broken up.

By then the possibilities of voluntary recruiting in Quebec were long past. In July 1916, the government had arranged for wide publication of a letter from Captain Talbot Papineau to his cousin, Henri Bourassa. It was an eloquent appeal, but Papineau, an officer in Princess Patricia's Canadian Light Infantry, and who was then writing news stories for the Canadian War Records Office, had little but his name to use to appeal to French Canada. Bourassa's reply, a cool but impressive summary of his arguments against the Canadian war effort, was an expression of what a majority of his compatriots were now feeling. Throughout Quebec and particularly in the major

[43]Lanctot to Borden, March 17, 1916, R.L. Borden Papers, O.C. 209, ff. 21285-88.

centres, the influence of the Nationalist leaders was in the ascendant in the summer of 1916. French Canada was no longer listening quietly to its established leaders. In August there were anti-recruiting riots in Montreal. In the spring of 1917, P.-E. Blondin, one of Borden's last remaining French Canadian cabinet ministers, resigned his portfolio and, aided by the aged General Lessard, tried to raise a 258th Battalion. A series of meetings, sometimes disrupted, a cold response from the village curés, and a total of 92 recruits were all the two men could show for their efforts.

The period of voluntary recruiting was over. The government would now turn to conscription. French Canadians, who had been converted from sympathy through neutrality to hostility to their fellow countrymen's war, would now be compelled to go along. Canada, for generations to come, would pay the price.

*   *   *

After the war, at least one French Canadian was converted to the merits of conscription: "le volontariat tel qu'il est pratiqué chez nous est pour plusieurs raisons un mode d'enrôlement à la fois inéquitable et ruineux," wrote Olivar Asselin.[44] It was a conclusion which Sir Etienne Taché, at least, would have acknowledged with a sense of vindication. The voluntary nature of the Canadian war effort until 1917 was inevitable. The kind of foresight that could anticipate the dimensions of the eventual Canadian military commitment would not have been politically influential in 1914. However, the frenzied patriotism, frequently from non-combatants of both sexes, which accompanied voluntary recruiting, the head-counting and the comparisons, the contradictions about whether or not French Canada was playing her part, all tied in with the completely emotional debate about Ontario French-language schools, were what really drove Canada apart in 1915 and 1916. By 1917 conscription could seem to many in English-speaking Canada as a vengeance which, with its carefully adjusted exemptions, would fall exclusively on Quebec.

There was also division within French Canada between those who moved to Bourassa's position of standing apart from the war and those who, like Laurier, the higher clergy and even Talbot

---

[44]Gagnon, *Asselin*, p. 193.

Papineau, were terrified of the consequences for Quebec of isolating herself and who therefore struggled, by making speeches, trying to raise troops and, in the case of Papineau, actually fighting and dying, to prove that French Canada was really playing her part.

In all of this, the military institutions of Canada really gave very little help. By 1914 French Canadian representation in the Militia was a mere formality. Thanks to Sam Hughes, even the formality was forgotten when the moment of crisis came. A weak prime minister, a minister of militia who behaved like a stage generalissimo, a recruiting campaign based on confusion and deception, these were no instruments for persuading French Canadians to enlist in a war for which they had little basic inclination.

"Whither are we being shoved?" Political Leadership in Canada during World War I

Robert Craig Brown

"Whither are we being shoved?" F. J. Dixon asked in an angry letter to Thomas Crerar, the Minister of Agriculture.[1] Protesting against Orders in Council in the autumn of 1918 which banned the Industrial Workers of the World and the Social Democratic Party, and which prohibited strikes and lockouts for the duration of the war, Dixon complained that excessive use by the Canadian government of its wartime powers had "taken away so much of the partial liberty we once enjoyed."[2] Simultaneously another correspondent, unable to understand why Sir Robert Borden spent so much time in London, leaving a captainless ship-of-state in Ottawa, bitterly noted that "Borden fiddles while Canada burns."[3] The effectiveness of Canada's war leadership was being questioned from both sides. To a few, mainly on the Left, the government's capacity for repression seemed unlimited and unchecked. To many more, it appeared that

---

[1] Queen's University, Douglas Library, T. A. Crerar Papers, Dixon to Crerar, 12 October, 1918.

[2] See David Edward Smith, "Emergency Government in Canada," *Canadian Historical Review*, L, (Dec., 1969) , 438-39 and Crerar Papers, Dixon to Crerar, 9 November, 1918.

[3] Crerar Papers, Montgomery to Crerar, 23 August, 1918.

the government's war effort was at best uninspired, more likely inefficient and purposeless.

Naturally, criticism focused on the Prime Minister. It was he who bore the burden of responsibility in the eyes of both his contemporaries and later historians for the Shell Committee scandal and the division of the country over conscription, to mention but two of the more notorious incidents of his wartime administration. Viewed even in the most favourable light, we have been told, they were political blunders of the first magnitude, classic illustrations of his, and his government's inept leadership. And contemporaries on all sides asserted that neither was an exceptional case. Rather, they were characteristic of the general ineffectiveness of Borden's leadership.

Michael Bliss has noted that Sir Robert simply did not measure up to the quality of leadership demanded by Sir Joseph Flavelle. To the Czar of the IMB, the Prime Minister lacked a "prophet's vision"; he had no "grip," no "vigour," no "application." Borden's own Minister of Trade and Commerce, Sir George Foster, often agreed. "The Prime Minister is undecided as usual," he noted after one Cabinet meeting, adding the next day the simple condemnation, "Drift-Corroding drift."[4] A few days before entering the Union Government, businessman Crerar observed that "the Borden Government has been the most inefficient and incapable administration we have had since the time of Confederation." Initially Crerar and his western friends had demanded Borden's retirement as a condition of Union.[5]

---

[4]Public Archives of Canada, G. E. Foster Papers, Diary, 7 & 8 October, 1915.

[5]Crerar Papers, Crerar to Parker, 3 October, 1917. Borden sincerely offered his resignation to his caucus which, led by Foster, flatly refused to accept it. See Henry Borden, ed., *Robert Laird Borden: His Memoirs,* II, (Toronto, 1938), ch. XXXII. ". . . went to caucus (the largest I have ever seen) at 11. . . . I described the negotiations, stated purport of messages from western Liberals, emphasized the overmastering purpose of winning the war, paid a tribute to Foster, offered to retire or to serve under him or in any other capacity to win the war. He spoke strongly conviction that I must remain leader and declined. Taylor moved resolution, since made public. There were several other speakers and then res'n carried by unanimous standing vote. There were calls for me and I rose and began when suddenly my heart became very full and I could not speak. I stood silent, almost sobbing, when Sam Donaldson suddenly sprang to his feet and began, "For he's a jolly good fellow." When it was finished I was able to go on for a few minutes. Then we discussed Franchise Bill." Borden Papers, Private, Diary, 29 August, 1917. "The Caucus . . . affirmed its desire for united

Sir Robert Borden lacked what our journalist friends incorrectly call "charisma" — as Roger Graham asks, "Sir Robert Borden in goggles and flippers?"[6] Bob Edwards made the point in the *Eye-Opener* a few weeks after Sir Robert's retirement.[7]

> Sir Robert Borden may have been an outstanding figure in Canadian public life, being even a leader in Imperial councils during the war, but he seems to have lacked the arts which most appeal to the popular imagination. For example, one never hears and never will hear a personal anecdote about Borden. His biography, when written, will be dull. It will read like the 'Life of the Prince Consort' and bore the people to death. A well-meaning, but torpid person.

That was exactly it; he "lacked the arts which most appeal to the popular imagination." His private life he kept strictly to himself; his public life, as he often made clear, was always a "duty," seldom a joy. Compared to the flamboyant and impulsive Lloyd George, he was colourless. Compared to Laurier, he was cold. Compared to Woodrow Wilson — well, as Wilson often made clear, no one compared favourably to Wilson!

The historical record upon which we might base a sound judgment of Borden's leadership is embarrassingly incomplete. Unlike our American friends, Canadian historians are just beginning the serious study of most of the complex story of Canada's rôle in the Great War. Ramsay Cook's fine study of Dafoe ventured into some aspects of wartime politics, and excellent work has been done on the Canadian Corps. Roger Graham has ably written the only modern biography of a member of the wartime government. Our ignorance of wartime administration, economics and finance, and of the impact of the war upon Canadian society, is appalling. Even in the much discussed area of Anglo-Canadian constitutional relations the recent opening of British and Canadian official records has made it necessary to re-evaluate some of the accepted conventions of our historiography.[8] It is possible that when this work is done the image

---

national action & its unwavering loyalty to the Premier as the natural & necessary leader of the Govt. new Union or otherwise. The emotional side of the Caucus was wonderful." Foster Papers, Diary, 29 August, 1917.

[6] See Roger Graham, "Charisma and Canadian Politics," in John S. Moir, ed., *Character and Circumstance* (Toronto, 1970) , pp. 22-36.

[7] *Calgary Eye-Opener*, September 11, 1920. Mr. Gerald Friesen of St. Paul's College, University of Manitoba, has kindly given me this quotation.

[8] See, for example, Stephen Roskill, *Hankey, Man of Secrets, I, 1877-1918*,

of Sir Robert Borden as a bumbling and ineffective wartime leader may be modified.

We might now recall that when the war broke out Borden's political support was uncertain. Since the early summer of 1914 he had been sounding his advisors about an election. He led a divided government and a divided party. Generally, his legislative program had been cautiously innovative and reforming in spirit, but unspectacular. The emergency Naval Aid Bill, however, had fractured the fragile unity of his French- and English-speaking supporters, deprived him of the possibility of either present or future significant support from French Canada, and ended with humiliating rejection in the Senate. Moreover, English-speaking Conservatives who bridled at the presence of French Canadians of dubious "loyalty" in the Cabinet were equally concerned at the appointment of a renegade Liberal, W. T. White, to the Finance portfolio, and some of them interpreted it as evidence of lack of loyalty to Conservatism in the Prime Minister himself. By 1914 the country was suffering from severe depression and the voters, remembering the prosperous Laurier years, all too easily blamed the Borden government for their economic plight. As the Prime Minister pondered, the necessity of an appeal to the people seemed as clear as the path to victory was clouded. The coming of war pushed election plans into the background but left the country with a fractious Cabinet, a quarrelsome party, and a public doubtful of either's capacities for leadership.

Two general policy decisions further detracted from the image of Borden as a dynamic war leader, though the Prime Minister thought them essential to the successful prosecution of the war. The first concerned the use of emergency powers. The War Measures Act, which gave the government enormous potential power to rule by Order in Council, was deliberately designed to be "blanket" in character.[9] And in the later stages of the war the government certainly did use the power conveyed in the Act to curb the activities

---

(London, 1970) ; Ramsay Cook, "From Lord Grey to Lloyd George," a review essay of the first two volumes of Canada, Department of External Affairs, *Documents on Canadian External Relations*, to appear in *International Journal*, (Winter, 1970-71) ; and Robert Craig Brown, "Sir Robert Borden, the Great War and Anglo-Canadian Relations," in Moir, *Character and Circumstance*, pp. 201-24.

[9]See Robert Craig Brown, "The Political Ideas of Robert Borden," in M. Hamelin, ed., *The Political Ideas of the Prime Ministers of Canada*, (Ottawa, 1969) , p. 94.

of dissenters from its policy. But, as Professor Smith has concluded, "the government acted with remarkable restraint" throughout the war. Wherever possible the authority of other existing legislation was exercised and Borden and his colleagues "consistently refused to use its delegated powers to solve problems which were basically unrelated to the war."[10]

Secondly, the government was convinced that it was necessary to distribute the responsibility and the authority for the war effort throughout all levels of government. Professor Smith notes that the reason for this was constitutional; "federalism . . . acted as an antidote to the centripetal impulses of emergency rule."[11] But there was more to it than legalism. Borden believed that the practical effect of this policy would be to bring the impact of the war more directly home to all Canadians and engage them more actively in the war effort. As the war dragged on voluntarism and persuasion were supplanted by control and coercion at all levels of Canadian life. Regulatory power was established over the production, distribution and consumption of food and fuel, and recruiting gave way to conscription of manpower. In all these cases policy initiative and general administration came from Ottawa. But the responsibility for enforcement and local administration was either delegated to or shared with subordinate levels of government. Characteristic was a 1918 Order in Council known as the "Anti-loafing law," potentially among the most coercive of all of Ottawa's exercises of emergency powers. Sir Robert told a British audience that it was "a very good law in time of war. I am not absolutely sure whether it would not be a pretty good law in time of peace. It provides that every man in Canada from the age of 16 to 60 . . . regardless of his financial position, . . . must be engaged in some useful occupation."[12] Enforcement was delegated to the municipal authorities across Canada.

Both decisions were open to varying interpretations. As Borden saw it, cautious restraint in the use of emergency powers and continued observance of the niceties of parliamentary procedure were the only consistent course for a government fighting for the preservation of democratic institutions and constitutional liberties against the forces of autocracy and despotism. But if the criteria for leader-

[10]David Edward Smith, "Emergency Government in Canada," pp. 447-48.
[11]*Ibid.*, pp. 442-44.
[12]P.A.C., Borden Papers, OC 569, Speech, June 21, 1918.

ship were the *apparent* exercises of "grip," "vigour," and "application," then his leadership smacked of inefficiency, indecision, partisan squabbling and inertia. Similarly, the diffusion of responsibility for the war effort implied bureaucracy, the extensive distribution of patronage, and lack of conviction. Or, from the other side of the political fence, just because the exercise of war powers was brought down to the local level, the governing institutions of the country appeared to have become all the more repressive. In either case the image of leadership was compromised.

Even more important in considering the nature of Borden's war leadership is the obvious fact that in almost every phase of war activity the Canadian leader was a frustrated follower. "Canada's war" was directed from London, not Ottawa. This was as true, ultimately, of the production of material as it was of the contribution of men. The IMB, the largest producer of war material, was an agent of the British Ministry of Munitions and, late in the war, of the United States Ordnance Department. It was autonomous enough in Ottawa for Flavelle to ignore pressure from Borden in 1916 to insert fair-wage clauses in IMB contracts as the Canadian government had done with its war purchases.[13] The Canadian government's own contributions of material and manpower were equally dependent upon policy made in London.

Nor was Lloyd George's enthusiasm for bringing the Dominion's leaders into the War Cabinet in 1917 shared by its secretary or his colleagues, who regarded them as bothersome intruders. Hankey wrote that

> The new Govt amused me much by their telegram to the Dominion Govts. inviting the Prime Ministers to attend meetings of the War Cabinet to discuss "questions" of great urgency. As a matter of fact they have not a notion what they are to discuss, and as Bonar Law said, "When they get here, you will wish to goodness you could get rid of them."[14]

In fact, with the exception of Smuts who remained in London to become a member of the British War Cabinet, it was not until the

[13]See "Report of the Chairman of Imperial Munitions Board to the Minister of Munitions," August 17, 1921, Appendix I; David Carnegie, *The History of Munitions Supply in Canada, 1914-1918,* (Toronto, 1925) ; Borden Papers, OC 235 and R.L.B. 1419; P.A.C., Flavelle Papers, Harper to Flavelle, March 23, 1916, Flavelle to Harper, March 29, 1916, Memo of March 3, 1916.
[14]Cited in Roskill, p. 348.

formation of the Prime Ministers Committee in the summer of 1918 that the Dominion leaders really took part in the determination of war policy.[15]

Needless to say, decisions made in London to take over Canadian merchant shipping, thus disrupting Canadian war production, or to engage in offensive operations on the Western front at the cost of thousands of Canadian casualties for no apparent purpose, reflected adversely upon the image of leadership in Ottawa. Private protests to the Imperial authorities could be and were vigorous, though usually with little effect. Of necessity, the Canadian public had to be content with general and unconvincing assurances from the Prime Minister of the well-being of the united Imperial war effort. "To-day we are thankful so much has been done," Borden told a Toronto audience after his disillusioning London visit in 1915.[16]

> I have it on the highest authority and from the best sources that what ought to be done is now being done. I believe that the steps now being taken are all that could be desired for the purpose. While results may not materialize as soon as we would desire splendid work is now being done and will be done, and, I think I may add, work that will bear great results in the almost immediate future.

Of course, Sir Robert Borden had to explain to Canadians why Canada was at war. The simple notion that Canada was at war when Britain was at war was not sufficient justification. It had too many connotations of easy colonial dependence and ran against the grain of the image of a vigorous foreign policy which Borden had propounded during the struggle over the Naval Aid Bill. It was out of tune with the loud chorus of enthusiasm for the war that arose across the country in the fall of 1914 and with his own pledge of "every effort" and "every sacrifice." For these reasons, and to unite a divided country behind the government's pledge, much time and effort was spent in elaborating a distinctively Canadian set of war aims and objectives. This was not to be just another Canadian contribution to an Imperial War, World War I was going to be "Canada's war."[17]

[15]See Brown, "Sir Robert Borden, the Great War and Anglo-Canadian Relations"; Borden, *Memoirs,* II, 808-817.

[24]P.A.C., Borden Papers, no. 15744, Borden to Hughes, 24 September, 1915.

[17]See Brown, "Sir Robert Borden, the Great War and Anglo-Canadian Relations," pp. 203-207.

The Prime Minister recognized that the initial enthusiasm would soon wane, and that it did not reflect any substantial realization of the economic and social consequences of war upon the Canadian people. It was up to him to bring that home to them. He was particularly apt at pointing out the grave implications of war policy. His serious platform appearance and his speeches, heavily laden with references to "duty," "earnestness," and the necessity of "sacrifice," conveyed a message of "the ideal of service." But he knew his limitations as a public speaker and usually brought with him a hearty tub-thumper who could stir the audience from grim sacrifice to enthusiastic patriotism. In 1915 in Toronto, for example, R. B. "Bonfire" Bennett loudly proclaimed: "It is the duty of Canadians everywhere to fight or pay."[18]

For you who can't fight — what? Pay, pay and then pay. How did you make your great wealth? You made it because the State gave you protection. Now what are you going to do for the State? Pay! . . . We are going to permit those who accumulated money to pay some of it back to the State which permitted them to make it. I make no appeal to dead men, but I expect the live ones to hear me, and pay. You women who are contemplating a new hat, or a new ball gown, forget it. You men who use tobacco, cut it out, and give.

If one of the tasks of the leader was to encourage participation in the war effort, another was to dispel the public's uncertainties and calm their fears. As confident as everyone else in Canada and Britain that the war would be quickly won, Sir Robert promised in December 1914 that "there has not been, there will not be, compulsion or conscription. Freely and voluntarily the manhood of Canada stands ready to fight beyond the seas."[19] And recognizing that the great number of Canadian immigrants who came from enemy lands might fear that they would become objects of persecution, he pledged that "so long as they do not attempt to aid the enemy they are entitled to the protection of the law . . . having invited them to become citizens of this country, we owe to them in the trying circumstances in which they are placed the duty of fairness and consideration."[20] Great efforts to secure substantial war orders for

[18]P.A.C., Borden Papers, v. 333, Speech, Toronto Arena, 27 September, 1915.
[19]P.A.C., Borden Papers, no. 177022, Speech, Canadian Club of Halifax, 18 December, 1914.
[20]*Ibid.*, no. 177074-5, Speech, Canadian Club of Montreal, 7 December, 1914.

depressed Canadian industries, initially unrewarded, were coupled with an assurance to Canadian businessmen that was carefully qualified. "The policy," Borden said, "is not to interfere with the business activities of the country, except in so far as this is absolutely and imperatively demanded . . . by reason of the war or by reason of conditions arising out of the war."[21]

Another phase of Borden's public activity, which he took very seriously, was to explain the Allied and especially the British Empire's case for war to the Americans. He often spoke to elite groups in New York who Borden and his advisor, Loring Christie, thought were influential in the formulation of United States foreign policy. In December of 1915 he told the New England Society that an inconclusive peace would be no peace at all, that the "curse of militarism" would continue. The British Empire was not in the war for self-aggrandizement, he added, "It is for the future peace of the world that we fight to the end."[22] Anticipating another Prime Minister in the conviction that Canada could effectively play the rôle of linch-pin in Anglo-American relations, Borden found these excursions in international persuasion very rewarding. After a similar message to the Pilgrims' Club the following day he recorded that he had "had magnificent reception and very warm congratulations. . . . Wonderful spirit for allies in everyone I meet. Many are ashamed that America not in war."[23]

These public appearances were infrequent, however. Until 1917, most of Sir Robert's time was devoted to solving the detailed and sometimes petty problems of Ottawa's war effort. Though he admired the energy and force of Sam Hughes, he despaired of the chaos left in his wake in the Militia Department. Hughes, whose capacity for detailed work was limited to the appointment of political colonels, was constantly "on tour" of military camps at home and abroad, heedless of Borden's repeated sharp reminders that "your first duty is to administer the Department."[24] The Prime Minister also had a long sparring match with the Governor-General, who had the misguided impression that his office and military experience entitled him to run the war from Rideau Hall. And he and

[21]Canada, House of Commons, *Debates,* March 1, 1915, p. 552.
[22]P.A.C., Borden Papers, no. 175538, Speech, 22 December, 1915.
[23]Borden Papers, Private, Diary, 23 December, 1915.
[24]P.A.C., Borden Papers, no. 15744, Borden to Hughes, 24 September, 1915.

112

Foster were plagued with reports of war contracts of doubtful propriety over which they had no control. The contracts had been let through middlemen, at a substantial rake-off, from the office of British purchasing agents in New York, working in concert with Morgan's financial house. The manufacturers, desperate for orders, appealed to Ottawa, and Ottawa to London, for direct Anglo-Canadian war purchasing, but received negative responses from London. Contracting through foreign sources continued, creating the impression of widespread corruption in Canada. But Borden and his government were powerless to stamp out the "graft . . . that was at the bottom of the affair."[25]

These were bothersome details symptomatic of a much larger problem. In fact, in 1914 the Ottawa government, like its counterpart in London, was totally incapable of carrying out the necessary administrative functions of wartime government. Building an adequate administrative machinery was Borden's most essential task, and he was as inexperienced in these matters as was every other British or Canadian politician. Inevitably there were quarrelsome disputes among his colleagues, jealous of their departmental jurisdictions. Inevitably a number of Ministers, of whom Hughes is only the best known, were found wanting at the time of testing. Inevitably there were blunders, political and administrative, in organization and execution. And inevitably the Prime Minister was out of the public's view, surrounded at his desk by a sea of paper and proposals, inaccessible to the press and so deluged in minutiae that little time was spared for either overall planning or public policy statements.

By 1917 the semblance of a functioning war machine had been established. And the Prime Minister's speeches, the efforts of numerous patriotic associations,[26] and the disheartening facts of the war had combined to make sacrifice politically acceptable to the public. New taxes on business profits and on incomes had been introduced in a hesitant attempt to cure inflation.[27] War production was at a

[25]P.A.C., Willison Papers, no. 1090607, Ford to Willison, 10 June, 1915.
[26]See J. C. Hopkins, *Canada at War*, (Toronto, 1919) , ch. XIII.
[27]J. Harvey Perry, *Taxes, Tariffs and Subsidies*, I (Toronto, 1955) , chs. IX-X. Professor Smith, I think, is incorrect in suggesting that these taxes "stimulated a certain amount of government-desired inflation." ("Emergency Government in Canada," p. 454) . The Government desired just the reverse.

peak, Flavelle's IMB had replaced the experimental, inefficient and scandal-tainted Shell Committee. Labour shortages had replaced wide-spread unemployment and had contributed to the revocation of the no-conscription pledge. In the fall the Cabinet had been re-constructed as a Union government, weeding out the less able Cabinet ministers and those, like Rogers, who were distinctly political liabilities to the government. A number of prominent Liberals, some of proven business capacity, and others with promise of ad-ministrative talent, had joined the government. And the Cabinet itself had been restructured into two functional committees to over-see the conduct of the war and to plan for reconstruction.

In that same year Sir Robert had become a member of the Imperial War Cabinet. For two and a half years he had tried to lead a war effort in Ottawa with only the slightest indications that Cana-dian problems or counsel made any impact at all on war policy in London. He eagerly seized the opportunity Lloyd George's invita-tion offered to exercise whatever influence he had over the conduct of the war. It was clear, however, that to be effective his presence in London would have to be prolonged. That fact, as much as the im-plementation of conscription and the growing Canadian clamour for "National Government," convinced him of the necessity to form a union government despite the nearly unanimous objections from his Cabinet colleagues. Once that had been done and confirmed in what he regarded as a fresh and united mandate in the 1917 elec-tion, Borden believed that his proper rôle as leader was to be a present and active member of Lloyd George's informal council of the Empire. After all, Canada's war was still being run from Lon-don. The difference was that Ottawa now had a spokesman in London who would be listened to. Of course, there was an element of pride and self-flattery in this decision. Borden was fêted through-out Britain as a great leader who had brought his people to the aid of the mother country; he walked with, talked with, planned with the mighty of the Empire — and was counted as one of them. It must have been a pleasant change from the dreary days in Ottawa where he was often regarded as the leader of a confused coalition of oppo-sites in 1911, and of a government responsible for a disgraceful 'gerrymander' and an uncommonly vicious election campaign in 1917. Then too, there was the satisfaction of interpreting the United States he thought he knew so well to the Imperial War Cabinet.

But still, there was much more to this decision than frills and pretence. He worked hard at the Cabinet and, unlike some others, took its purpose seriously. He faithfully supported Lloyd George in his fight against wavering and doubt among the British Ministers and High Command over the conduct of the war. He agreed with the British Prime Minister about the futility of endless slaughter on the impenetrable western front, and raised sufficient complaints in the War Cabinet to force a thorough re-examination of strategy by the Prime Ministers Committee in the summer of 1918. Again, his was one of the strongest of voices in the War Cabinet against the numerous proposals for Imperial aggrandizement in the captured German colonies. Whether, in the light of subsequent events, the positions Borden took and the decisions emanating from them — the Canadian part in the Siberian intervention, for example — were entirely wise is, of course, an open question. That he should have been in London — and later in Paris — to make the decisions seems to be less a matter of debate. Lloyd George's decision opened the door to consultation *and cooperation* with the Dominions in the determination of high policy for war and for peace. It is most unlikely that anyone other than the Prime Minister could have spoken with the same authority or commanded the same respect for his country that Borden did in the War Cabinet and the subsequent British Empire Delegation.

Obviously, there was a price to be paid for playing the rôle of Imperial Statesman. Sir Robert fretted at being out of touch with events in Ottawa. "I should judge that matters are somewhat confused," he wrote to his wife in 1917. "When I left I asked Blount to report to me weekly but he has done so only very irregularly . . . I am sending him a sharp telegram tomorrow." On the other hand, more frequently his Ministers seemed incapable of making any decisions themselves, referring all matters to London or Paris for his determination. "They shower telegrams from Ottawa upon me in great profusion. It takes the time of two decoding clerks all day to decipher them," he complained.[28]

More aggravating, his colleagues seemed to place a lower priority on his services overseas than he himself did. In 1918 he was away from May throughout August, and left again two days before the

[28]Borden Papers, Private, R.L.B. to Laura, 15 April, 1917, 1 December, 1918.

Armistice. His Conservative colleagues thought that Canadian representation at the Peace Conference was relatively unimportant — a view not shared by the Liberal ministers or Borden — and could quickly be settled. After the Armistice all of them were under intense pressure, and the Cabinet seemed unable to cope with the threat of growing social unrest without their leader. Meighen relayed their fears in an apprehensive letter in mid-December.

> The letters I get from Winnipeg, are however, indicative of very great unrest and the same may be said of practically the whole country . . . really, the public mind seems to have got to such a stage of sensitiveness and soreness, that makes the carrying on of Government increasingly difficult. . . . We cannot sustain indefinitely a sufficient measure of public confidence to enable us to effectively do what we have to do through these times without . . . an organization. We cannot indefinitely remain a Government at large, the sport of every sniper, of every liar and of every disappointed partisan. I think the Unionist party should be formally and definitely launched. . . .
>
> For this purpose, I consider it essential that you should return for the Session. . . . I do not think the period of this session can be encountered without you.[29]

"The Acting Prime Minister sent me a telegram yesterday that they propose an early session and that I must return," Sir Robert told his wife. It was proposed that he go to Ottawa to put things in order and then, if necessary, return to the Peace Conference. "I am willing to go on with my work here, which is much more difficult and important than they seem to realize," he added, "or I can undertake the session. I cannot, however, do both."[30] To Meighen he coldly replied, a month later, that the "serious political situation" in Canada "is no worse there than elsewhere," suggesting that the Cabinet pull themselves together and get on with the job. He was unimpressed by any suggestion that he go home to organize a Unionist party.

> If Parliament reaches the conclusion that Union Government has served its purpose and should no longer be continued, I do not know that any of us would have any right to complain. Certainly I should greatly

[29]P.A.C., Meighen Papers, 8, Meighen to Borden, 17 December, 1918.
[30]Borden Papers, Private, R.L.B. to Laura, 22 December, 1918.

116

welcome any respite from the burdens which I have sustained during the past four and a half years.[31]

This seemingly callous indifference to the growing problem of social unrest within his nation and to the political fortunes of his colleagues who, from both sides of the House, had forsaken deeply rooted political allegiances to rally round him for the sole cause of a successful prosecution of the war, goes to the heart of the dilemma of Borden's wartime leadership. He might have been able to "do both." He chose to stay in Paris to enhance the rôle of Canada in international affairs.[32] There was no consolation for his Cabinet in a reminder that economic instability and social discord were a world-wide problem. The Ministers lacked a guiding hand; some reacted to the crisis with more of an eye to politics than policy, all vacillated between hesitancy and extremism. The public, knowing little and understanding less of what Borden was doing in Paris, placing a higher value on the settlement of a strike in Winnipeg than on the determination of the boundaries of Greece, responded predictably: "Borden fiddles while Canada burns."

Many years later Sir Robert observed that the Prime Minister was not only the leader of the nation but "the trustee of the policies and the welfare of his party."[33] In 1917 he sacrificed the interests of his party for Union government, placing, he said, "the winning of the war above every other consideration."[34] In effect, he went so far as to offer a veto over the Conservative appointments if Sir Wilfrid Laurier would only join the Cabinet. It was a noble gesture, to be

---

[31]Meighen Papers, 8, Borden to Reid, 25 January, 1919 in Borden to Meighen, same date.

[32]The decisive factor was Lloyd George's request that he lead the British delegation at the proposed Prinkipo Conference. "Lloyd George asked me to go as Chief British delegate to the proposed meeting with delegates of all the defacto Russian Governments at Prince's Island, Sea of Marmora, on the 15th February. Lord Robert Cecil will accompany me as the second delegate. I have telegraphed to obtain the views of my colleagues as this mission will entail a longer absence from home than I contemplated. It is of course a great honour both to my country and to myself for so important a duty which concerns the peace and future destiny of half of Europe and of Asia." Borden Papers, Private, R.L.B. to Laura, 23 January, 1919. "Tlgm from White saying Council divided as to Prince's Island conference. Told L.G. I would accept. Afterwards tlgms from White and Calder saying I should not go." *ibid*. Diary, 25 January, 1919.

[33]Borden Papers, Private, Letters to Limbo, XXXII, August 13, 1934.

[34]*Ibid*., Diary, 29 September, 1917.

sure, and indicative of Borden's total commitment to the war effort. But there is another side to Union government. For it is equally true that it was both an attempt to destroy the Liberals as a political force and the ultimate confession of failure by the Conservatives of their ability, as a party, to lead a united war effort. Union government did achieve a fair measure of unity among English-speaking Canadians behind the war. The price was very high: the final alienation of a third of the nation from its declared national purpose. Again, in the winter of 1918-1919, the Unionists found themselves politically homeless and were anxious to construct a house of their own. Borden's response was characteristic. Party interest might demand his presence in Ottawa, but national interest dictated his staying in Paris. After all, the fighting was stopped but the war was not over until the peace had been won. By refusing to go home Borden may well have signed the death warrant of the Unionist party while he attended the birth of Canada as an international person.

Ideally, the functions of a wartime national leader might be two. First he should instill in his people the will to fight, arouse their patriotism and commitment to sacrifice. By the measuring stick of mobilization of Canada's fiscal and economic resources and much of her manpower, Sir Robert Borden was generally successful. Where his own limitations were most evident, he turned to others to fill the gap. But a people so aroused can be dangerous to the welfare of the state, and the leader's second function is to restrain and channel their enthusiasms, check the abuses of patriotism, the slander of minorities, the harrassment of aliens and the exploitation of politically and economically powerless groups within the society. In this second function Borden was less successful. In part it was a matter of timing, for the exercise of this second, restraining rôle became most important when the war crisis was at its worst, when conscription had been passed and the Union government had been formed to enforce it. It was a government with a singleness of purpose, impatient and distrustful of minority views and insensitive to the plight of individuals or groups who stood in its way. It was the creature of the war psychology it should have held in check.

Finally, Union government was Borden's own government. And apparently inexplicably he formed it and abandoned it. But here an important qualification is necessary. It is natural to assume that

118

the leader of a national war effort is master of the effort he leads. Asquith, Lloyd George and Wilson were, and may be judged accordingly. But as we have seen, Borden was not. To achieve some measure of power and control he had to leave his government in the hands of others whom he trusted. Union government made that possible; he formed it so that he might with confidence abandon it.

The portrait of Sir Robert Borden's political leadership that emerges from these pages is not wholly attractive. It is decidedly contrary to all of our most cherished assumptions about political leadership. True, his leadership was partially responsible for the eventual creation of an impressive economic war machine, for the continuing supply of manpower to the heroic Canadian Corps, and for the emergence of Canada from colonial status to nationhood. But he destroyed his own party and gave scant encouragement to the party aspirations of the Unionist coalition which succeeded it. More than that, his policy, for conscription surely was *his* policy, divided the country just when it was most in need of unity. Union government was the vehicle of both the assets and liabilities of Borden's political leadership. It was a creature of the politics of war. It violated all the canons of traditional political leadership. At its base was no party nor any recognizable traditional constituency support. It substituted a wartime national purpose for a celebration of peacetime national unity. Its foundation was an artificially created "National" constituency and a singleness of purpose. Most important, by definition, its authority was temporary. When the war had been won, the Unionist mandate would run out and the compelling rationale for Unionism would vanish. Sir Robert Borden recognized that. As his letter to Meighen in January 1919 suggested, the price of victory in 1917 was the eventual surrender of power. That might be the ultimate heresy in Borden's concept of leadership during the Great War. But the heresy may be ours, not his; it may rest in our failure to appreciate the corrosive effect of war upon our traditional concepts of political leadership.

Franklin D. Roosevelt's Wartime Political Leadership

Richard Polenberg

The Second World War presented a serious challenge to Franklin Roosevelt's political leadership. Roosevelt, of course, had broad-gauged goals — to preserve unity among the partners in the Grand Alliance and commit the United States to membership in an international peacekeeping body, to enact a wartime economic program that would ensure a rough equality of sacrifice yet release the nation's productive energies, to protect New Deal reforms during the war and make possible their extension afterward. All of these objectives required that the President maintain his political support at home, that Congress be reasonably responsive to his wishes and, above all, that he win re-election in 1944. Holding the New Deal coalition together in time of war, however, demanded a juggling act of the first order.

The political coalition that had carried Roosevelt and the Democrats to victory during the 1930s had been built around bread-and-butter concerns. It had been composed of blue-collar workers, southern farmers, Negroes, various ethnic minority groups, and portions of the middle class. Although their interests sometimes clashed, so long as recovery was a chief concern they had a good deal in common. But the war subjected this alliance to intense strain, for as problems caused by the depression faded away the bonds uniting the alliance dissolved. In addition, the war raised issues relating to economic policy, race, civil liberties and foreign affairs that further threatened to rupture the New Deal coalition.

How these issues affected the different parts of Roosevelt's constituency, how he went about offsetting their centrifugal influence, and how much success he managed to achieve are the subjects this paper will consider.

Perhaps nothing better illustrated the way in which wartime pressures jeopardized Roosevelt's basis of support than conflicts between the administration and organized labor. This was not without its irony: during the war unemployment came to a virtual end, union membership climbed from 10.5 to 14.75 million, and workers' real wages rose very substantially. Yet even as conditions were improving, Roosevelt feared that runaway inflation could wreck the economy. When someone was incautious enough to suggest that "a little inflation would not hurt," the President replied that he was reminded of "a fellow who took a little cocaine and kept coming back for more until he was a drug addict."[1] Consequently, the administration felt obliged to control wages, restrict strikes, and regulate manpower. To do these things without hopelessly alienating sizeable numbers of workers was no simple task.

Disagreement over economic policy existed on both a theoretical and a practical plane. The administration subscribed to the "inflationary gap" theory, which held that as the difference between disposable income and available consumer goods grew, prices would skyrocket. Wage increases posed a dual danger: they increased production costs for each item and drove up prices by boosting purchasing power. If wage levels were determined by bargaining strength, one official explained, "the stronger bargainers will hold their standard of living at the expense of others, and these others will suffer a double burden, getting an even smaller piece of a smaller pie."[2] Trade unionists, however, rejected this line of reasoning. They denied that wage hikes were always inflationary since workers would put added earnings in the bank and employers could absorb increases out of profits. Similarly, leaders of the American Federation of Labor and the Congress of Industrial Organizations resented any derogation of collective bargaining. Once undermine that process, CIO president Philip Murray warned his executive board, "and see

[1] Harold D. Smith Diary, October 20, 1943, Harold D. Smith Mss (Franklin D. Roosevelt Library) .
[2] Minutes of the National War Labor Board, February 6, 1942, Franklin D. Roosevelt MSS, Official File 4710 (Franklin D. Roosevelt Library) .

how effective you will be with your people back home. You will find out how quick they will tell you to go to hell."[3]

Responsibility for putting a brake on spiralling wages fell to the National War Labor Board. In July 1942, faced with a demand by workers in the Bethlehem, Republic, Youngstown and Inland Steel companies for a dollar a day increase, the Board adopted the Little Steel formula. Taking January 1, 1941 as a starting point, the Board approved a 15 per cent increase to cover the rise in living costs to May 1942, but noted that in applying the formula to other workers larger increases would be granted where necessary to correct substandard wages or other inequalities. But while the formula cooled wages off it by no means froze them and, as a result, unions at first found it possible to live with the decision. Not only did the ruling permit some increases, but it also applied to hourly rates rather than weekly earnings. A fatter pay envelope could still be obtained through overtime, fringe benefits, and travel allowances. Then, too, wage boosts resulting from upgrading of job classifications commonly occurred and were not restricted. Finally, the formula only affected disputed cases. Where war contracts were involved and the government was footing the bill, employers were often quite willing to pay higher wages to attract labor.

In time the administration moved to close some of these loopholes. In October 1942 Roosevelt extended the jurisdiction of the War Labor Board over voluntary wage increases. When even this proved inadequate, the President issued the "Hold the Line" order in April 1943, which deprived the Board of the power to revise the Little Steel formula upward. The Board, however, retained the right to grant increases in "rare and unusual cases affecting critical war production" and in cases of substandard conditions. Consequently, while wages were largely removed from the realm of collective bargaining, they were not bound by iron-clad rules. Labor leaders continued to assail the stabilization program, but the administration, by imposing wage ceilings in a selective, piecemeal fashion and by removing some of the sting with rent and price controls, blunted labor's dissatisfaction.

In some respects, strikes posed an even more ticklish problem than did wage control. On December 23, 1941 spokesmen for labor and

[3]Cited in Paul A. C. Koistinen, "The Hammer and the Sword" (unpub. Ph. D. diss., Univ. of California, 1964), pp. 165-66.

business had agreed to refrain from strikes and lockouts, but the pledge was not legally binding on either side. As their indignation over rising living costs mounted, workers rode roughshod over the agreement. During 1943, 3.1 million men took part in stoppages compared with fewer than 1 million the year before. Of course, this figure was much inflated by the inclusion of 400,000 bituminous coal miners who walked out on four separate occasions. Led by John L. Lewis, the United Mine Workers struck for higher wages and improved safety conditions. The coal strike represented the most determined effort by any group of workers to throw off the yoke of regulation, and it caused terrific public indignation. By mid-1943 John L. Lewis had apparently become the most hated public figure in the United States, and Roosevelt remarked venomously that he would be glad to resign as President if only Lewis would commit suicide.

Yet Roosevelt could not allow his actions to be dictated by personal resentment. Even though Congress in June 1943 passed the War Labor Disputes Act, making it a crime to encourage strikes in plants taken over by the government, an overly harsh response— such as an attempt to draft miners or send them to jail — might easily boomerang. Coal could not be mined without the UMW's cooperation, and besides, drastic measures would offend most of organized labor. Many union leaders who opposed wartime strikes had been placed in an uncomfortable position by Lewis's boldness, and Roosevelt, if he were not to forfeit their backing, had to draw a sharp line between the coal miners and other workers. As one official noted, "The only successful strategy is to isolate Mr. Lewis and his assistants from other more responsible labor leaders."[4] To do this, the administration had to avoid taking any step that might cause labor to close ranks behind the coal miners yet not allow so attractive a settlement that other workers would follow them to the picket lines.

Pulled in one direction by a desire to appease his labor constituency and pushed in the other by public opinion, the President charted a hazardous course between the two. He had the government take over the coal mines, but placed them under Secretary of the

[4]Boris I. Bittker to Oscar Cox, April 27, 1943, Oscar Cox Mss (Franklin D. Roosevelt Library) .

Interior Harold Ickes whose relationship with Lewis was reasonably cordial. He appealed to the miners to return to work but permitted bargaining to continue even while they stayed off the job. He approved a new contract which held hourly rates steady yet granted a substantial increase by paying the miners for portal-to-portal travel. He vetoed the War Labor Disputes Act but asked Congress to authorize the government to draft strikers up to the age of 65 as noncombatants. Roosevelt managed to retain the good will of most labor leaders who applauded his veto — which was promptly overridden by Congress — and paid scant attention to his alternate proposal.

No less than the need to limit wages and curb strikes, the need to control manpower imperilled Roosevelt's standing with labor. In 1943, as the manpower pinch became tighter, the administration experimented with a variety of solutions, but relied wherever possible on voluntarism rather than compulsion. A system of controlled referrals adopted in major cities ensured that new hiring would be done with the approval of a central employment service. Workers could not switch jobs at will, but no worker was forced to change his job and no employer obliged to hire anyone to whom he objected. When these measures failed to halt the deepening manpower deficit, Roosevelt, in January 1944, came out in favor of national service. This legislation — which in its original form would have placed all citizens, men and women alike, at the government's disposal for assignment to whatever job seemed necessary — was a red flag to organized labor.

From the time the scheme was first mentioned until its ghost was laid to rest, labor regarded national service as the worst of all possible solutions to the manpower problem. To union leaders it was a disguised form of "involuntary servitude" that would put the United States on "the high road to fascism."[5] Convinced that most men in the shops would violently resent being told by the government where they must work, labor officials feared that to endorse national service was to betray the rank-and-file. More than this, they opposed national service because its potential as an anti-strike weapon was

[5]Joel Seidman, *American Labor from Defense to Reconversion* (Chicago, 1953), pp. 162-64; *National War Service Bill,* Hearings before the Committee on Military Affairs, United States Senate, 78th Congress, 2nd Session (Washington, 1944), pp. 177-232; Byron Fairchild and Jonathan Grossman, *The Army and Industrial Manpower* (Washington, 1959), pp. 226-237.

all too plain, and because it raised a threat to the closed shop. If the government ordered a worker to leave his job and report elsewhere, it could hardly require him to join a union before starting work. The plan, therefore, seemed to imply a frontal assault on union security.

The battle over national service cut across traditional political divisions. Advocates of the measure included the American Legion and the Communist Party. The communists, of course, were above all interested in stepping up production: members of the Young Communist League referred to themselves as "Production Commandos," and a YCL newspaper ran a comic strip whose hero was not Superman or Dick Tracy but someone who combined the virtues of both — "Production Yank." Joining organized labor in opposition were die-hard reactionaries who had always suspected that Roosevelt wanted dictatorial power and now saw their worst fears confirmed, women's organizations which claimed that the plan, by tearing mothers from their children, would destroy home and family, and businessmen who feared a loss of autonomy. Just as union members did not want to be told where to work, businessmen did not want to be told whom to hire. Given the forces arrayed against it, even a badly watered-down version of national service made little headway in Congress during 1944. Besides, Roosevelt had protected his labor flank to some extent by making support conditional upon Congressional willingness to impose higher taxes on corporations, scale down profits on defense contracts, and authorize effective consumer price ceilings. Consequently, his advocacy of the plan, while it annoyed labor, did not cause many workers to desert the Democratic party.

Not only did Roosevelt's policies with respect to wages, strikes and manpower run an unavoidable risk of offending labor, but widespread migration of workers to war production centers also worked to the administration's disadvantage. This was apparent in the Congressional elections of 1942, which saw the Republicans capture 44 additional seats in the House of Representatives and 9 in the Senate. Democrats suffered more from an astonishingly low turnout than from anything else. Only 28 million people bothered to vote, 8 million fewer than in 1938 and nearly 22 million fewer than in 1940. In district after district the Republican vote fell off slightly or remained stable, but the Democratic vote dropped precipitously.

While this was in part a result of the waning interest in traditional economic issues, to an even greater extent it reflected wartime social upheaval: young men in the armed forces lacked the opportunity or incentive to cast absentee ballots, and war workers who had recently taken jobs in different states could not meet residency requirements. At the time, five states demanded two years' residence and thirty-two others insisted on at least one year. Even when workers met these standards they were often reluctant to forfeit wages by taking time off, and those working night shifts or overtime found voting an inconvenience. Since many war plants were built on the outskirts of cities, commuting back and forth to the polling booths was more time-consuming than ever before.

Issues of economic policy were not the only ones that arose to plague the Roosevelt administration during the war. The President, after all, was trying to hold together a coalition comprising Negroes living in New York City, Chicago, and Detroit, as well as white farmers living in Mississippi, Georgia, and Alabama. During the depression racial concerns had to some extent been submerged; New Deal relief programs had cemented the loyalty of Negro voters in the North despite the administration's lack of attention to civil rights. But the war spurred Negroes to insist more strongly on racial equality, while the South, at the same time, clung more stubbornly than ever to white supremacy. If the Democratic party had an Achilles heel, it was the issue of racial justice.

During the First World War, most Negro leaders — conscious that their position was weak, that President Wilson had proven unfriendly to their cause, and that widespread anxiety over divided loyalties might victimize blacks as well as immigrants — counseled unqualified support for the war. By demonstrating their loyalty, the argument ran, Negroes would earn the good will of white America. But this had not worked very well: at the end of the war most of the economic gains made by Negroes evaporated and a wave of race riots swept the country. Even in 1918 the policy of accommodation had come under sharp attack, and by the 1940s it commanded little support. Not only had experience demonstrated its inadequacies, but most black leaders believed that a militant posture would be more likely to win concessions from the Roosevelt administration. The theme that ran most insistently through the Negro press was that the war must not be allowed to divert energy from the struggle for equality. Nothing less than the end of racial oppression, it was said, would ensure Negro backing for the war, since "only a fool would fight for continued enslavement, starvation, humiliation and lynching."[6]

As a result, civil rights groups stepped up their activities and developed new forms of protest. In the summer of 1941 A. Philip Randolph of the Brotherhood of Sleeping Car Porters called for a march on Washington to protest discrimination against Negroes in defense industry and the armed services. Randolph's movement differed from existing forms of protest in important respects: it attempted to mobilize the Negro masses rather than the middle class, it sought concessions through direct action and publicity rather than quiet back-stage negotiations, and it worked for reforms that would benefit Northern urban Negroes as much as those living in the South. But it departed most radically from the practice of other civil rights organizations by excluding whites altogether on the grounds that "Negroes are the only people who are the victims of Jim Crow, and it is they who must take the initiative and assume the responsibility to abolish it."[7] While the movement adopted a separatist organizational structure its goal was in every respect to achieve full integration. It demanded that the President withhold defense contracts from employers who practised discrimination, and abolish discrimination and segregation in the armed forces and federal agencies. Anxious to have the march cancelled, Roosevelt compromised: on June 25, 1941 he issued an executive order providing that government agencies, job training programs, and defense contractors put an end to discrimination, and creating a Fair Employment Practices Committee to investigate violations.

By 1943 Randolph was advocating disciplined acts of civil disobedience to bring Jim Crow to its knees, and at least one organization, the Congress of Racial Equality, took action along those lines. Founded by pacifists associated with the Fellowship of Reconciliation, CORE endeavored to apply the same tactics of non-violent resistance to the cause of racial justice that Gandhi had to Indian independence. Unlike the March on Washington movement, CORE

[6]*Amsterdam News,* June 7, 1941.
[7]A. Philip Randolph, "March on Washington Movement Presents Program for the Negro," in Rayford W. Logan (ed.) , *What the Negro Wants* (Chapel Hill, 1944) , pp. 135-62.

was inter-racial, but it too stressed "non-violent direct action" and concentrated on the economic aspects of racial injustice. In 1943 CORE sit-ins helped eliminate segregation in movie theatres and restaurants in Detroit, Denver and Chicago. Nevertheless, most civil rights activity during the war was channeled through the National Association for the Advancement of Colored People and the Urban League, which relied on more traditional means of protest: exposure, propaganda, political pressure, and legal action. By 1945 the NAACP had become a force to be reckoned with, and white liberals in the North were attaching new importance to civil rights.

Southern Democrats regarded these developments with horror. Devoted to the belief that the existing order was marked by harmony, yet at the same time made vaguely uneasy by charges that Jim Crow resembled the racial practices of the Nazis, Southerners explained away Negro dissatisfaction as the product of outside agitation. A Memphis, Tennessee newspaper claimed in 1943: "Anyone who hears Delta Negroes singing at their work, who sees them dancing in the streets, who listens to their rich laughter, knows that the Southern Negro is not mistreated. He has a care-free, child-like mentality, and looks to the white man to solve his problems and to take care of him. To stir up sullen discontent and misguided hatreds is wrong."[8] The Southern obsession with race sometimes took forms bordering on paranoia. During the war a tidal wave of rumors swept over the region, playing on fears of sexual inadequacy, race warfare, and the unwillingness of Negroes to accept an inferior status. As white men were drafted, people said, blacks would take control of the South and of white women; blacks, people whispered, were purchasing ice picks and storing them in order to massacre whites during the next blackout; Negro women, it was commonly thought, would no longer work as domestic servants but were forming "Eleanor clubs," named after the President's wife, whose goal was "a white woman in every kitchen by 1943."[9]

Because Southerners played so pivotal a role in the Democratic coalition they demanded that the President pay attention to their grievances. Without the South, one Congressman reminded the White House, "there would be no Democratic Party now and Presi-

[8]*Race Relations,* I (September, 1943) , 22.
[9]Howard W. Odum, *Race and Rumors of Race* (Chapel Hill, 1943) , pp. 57, 69, 73.

dent Roosevelt would not have his position as President and I would not be in Congress. It will be very difficult to break up a solid South and there is only one thing that will really do it, and that is this race question." An Alabaman warned Roosevelt that if the government tolerated challenges to segregation "we are going to face a crisis in the South, [and] witness the annihilation of the Democratic party in this section."[10] There was little variation in the theme: the South could settle its own racial problems, Northern meddling would do no good, law-abiding citizens of both races were making slow but visible progress, the South could only fight one war at a time.

The President's sympathy for victims of discrimination had always been tempered by the conviction that racial problems could be solved only through a gradual process of education, that progress hinged on the Democratic party's ability to win votes from Southern whites and Northern blacks, and that military needs took priority over everything else. He attempted with limited success to mediate between the conflicting claims of Southerners and civil rights activists. He created a Fair Employment Practices Committee, but refused to back up its efforts to weed discrimination out of railway unions; government agencies outlawed wage differentials based on race but made little effort to enforce the ruling; new opportunities were opened up for Negroes in the armed forces, but the army's system of segregation was not seriously challenged. Always Roosevelt endeavored to soothe Southern sensibilities. When someone proposed using "The Battle Hymn of the Republic" as a national rallying-cry, Roosevelt responded: "There is still real objection in the south to some of the words. . . . I wish somebody would eliminate those verses and substitute something else."[11]

A few Southerners actually bolted the Democratic party, but a great many more preferred to snipe at the President's program from a vantage point within Congress. After the elections of 1942, as overall Democratic strength in Congress shrunk, the relative importance of the South increased. The changed complexion of Congress also enabled Southern Democrats to solidify their alliance with Republi-

[10]Frank Boykin to Roosevelt, March 6, 1943, Roosevelt Mss, Official File 93; Eugene Connor to Roosevelt, August 7, 1942, *ibid.*, Official File 4245-G.
[11]Roosevelt to Frederick M. Davenport, May 4, 1942, Roosevelt Mss, President's Personal File 5485.

cans, an alliance which, while it had originated in the late 1930s, became at once more powerful and cohesive during the war. In 1943 Southern Democrats and Republicans tasted blood by liquidating such New Deal agencies as the National Youth Administration and the National Resources Planning Board, cutting the budget of the Farm Security Administration, and passing the War Labor Disputes Act. In 1944 they were instrumental in blocking Roosevelt's proposals for soldier voting and for raising taxes. According to Budget Director Harold D. Smith, Roosevelt commented in February "that he had made up his mind that it is impossible to get along with the present Congress; . . . that for all practical purposes we have a Republican Congress now."[12]

Just as issues of race and the economy affected Roosevelt's hold on Southerners, Negroes and workers, so issues concerning foreign policy and civil liberties affected the political loyalties of ethnic groups. In 1944 more than 25 million people — better than one out of every three eligible voters — were either immigrants or the children of immigrants. The Democrats had always drawn heavy support from these groups, particularly from Irish-Catholics, Germans, Italians, Eastern Europeans and Jews. Several points are worth noting at the start: first, immigrants were heavily concentrated among the working classes and often backed the Democrats out of gratitude for New Deal economic programs; second, conflicts over foreign policy had existed before the United States entered the war, and had influenced the way some immigrants, particularly Germans, voted in 1940; third, the war enabled Roosevelt to solidify his support among voters who strongly identified with his foreign policy (in heavily Jewish precincts in New York City, for example, even some Republican poll-watchers voted Democratic in 1944).

The President, however, was faced with a falling away of support among German-Americans who had grown increasingly isolationist during the 1930s, Italian-Americans who feared that harsh terms would be imposed upon their homeland, Polish-Americans who feared that in planning for peace Roosevelt might allow Russia a free hand in Poland, and Irish-Americans who not only objected to what they regarded as the subservience of the United States to Great Britain, but also were angered by the extent of Roosevelt's collabora-

[12]Harold D. Smith Diary, February 16, 1944, Smith Mss.

130

tion with Stalin. As one Catholic put it, "the American Hierarchy is not in accord with the President due mainly to the Russian situation."[13] Those who took the public pulse found signs of ethnic group disaffection all around. One report sent to the White House detected substantial Republican strength and "apathy among . . . workers who are Italians and among those of the Catholic faith."[14] In August 1944 an opinion poll in New York City turned up a surprising amount of anti-Roosevelt sentiment among lower class voters; the survey concluded that when a closed ballot was used "what apparently happens is that the anti-Roosevelt sentiment of the Irish Catholics, Italians and Germans . . . is brought out."[15]

To stem this drift away from the Democratic party, Roosevelt offered assurances that a vindictive peace would not be sought, pledged his support for self-determination, praised the loyalty of German and Italian citizens, and took pains to build a good civil liberties record. "We know in our own land," he said in the midst of the 1944 campaign, "how many good men and women of German ancestry have proved loyal, freedom-loving, and peace-loving citizens."[16] Significantly, the only group of immigrants to lose its rights — Japanese-Americans on the West Coast — was politically powerless because foreign-born Japanese who had migrated before 1924 were barred from citizenship and most of their children — although born in the United States and therefore citizens — were too young to vote. During the First World War Woodrow Wilson had warned of the dangers posed by hyphenated Americans, and the nation had stressed the importance of assimilation and uniformity; but during the 1940s positive values were more often attached to pluralism and ethnic diversity.

Tolerance toward persons of foreign ancestry was displayed in a number of ways. Minimal restraints were placed on enemy aliens: they could not travel without permission, were barred from areas near strategic installations, and could not possess arms, short wave

[13]Michael F. Doyle to Steve Early, October 28, 1944, Roosevelt Papers, President's Personal File 1771.

[14]Isadore Lubin to Samuel I. Rosenman, October 17, 1944, Samuel I. Rosenman Mss, Box 5 (Franklin D. Roosevelt Library).

[15]Hadley Cantril to David Niles and Samuel Rosenman, August 4, 1944, Rosenman Mss, Box 4.

[16]Samuel I. Rosenman (ed.) *The Public Papers and Addresses of Franklin D. Roosevelt* (13 vols., New York, 1938-1950), XIII, 353.

receivers or maps. But as the war progressed restrictions tended to be relaxed, and on Columbus Day in 1942 Attorney General Francis Biddle announced that Italian aliens would no longer be classified as "aliens of enemy nationality." Aliens could work in factories with defense contracts if they obtained clearance, and forty applications were approved for every one rejected. The contrast with 1917 could sometimes be startling: when a Lutheran minister in Illinois asked permission to conduct services in German he was advised to do so by the Governor, who made appropriate references to the help Baron von Steuben had given Washington's army at Valley Forge.

Roosevelt's efforts to hold the shaky Democratic coalition together culminated in his campaign for re-election against Thomas E. Dewey in 1944. At the outset, the President permitted each faction in the party to operate as a veto group in choosing a vice-presidential candidate; in large part, Harry Truman was named over James F. Byrnes and Henry A. Wallace because he alone was acceptable to the South, Negroes, organized labor and Catholics. During the campaign Roosevelt sought to breathe new life into old loyalties by stressing jobs and economic security after the war, and reminding voters that the Republicans were the party of breadlines and Hoovervilles. Finally, the President attempted to exploit his prestige as Commander-in-Chief and architect of the D-Day invasion. Nevertheless, Roosevelt won his narrowest victory: he obtained 53.4 per cent of the vote and had a margin of 3.6 million votes compared with 5 million in 1940. His continued strength in working class districts, even if somewhat diminished, was reflected in big city returns. In cities with a population over 100,000 Roosevelt garnered 60.7 per cent of the vote. In seven states with enough electoral college strength to have reversed the outcome, Roosevelt's plurality in the largest city overcame a Republican majority in the rest of the state.

The party's urban cast was even more pronounced in Congress where, outside the South, the overwhelming majority of Democratic representatives were elected from urban constituencies. Of the House seats they took from Republicans, fully two-thirds were in districts with a city of 100,000, and one-third were in districts with a city of 500,000. Unlike 1942, when migration and a correspondingly low turnout had hurt the Democrats, in 1944, as the CIO's Political Action Committee launched an energetic registration drive and more war workers were able to meet residency qualifications, safe Republican districts were suddenly thrown up for grabs. This was particularly true in cities in the midwest and on the Pacific Coast which had received a large influx of workers from the South. One Republican in Washington explained, "I was beaten by the votes of several thousand war-workers who had recently come into my district;" in Illinois, another candidate ascribed his downfall to "registration of all voters, thousands of whom had migrated from Southern States during the past two years to seek employment in steel mills and defense plants."[17]

Despite his popularity among working-class minority group voters, Roosevelt was criticized during the war on the grounds that he sacrificed liberal interests on the altar of military expediency— that his economic policy ignored the needs of the underprivileged, that he acquiesced in depriving Japanese-Americans of their freedom, that his commitment to racial equality was at best half-hearted. Historians have, sometimes with good cause, made similar accusations. Yet in condemning Roosevelt because he did not pursue a reformist or libertarian course in wartime, historians should avoid judging the past either by present-day standards or on the basis of information that is available now but was not available then. Today it is evident that Roosevelt might have done some things differently, that, for example, the danger presented by the West Coast Nisei was blown all out of proportion; in 1942 this seemed much less certain.

Moreover, any assessment of Roosevelt's leadership must not ignore certain harsh political realities. Roosevelt believed that his task was to satisfy disparate groups in the Democratic coalition, and this often required him to trim his sails. Nor was he ever a free agent; as the defeat of his plan for a more equitable system of taxation in 1944 showed, Roosevelt was always hemmed in by Congressional conservatives. Then too, Roosevelt took for granted that every act should be judged by its probable effect on the war effort. If the President was unwilling to support liberal measures which he believed might weaken the nation's military capability, could he have done otherwise? To take one instance, should he have supported the FEPC's efforts to eliminate discrimination in railway unions if by so doing he risked a crippling transportation strike?

[17]Fred Norman, Calvin D. Johnson questionnaires, [December, 1944], Emil Hurja Mss (Franklin D. Roosevelt Library).

There were those during the 1940s who would have answered in the affirmative, who conceded that a continued struggle for social gains might involve the risk of a Nazi victory but held that the risk was worth taking. Not only Roosevelt, but the overwhelming majority of Americans, thought otherwise.

Several conclusions, however, may be drawn from a study of Franklin Roosevelt's wartime political leadership. First, to the extent that the war replaced traditional concerns over economic security with problems of inflation, civil rights, foreign policy and civil liberties, it tended to erode Democratic strength. Second, not all of these new issues had equal saliency or posed difficulties of the same magnitude. Wartime economic policy, for example, affected more potential voters, and affected them more deeply, than did foreign policy decisions. Third, in attempting to placate diverse groups of voters, the President had more room to maneuver in some cases than in others. It was much easier to protect the civil liberties of immigrants than the civil rights of Negroes, since the latter forced the President to choose between two groups upon whose support he relied. Fourth, the victory of Democratic candidates for the House and Senate, while often an essential condition for fulfilling Roosevelt's broader goals, gave no assurance that they would in fact be fulfilled. As in the case of Southern Democrats, opposition from within could be as destructive as opposition from outside the party. Finally, by the end of the war the basis of the President's support had undergone certain changes. The Democrats still depended heavily on urban voters but had less strength in the countryside, still drew widespread support from the working classes but witnessed some defection to the Republicans, still relied on ethnic minority groups but were more heavily favored by Jewish than Irish voters, still could count on the Solid South but with less confidence every day. Although Roosevelt's political coalition retained the same broad features, it was not precisely what it once had been.

Hemingway's Unpublished Remarks on War and Warriors

Bickford Sylvester

Ernest Hemingway is obviously the one creative writer whose
name could not be excluded from any interdisciplinary consideration of war and American society. His is the most celebrated
fictional treatment of the impact of war on the American consciousness during the first half of our century. That impact is, of course,
the explicit subject of most of his fiction, including, we know now,
his posthumous *Islands in the Stream;* his response to combat is
reflected even in *The Old Man and the Sea,* in ways not often recognized. Hemingway's twentieth-century Americans abroad learn
largely through war the European lesson Henry James' protagonists
learned through social experience: that destiny governs man and
not the other way around, that our only freedom is an ironic
awareness of the trap and our only triumph an ability to exploit
certain strategies for grace and occasional pleasure in the face of
absolute knowledge that there is nothing we will not lose except our
dignity. Those strategies for exploiting adversity Hemingway had
always seen as working prerequisites for fighting men, whether
they opposed bulls, dangerous game, or other men. But it was
the very best combat soldier—modern society's gladiator about to
die and bearing his lot with élan—who lived out most consistently
and intensely the "distilled essence" of Hemingway's vision of
human existence.

While still in his 'teens in Italy Hemingway had met one such
man, Eric Dorman-O'Gowan, later a Major-General in the British

Army. It was Dorman-O'Gowan who impressed upon Hemingway the lines from Shakespeare's *Henry IV* which were later to appear in "The Short Happy Life of Francis Macomber": "By my troth, I care not; a man can die but once; we owe God a death and let it go which way it will he that dies this year is quit for the next." Another soldier early incorporated into the Hemingway myth was Colonel Charles Sweeny of the Foreign Legion, whom he first encountered in 1922. But despite his life-long admiration for Dorman-O'Gowan and Sweeny, it was in 1944 as a *Collier's* correspondent visiting the American 1st Army's Fourth Infantry Division in France that Hemingway met the commander of its 22nd Regiment, Colonel Charles T. Lanham (now Major General, Ret.), and began what was possibly the most important male relationship in his adult life. To put it in rather facile psychological terms, one might say that at the age of forty-five Ernest Hemingway met his spiritual father, the living embodiment of a masculine role-model he felt had been lacking in his own background, but which he had created in fantasy and had emulated in his work through the medium of fictional protagonists who served as his own idealized alter-egos. More simply, "Buck" Lanham, so genuinely confident that he required no compensatory display, represented the self Hemingway felt potentially his own, the self his personal conflicts often forced him to obscure, but that he had been obliquely proclaiming throughout his artistic career.

This admittedly tentative analysis of the psychology involved is based largely upon a voluminous run of letters from Hemingway to Lanham.[1] These letters were part of Carlos Baker's working material as he prepared his biography of Hemingway, and as such will eventually be accessible to scholars at the Kennedy Library. The correspondence was particularly heavy for a decade following the meeting of the two men in 1944 and continued until Hemingway's suicide in 1961. This paper will confine itself to illustrations, primarily from these letters, of Hemingway's attitudes toward what

[1] I am indebted to Carlos Baker and General Lanham for permission to examine these letters and to General Lanham for considerable help with the background and preparation of this manuscript, although I alone am responsible for its contents. It should particularly be emphasized that in General Lanham's own opinion my analysis "vastly" overstates what he meant to Hemingway.

he called the "sad science" of war and the men who practised it. The purpose is to present rather more information than analysis, in some cases duplicating Baker's account of this period in Hemingway's life and in others providing supplementary details which illuminate much of what appears in Baker's flatly factual rendition,[2] qualifying and possibly correcting in matters of emphasis. We can gain some fresh sense of the personal reasons why war particularly lent itself to Hemingway's monolithic, myth-making imagination. And for those whose concerns are not essentially literary, there should be some incidental interest in the anecdotal references to recent history in the making as viewed by an observer as celebrated as the figures and events themselves.

When Helen Kirkpatrick was asked to write Lanham up for *The Saturday Evening Post* she turned to Hemingway for his estimation of his friend. He sent a copy of his reply to Lanham, so that it is included in the letters. For Hemingway, Lanham in action personified absolute purity of professional purpose — unbroken resolution and endurance in the face of exhaustion, together with the ability to maintain intelligent efficiency without tightening up, and to sustain wit and gaiety in the face of the most terrible odds. The combination, familiar to any reader of Hemingway's fiction, would serve aptly to describe Santiago in *The Old Man and the Sea,* for whom Lanham was a primary model. We find the same pattern in Hemingway's admiration for British Air Group Captain Wykeham Barnes, whom he had earlier observed on some especially perilous missions and whom he described in a letter to Lanham. Again, what Hemingway remarked was the complete accuracy of performance managed with calmness and utter lack of pretension or self-consciousness. And again there was the reference to gayness before the imminent likelihood of death. One thinks of Yeats' description in "Lapis Lazuli" of those carved figures from a wise civilization that had passed all concern for individual survival: "their eyes, / Their ancient glittering eyes, are gay." Men like Lanham had moved into what Hemingway elsewhere called "another country," where the ultimate mortal distraction has no

[2]Careful consultation of Professor Baker's biography, *Ernest Hemingway: A Life Story* (New York, 1969) is essential to any full consideration of the material in this article. The biography is dedicated, in part, to Buck Lanham.

meaning, so that adversity merely intensifies the richness of existence. When you have been hit hard, he later wrote of Buck and
himself, and have seen your heart drive your blood out before you,
you are inured to everything. Possession of this secret earned praise
even for General Barton, Lanham's divisional commander, whom
Hemingway sometimes thought of as an impure soldier and parodied as "The Lost Leader." Hemingway remembered once seeing
Barton talking on the phone when an 88 shell ripped through the
command post taking off an attendant's leg, the heated round
searing the wound on the spot. Barton's voice on the phone never
changed in spite of the sound and the sight, and Hemingway
marked this forever in his favour. And there was Jean, Hemingway's
devoted Free French scout during the impromptu and technically
illegal reconnaissance missions he organized in France. Jean had
the ability to exercise an inborn talent for terrain and observation
with cheerful efficiency under all conditions. Hemingway found this
performance aesthetically attractive, like that of a fine animal.[3]

But Jean was too entirely instinctive to represent the ideal. The
"wonderfuls," "the more than merely mortal" (the latter is Buck
Lanham's phrase) , were those soldiers who possessed their equa-
nimity despite a full awareness of all the futilities involved in war
and an intellectual grasp of the frequent stupidities of the big
picture. For Hemingway the ability to overcome a sophisiticated
consciousness of inevitable injustice was the dimension that gave
man his unique dignity among all the creatures, as *The Old Man
and the Sea* dramatizes, and as I have suggested on other occasions.[4] Thus when he wrote to Lanham that that novel had in it

---

[3]Hemingway simply could not believe, at first, the charges later brought against
Jean for collaborating with the Germans after Hemingway's departure. When
the charges were confirmed, and Hemingway learned of the extreme duress that
occasioned the lapse, he was immediately sympathetic. According to General
Lanham, the horrifying story of Jean's ordeal is one of the major portions of a
book by C. Sulzberger entitled *The Resistentialists*, being prepared for publication.

[4]"Hemingway's Extended Vision: *The Old Man and the Sea*," *PMLA*, 81
(March 1966) , 130-138; " 'They Went Through This Fiction Every Day';
Informed Illusion in *The Old Man and the Sea*," *Modern Fiction Studies*, XII
(Winter 1966-1967) , 473-477. The former article, exposing Hemingway's final
vision of a natural order based upon harmonious opposition, would be useful
to those wishing to consider further the various references above and below
to Hemingway's positive attitude towards struggle and adversity.

all the things he and Buck believed in, he probably referred to their conviction that no one has a more consistent need to meet this human obstacle to resolution than the military man. As he had written earlier to Lanham, he had always considered injustice the central characteristic of a soldier's life. But the pure soldier, as Hemingway's ideal man, was the purer for adversity; and intelligence made things all the harder. Hemingway wrote that he would need a novel to characterize Buck, and when he was later creating the demoted General, Colonel Cantwell of *Across the River and Into the Trees* — like Santiago, modelled on Buck, Charles Sweeny and himself, he claimed — Hemingway wrote that it was about an intelligent, well-rounded fighting man opposed by the world (as Hemingway saw Lanham to be thwarted by military bureaucracy). He emphasized the word "intelligent." Very little is apparently known about his other model, Charles Sweeny. But, significantly, Hemingway's earliest personal military hero, Eric Dorman-O'Gowan, whom the distinguished military historian, Sir Basil Liddell Hart, called "one of the most brilliant soldiers that the British army has produced in modern times," encountered a disastrous reverse in his career upon the miserable sacking of his chief, Auchinleck, in North Africa in 1942. Both Sir Basil and the author R. W. Thompson have written to me with some heat that Dorman-O'Gowan's original, strategic mind and his scintillating personality were clearly penalized by threatened bureaucratic superiors. And Hemingway would have agreed. He wrote in one of his letters that Sir Eric would have had the highest command if there were any justice in the world.

There is emphasis on military adversity and injustice throughout the letters. The greatest fight in that part of Lanham's career experienced by Hemingway was the Hürtgen Forest siege in November and December of 1944, Passchendaele with treebursts, as Hemingway described it. Lanham lost a great many men. His bitterness over the decimation is obliquely alluded to, one suspects, in some of Cantwell's sourest ruminations in *Across the River;* it is perhaps the Colonel's "secret sorrow" that has perplexed critics. Yet as Hemingway wrote to Lanham, the blame was not his but that of those who conceived the plan at SHAEF. In other cases he complained that the 4th Division was twenty-five minutes ahead of the 16th infantry at Omaha Beach, first into Paris, and first into Germany, all without the slightest public or Allied appreciation.

The lot of the infantryman was for such reasons more emblematic of sacrifice than that of Christ on the Cross. (Charles Scribner's judgment was at one point disparaged because as a former cavalryman he was in Hemingway's view limited in his knowledge of true fighters. Scribner, Hemingway's publisher, had claimed no officer and gentleman could possibly speak to a woman as Cantwell speaks to Renata.) The engagements that interested Hemingway were fought for territory that was the roughest to defend: in Spain the defense of the road to Valencia and the taking of Guadalajara had it all over the more publicized "name fights" like University City. And the unbelievable stupidity of high command always increased the odds. It was the distilled essence of such extreme, unrecognized adversity, Hemingway later vowed, that he hoped to universalize in his long novel on the land, sea and air, as he felt he had done in *Across the River* and *The Old Man and the Sea* (where he said it had been distilled and then redistilled).

It is extremely revealing that of all the leaders in earlier military history Michel Ney, Napoleon's rearguard commander on the French retreat from Moscow, who was later executed by the monarchy as a traitor while confirmed turncoats like Bourmont were honoured, was Hemingway's favourite and the one he most identified with. His statue near the Closerie des Lilas was a Hemingway shrine. (And he consistently referred to him in the letters as "Mike" Ney, indicating his feeling of intimacy and giving us a glimpse into the way he personalized history.) For Hemingway, as we know from his fiction, man's life is a retreat from birth to death before the invincible forces of destiny. We are beaten whether we realize it or not, "winner take nothing." And the man in retreat, resolutely fighting backwards like Ney, making the enemy pay for every inch of ground, is most consciously engaged in the archetypal act. Free of the illusion that his struggle can achieve practical victory, he gains confidence in the things he can salvage: the pure satisfaction of performance for its own sake, and the vital intensity of experience born of opposing overwhelming adversity. We think here of Hemingway's protagonists in the latter part of his career especially, including both Thomas Hudson and his German opponent in *Islands in the Stream;* and the letters show how closely those figures reflect his sense of his own life. He got his confidence, he wrote, in Spain in the 'thirties when he learned how to "fight backwards," just as his wife Mary got hers in Casper, Wyoming when it had been completely accepted by everyone except Hemingway himself that she would die of a hemorrhaging tubular pregnancy. Hemingway had a great advantage when pursuing in battle, he wryly remarked, because he was so familiar with retreat that he could think like the victim. His father's suicide, he noticed, had happened at just the time to complicate his efforts to rewrite the manuscript of *A Farewell to Arms*; and his second wife Pauline's attempts to smother him emotionally had intensified his struggle as he wrote *For Whom the Bell Tolls*. But if you got rid of the misplaced youthful illusions of success, as he had after his early experiences in Italy, you could calmly pronounce an obscenity in the faces of your universal antagonists and coolly prepare a counter-punch. That way you could at least earn the right to hold your head up when you returned to the scenes of your defeats. He had now been back to every place he had ever lost, he wrote in 1953, and had been respected there by those in a position to know the score. He would rather have that than all the battle decorations he had never won.

Hemingway's definition of the impure soldier is predictable enough from the foregoing. Only the first two stars of a general's rank meant anything, he wrote, because they were the ones for crafts-manship. The rest were for politics. He detested the uncommitted professional, the rear-echelon, pistol-slapping officer who sought command to gain status rather than to satisfy his craft passion, and whose angling for position involved intrigue, military officiousness, and callousness toward enlisted men. But he also detested what he felt was the feminine psychology of those who foolishly believed in military democracy. For he agreed with an article by Bruce Bliven in *American Mercury* (July 1946) that democracy was in-imical to efficient performance and that the pure purpose of the craft had to come first. Partially for this reason he had contempt for military psychiatrists and for all the sentimental hypocrites who forgot that the business of war involved risk and death. He sneered at Ernie Pyle dying a thousand deaths for our noble troops killed by their own artillery barrage, when (according to a statistic ap-parently of his own invention) it was technically required that twenty per cent casualties be allowed on your own side if the artillery cover was to be close enough in to save a far greater number of lives. He disparaged what he claimed was a Geneva Convention rule against night fighting. Anything that shackled the craftsman violated his philosophy that death and killing must be accepted and then discounted in this world, and that for the military man to forget this was especially absurd. It was ridiculous, for example, not to live off the enemy in his own country but to eat K rations in Germany as though on a YMCA outing.

Accordingly, he derided alleged fighting men who did not understand the ultimate kindness of discipline. When Lanham was on a postwar inspection tour, Hemingway (who never volunteered advice on any aspect of command) offered his approval after Buck had performed the surgery required to root out incompetent officers. It was necessary in the name of compassion for those who would fight under them in the inevitable next conflict, Hemingway thought. He declared that he himself would relieve Christ on the Cross if He was losing His touch, although (one is glad to report) he allowed that for a man like that he would try to find another good job. Soldiers may hate a disciplinary commander during a fight, he observed, but afterwards they may love him for the feats his discipline has allowed them to accomplish. In this connection he often thought of Stonewall Jackson, whose death from a stray bullet from his own side nudged Hemingway's sense of irony, since Jackson was so prone to use a firing squad to maintain discipline. But Jackson was a marvel at manoeuvering, and he got that speed only by discipline. Hemingway proposed a toast to him as a master craftsman who could manoeuver — the ultimate compliment from Hemingway. (Indeed, the critics should make more than they have of the Jackson parallels in *Across the River*.)

This is not to say, however, that Hemingway's ideal commander had the impassioned tunnel vision portrayed in the recent movie on George Patton. Hemingway admired, after all, purity of purpose specifically conditioned by the widest perspective on reality, and he spoke favourably of such balanced leaders as Omar Bradley and Pete Quesada. It was false sentiment he deplored, because it showed lack of real combat knowledge. He winced at Faulkner's picture of Christ as a corporal in *A Fable*. And he dismissed the uninformed mewling of Saroyan's war novel *The Adventures of Wesley Jackson* as the predictable product of a correspondent who had carefully avoided combat. Baker attributes Hemingway's hostility toward

Saroyan when the two writers were observing the war in 1945 to some unflattering remarks Saroyan had made about Hemingway years earlier in *The Daring Young Man on the Flying Trapeze*. But we have only to read Saroyan's *Wesley Jackson,* which appeared in 1946, to see why Hemingway had found it easy to rationalize this grudge and therefore to snub and taunt Saroyan when Saroyan was supposed to be covering the war. "Jill," says Saroyan's supposedly battle-tested protagonist to his wife at the end of the novel, "I died tonight when I saw our house in London gone, because I was afraid you were gone too, and that killed me — and Joe's dead — yes, he's dead, Jill — and your brother Mike's dead — all these things killed me." But he's not been killed, we notice; he's standing there clasping his healthy wife, and nobody who truly knew about dying and loss — I am sure Hemingway would say — could refer to death so meretriciously. "Human beings must not murder one another," Wesley declares at the end. But he hasn't paid the dues to make such a proclamation. Joe and Mike could tell him that human beings *will* murder one another and that that's where you begin, not where you end. But Wesley has all he wants in his arms (no farewells for him) and he wouldn't understand. At any rate, Saroyan might have known something of war, Hemingway hints in mentioning the novel, had he gone where the killing was; but he betrayed his writer's trust to seek out the truth, at least in Hemingway's view, and that was his crime. Hemingway accordingly suggests that we might well kill all Armenians.

By the same token, *The Gallery,* by John Horne Burns, Hemingway thought beautifully written and true. And again a glance at the novel tells why. It contains more compassion for the victims of war than Saroyan's book, for Moe (the subject of the last portrait in the gallery) grasps love briefly at the end only to die capriciously on the final page. *That* is the way it was; that is sentiment rather than sentimentality.

Hemingway's view of one further war novel helps us to see what he considered perhaps the worst result of perverted military thinking as reflected in the fiction of correspondents who got their war secondhand from those uncommitted soldiers who made life hard for men at the front by contributing to the public's false picture of war. Hemingway deplored Irwin Shaw's *The Young Lions* only partially because, as Baker tells us, he thought Mary and himself maligned as two of the characters in the book. His deeper reason is revealed in the letters, which are especially vituperative here. In view of the popular conception of Hemingway's blood lust, we should note his hatred of that perverted vision of combat that leads to atrocity fiction. He detested atrocity stories, he said, because of the false sentiment for the victims and for the sadistic relish they concealed. Shaw knew nothing of combat but he did have instead a frustrated sadism which was repulsive. (Hemingway disliked Robert Ruark's *Something of Value,* possibly for the same reason. At any rate, he considered the book a compilation of fraudulent stories that phony white hunters had been telling since Hemingway's first trip to Africa, so that only an untested observer could credit them and, one infers, only a dishonest writer principally guided by sensationalism could apply them to the Mau Mau situation.) Shaw's novel contained erotic fantasies of beating up others, like the wishful yearnings of a bad SS man, he said. If Shaw had ever truly faced the gallows or genuine combat men like Buck and himself, he suggested, he would know real death and not need to indulge in perverse enhancements of the experience. Real killers killed for something beyond killing, he implied, and therefore thought nothing of the act itself — as Shaw would find out if he ever messed with Hemingway. He then went on to consider removing Shaw's facial and genital organs, disembowelling him, and more. No doubt Hemingway would defend this sadistic fantasy of his own as justified by its object — and make of it what we wish, we must admit that he reserved this sort of thing for his letters, not his novels.

With this intense and structured set of likes and dislikes, then, it is easy to see why Hemingway so revered Buck Lanham, the man who actually lived Hemingway's rigid paradigm for human behaviour. To top it off, there were certain shared personal interests, as General Lanham has remarked to me, interests that increased Hemingway's sense of affinity. They quoted Proust and Shakespeare to each other as Buck fought. And when Hemingway heard that high command had changed the time for an attack five times in one night during the siege of Paris (so that the French could catch up and be allowed into the city first), he remarked to Buck, "What did they think it was, a moveable feast?" According to General Lanham the two men came to use the phrase "for many things," an indication that the soldier responded to its complex implications in the mind of the artist who was later to use it as a title. Such a combination of sensibility and martial toughness must have been irresistible to Hemingway. And Buck shared his love for markets, for "all the beautiful fruits of earth and air," as Buck put it. Furthermore, Lanham was a sometime poet and practical linguist, as Hemingway prided himself in being. Then too, Buck appreciated Hemingway as a man. He let Hemingway know that he was deeply grateful when Hemingway rushed from a sick bed in Paris to be at his side during the Battle of the Bulge. And there is a revealing letter from Lanham to Hemingway in which Lanham says, "Nobody — none of your phony friends — has written of the Hemingway I know. We hear of the Maestro Hemingway, the soldier Hemingway, gamekiller Hemingway, the Hemingway wounded by life, but the real Hemingway was the one known to the 22nd Regiment."

In all the portrayals of Hemingway, he remarks, there is never the man he knows. Nobody has written of Hemingway's restraint in a world without restraint, of his remarkable personal discipline, which is his *central* characteristic and virtue. For Hemingway this must have been that rare gift, which any of us can appreciate, of having an idol see us as we secretly wish to see ourselves. Thus my opening reference to Hemingway's having discovered a father image. If Buck sometimes felt vicarious when thinking about Hemingway's life, Hemingway wrote, so did he when thinking about Buck's — and often, too. This explains why it was Lanham — the truly tough and tested man who could afford to be gentle — who finally made Hemingway most aware of his need to temper his overcompensating personal ruthlessness, his lack of tolerance and "kindness." And this explains, incidentally, that central conflict in *Across the River* that is usually overlooked by critics: Cantwell's conscious struggle to temper his ruthlessness. Hemingway had lacked in early life a male model strong enough to impress all this upon him. It took Lanham to get the message across by precept. And there is a poignant touch of almost boyish deference and reverence in Hemingway's declaration that he would get into history, not as a great writer, but because Buck Lanham had commanded the 22nd regiment and Hemingway was along with him. Indeed, as he once wrote, love would not be too strong a word for him to use.

Thus, although we have known that Hemingway frequently

longed to be a soldier himself, after these pronouncements we can see why that longing was surprisingly pronounced following his association with Lanham in battle. This point has never been made strongly enough, although Baker perhaps implies it. He never felt like a civilian, Hemingway wrote of himself after he returned from Europe. He had never preferred to shoot animals, but only the kind that shot back. He did not really believe in anything at all except in fighting for his country or its good. The things he wanted were first to be a soldier, then to give and receive love, and to raise happy children. The only animate things he loved were good soldiers, animals, and women — basically in that order. In war he had had the feeling of immortality, and now he had the feeling he might not live a year, which was something he hadn't had to cope with since 1936, when (he implied) he started in Spain a continuous series of involvements in combat. The likelihood of a natural death depressed him, he said, and he could only be relieved by occasional visits from true fighting men who helped him relive the war. If you could really read a map and think ahead of the opposition, he claimed, you got bored being a lonely writer with no comrades. It was like being a knuckle ball pitcher with a crippled outfield. He loved Miss Mary, he said, but he missed the sad science of war.

Accordingly, he experienced a conflict between fighting and writing. He couldn't write well after any war, he said; he must try not to think of the war so he could write. Finally there is a fundamental and rather startling confession: he had never wanted to be a chickenshit writer; he wanted to be a soldier like Buck Lanham. The old futile wish, he wrote with deep feeling.

This confession gives us a perspective for viewing Hemingway's repeated attempts to approximate actual service. His wish to serve as an official fighting man was worthless because of his faulty eyesight and other physical disabilities. But he had been an ambulance driver in the First World War, a sometime unofficial guerilla in the Spanish war, had organized "the crook factory," a rather bizarre semi-official counterintelligence organization in Cuba during the early part of the Second World War, and had got official permission to go sub hunting in the Caribbean after that had folded, using his fishing boat the *Pilar*. But while a correspondent with the 4th

Infantry Division, during the period when he was close to Lanham, he had found a way of playing soldier that was the most satisfying of all these peripheral functions. He had organized that unofficial reconnaissance group mentioned above. And while ostensibly covering the action for *Collier's* he had actually carried arms, probed enemy territory, and in fact often provided the 4th Division with valuable information. He took great pride in his role as an observer, for which he did in fact have extraordinary talent and learning. It is touching as well as significant that the combat role he found so fulfilling was that of the precise, realistic observer and analyst, exactly the role which as a chronicler of life he played so superbly but with nowhere near the same feeling of self-esteem. It is, indeed, rather pathetic to see him imagining the next war when he could again serve Buck as an observer and consultant — as a professional without portfolio, as he rather bitterly put it — all this at just the time when his sensibility was preparing itself to bring forth *The Old Man and the Sea,* a far greater contribution to everything he and Buck believed in than anything he could have done on the battlefield.

But he most wanted his observations to be applied on the field, and he sometimes sent them not to *Collier's* but to the command post, allowing others to put the material in writing for the press. He claimed that he fed information to Gorrell of the United Press and to Ira Wolfert of the North American Newspaper Alliance and Wertenbaker of *Time* and *Life,* because they could get it into print quicker than *Collier's* and thus better help the division's public image. Thus he excused himself for allowing a less accurate reporter to misrepresent the division in *Life* on one occasion, and at another time he similarly apologized for the inaccurate account he thought Barton and Richard Marr had given of the 22nd regiment in a military publication. Sometimes, of course, he held back details for his later creative use: he claimed he kept the story of Marigny for his own book, presumably Part III of *Islands in the Stream* or possibly *Across the River* (although any such material has been so transformed in the distillation that it is hard to identify it) . And he wrote that he deliberately withheld details of the Paris entry from Malcolm Cowley, when Cowley was preparing his Hemingway feature for a postwar issue of *Life,* because he wanted to use the story later himself. But far more often he was fundamentally motivated by his desire to follow his observations in battle rather than take the time to put them into copy.

It was partly the intensity of this desire for active duty that led him to fantasize those exaggerations and embellishments of fact, some of which Baker has recounted. He imagined, in the first place, that he might have got into the army had he gone to college and that he had unwisely given up a fighting career to be a writer, when, as we have seen, his physical problems had taken such a decision out of his hands. Then he claimed a family military tradition far more legitimate than Faulkner's (his two grandfathers, he said, fought in more battles than all of Faulkner's ancestors combined), and imagined that he himself had actually served within that tradition as well as he could. He had not only contributed a son to the fight and suffered the label of premature antifascist for his efforts in Spain, but had spent hours sub chasing and scouting in France and he hinted that this was legitimate combat. If Philip Wylie was so bitter about fascism, he remarked in another letter, why had he never fought? — as though Hemingway himself had done so. Wylie couldn't know people as well as he because unlike Hemingway he had never killed any. It was in killing men that you knew them, he said, and mentioned heights of human valour he considered beyond Wylie's conception, including the story of a captured soldier who refused to reveal information even when all his teeth were drilled without anaesthetic. Hemingway didn't say that he was actually present at this scene. But he did write in another letter of having shot a defector fleeing from an execution he had himself ordered and then having given the man the *coup de grâce* with a revolver. The man had thanked him for doing his duty. When you have grown up to that sort of thing, he said, it was ridiculous for critics to attack you for not having made the academy of letters. (This was when he was very bitter about the reception of *Across the River* and needed to compensate in fantasy by implying an authentic frame of reference for the story, in answer to charges that it was too bitter a book to be realistic.) Such pseudo-imaginary killings (probably heard of but not personally participated in) are referred to several times in the letters. He had shot men for less, he complained, when annoyed by inefficiency at the post office. He hadn't killed anyone for five years, he wrote in

1949, implying that he had killed in 1944, and that had been five idle years as far as he was concerned — in spite, we cannot help thinking, of all the writing he had been doing.

Our understanding of a frustrated desire to fight that could lead to such compensatory excesses of imagination can help us to accept with some compassion perhaps the most extreme of Hemingway's wishful distortions: his private feeling that he should somehow have been awarded the DSC for his services during an encounter at Rambouillet, France, even though as a civilian he was clearly ineligible.

It was recognition that he wanted, possibly to make up for his irrational feelings of guilt and worthlessness at not being able in every way to match the ideal of human accomplishment he saw in men like Buck. His feelings of frustration at being threatened with deportation rather than officially lauded for having exceeded his duties as a correspondent,[5] must be seen against the psychological background I have presented here. And we must particularly keep in mind the impact of Lanham's recent entry into his life. Hemingway felt embarrassed before Lanham at what he said were the excessive praising falsehoods of John Groth's *Studio: Europe* (see Chapter XII). He insisted that they were inserted after he had seen the proofs of the book. But he felt he deserved more than the Bronze Star, which could be awarded on an honorary basis since it is not exclusively for valour, and which he did receive for his "ability to evaluate campaigns and operations of both sides" while "circulating freely under fire" to get his information. He had done more than that, he said; he had made battle decisions. And the

[5]Hemingway had reason when recalling the action at Rambouillet to resort with particular intensity to whatever compensatory mechanisms he had at his disposal. For he had in fact performed very creditably; yet it was there of all places that fellow journalists observed his several violations of the Geneva Convention's rules for correspondents and planned the accusations that led to his humiliating investigation by the Inspector General, an investigation further humiliating because he could only remain in Europe by perjuring himself (see Baker, pp. 428-430 for details of the charges and investigation). His enforced civilian status, always a frustration, must have seemed all the more hateful a rebuke by destiny now that it required him to deny actual combat; and one can see why, in thinking of his activity at Rambouillet, he may have projected himself as far as one could go into the military, virtually assuming command, as we shall see below, and imagining himself to earn one of the highest awards a soldier can receive.

threat of having violated the Geneva Convention's rules for correspondents had forced him to deny it all. Ike could write his postwar book and enjoy tax exemption because of his service to the
country; but he, he wrote Buck, had to give most of his profits to
the government because he could not admit his activities. Accordingly, he complained, in one hundred years some bastard would
write a book claiming he was a coward and there would be no
record to show how wrong that would be. In one letter he said
facetiously that Comm. Lester Armour of the OSS got his DSC; but
in another he said flatly that it was Ernest Hemingway who should
have received the DSC that was in fact awarded to the commander
of the American forces at Rambouillet, Colonel David Bruce, recently the U.S. Ambassador to the Court of St. James and now the
American representative at the Paris Peace Talks. Hemingway
claimed that he had made more than a majority of Bruce's decisions,[6] when all that could be made officially known was that after
insisting on written orders from Bruce, Hemingway had managed
some partisans and had acted to maintain discipline among some
drunken correspondents and assorted stragglers from nearby military outfits. And Hemingway fumed in his letters at the unfairness
of it all, although in public and in his subsequent fiction he sought
to transmute his rage at such injustice into that sophisticated resignation he so firmly believed in and knew Buck approved of.

[6]Professor Baker's treatment of the episode, while not dealing with this part
of Hemingway's subjective estimate of his role, gives a full and objective account
of the events (Baker, pp. 408-414). Possibly Colonel Bruce, in his admiration
for Hemingway, and with the touch of a perfect diplomat, contributed to an
illusion fostered in Hemingway's mind primarily by the psychological pressures
discussed above. Indeed, this is suggested by the flattering entries in Bruce's
diary (Baker, p. 411).

Be that as it may, however, we should consider Hemingway's mode of discourse in the letters as I suspect he felt Buck to understand it. Many of Hemingway's private statements were implicitly metaphorical and were expected to be received as such. Thus in this instance, perhaps, the decisions he claims to have
made are intended to *represent* for Buck decisions Hemingway might well have
made had he been in command (perhaps he had thought along with Bruce,
privately). Perhaps Hemingway often assumed on the part of intimate audiences
a tacit understanding of some such metaphorical mode and motives and this
accounts for a good deal of the fabrication to which Baker constantly alludes.
Probably Buck was expected to recognize the Rambouillet affair as in part the
stuff of fiction, since it involved unacknowledged merit, a subject both men had
long agreed upon as universal.

The process of transformation is recorded in the work written in the late 'forties and early 'fifties. We have already noticed the struggle between bitterness and acceptance in Colonel Cantwell's *psychomachia*. In *Islands in the Stream,* composed during much of this period, Hemingway needed the satisfaction of proclaiming, via the obvious identification of Hudson's experiences with his own war effort aboard the *Pilar,* that even before going to the European front he had, after all, undertaken an authorized battle command that *might have involved* the kind of decisions and risks he could not be given credit for in France — that *might,* indeed, have led to his death in an official action replete with the ironic discrepancy between careful execution and ultimate practical futility he found characteristic of most engagements. But in *The Old Man and the Sea,* which immediately followed these compositions, we find Hemingway's anger almost perfectly transmuted. And in observing this progress — as in considering all the material from the letters presented here — we can perhaps learn something of this great writer's complex sensibility, particularly of his way of personalizing history and universalizing his experience according to the extraordinary unity of his mythic mind.

A word must be added. If we are understandably critical of the essential values in Hemingway's vision and reflected in his correspondence, perhaps we should remember the following lines spoken by a man about to die in a hopeless battle against vastly superior numbers: "Thought shall be the harder, heart the keener, courage the greater, as our might lessens. Here lies our leader all hewn down, the valiant man in the dust; may he lament forever who thinks to turn from this war-play. I am old in age; I will not hence, but I shall lie by the side of my lord, by the man so dearly loved." This is from a poem written soon after the battle of Maldon in 991. Hemingway's apotheosis of adversity, of the intensity of feeling and experience it provides, and of the human dignity it releases, is as old as the Anglo-Saxon world. And whatever our specific cultural allegiances in today's conflicts, it strikes a chord in most of us who have been educated in the Western tradition. For it is older than Anglo-Saxon England. It is Homeric.

This idealist disregard for individual survival, this assumption of transcendent value justifying the sacrifice of physical life, is rather unpopular during the current celebration of life at all costs in a world seen to contain nothing beyond the flesh. Thomas Hudson's dying assertion that "life is a cheap thing beside a man's work," and his relentless dedication to a violent chase finally devoid of any practical "use," will further alienate those already put off by the metaphysical cast of *The Old Man and the Sea*. Moreover, Hemingway's very success in impressing order upon the raw forces of so terrifying a phenomenon as war is itself an Apollonian victory antithetical to the resurgent Dionysianism in our time. But we might reflect that in their fashionable championship of peace and love many young people are experiencing the exaltation of placing these principles before their concern for their own survival. The names of the causes may change, but the human processes do not. And Hemingway saw deeply into something that is as new as it is old.

Norman Mailer's Civil War

Paul Levine

*"Like many another vain, empty, and bullying body of our time, I
have been running for President these last ten years in the privacy of
my mind, and it occurs to me that I am less close now than when I
began. Defeat has left my nature divided, my sense of timing is eccentric,
and I contain within myself the bitter exhaustions of an old man, and
the cocky arguments of a bright boy. So I am everything but my proper
age of thirty-six, and anger has brought me to the edge of the brutal.
In sitting down to write a sermon for this collection, I find arrogance
in much of my mood. It cannot be helped. The sour truth is that I am
imprisoned with a perception that will settle for nothing less than
making a revolution in the consciousness of our time. Whether rightly
or wrongly, it is then obvious that I would go so far as to think it is my
present and future work which will have the deepest influence of any
work being done by an American novelist in these years."*

Norman Mailer, *Advertisements for Myself*

Is it the present failure of politics or imagination that makes
Norman Mailer appear to be the most important, if not the best,
novelist of his generation? In a time when even Hans Morgenthau
is reflecting on the end of the Republic,[1] it is perhaps difficult to
take seriously any artist who is concerned with less than *"making
a revolution in the consciousness of our time."*[2] Surely, no one,
least of all the novelist himself, would accuse Mailer of false
modesty; yet Mailer's claim to our attention is based on more than

[1] Hans J. Morgenthau, "Reflections on the End of the Republic," *The New
York Review of Books*, September 24, 1970, pp. 38-41.
[2] Norman Mailer, *Advertisements for Myself* (New York, 1959), p. 17.

his self-advertisement. For, unlike many of his fellow artists, Mailer has been obsessed with the relationship between politics and imagination and with the dilemma of the contemporary artist caught between his dual roles of moral witness and social actor. The result has been his continuing dramatization of what one can call Norman Mailer's civil war. To put the matter succinctly, Mailer's work represents the crisis of the contemporary American artist-intellectual as he experiences his special cultural schizophrenia and recognizes at one and the same time that politics is not enough and that art is not enough either.

This drama has been present in Mailer's work since the beginning. Mailer's famous first novel, *The Naked and the Dead,* follows consciously in the great tradition of modern American fiction in its concern for individual responsibility in a mass society. From Hemingway, Mailer took an obsession with the possibilities of individual heroism, and from Dos Passos, his analysis of modern society. Though much has been said about his debt to Hemingway — Mailer himself keeps making the comparison — it was Dos Passos who provided the structural model as well as the sensitive Harvard hero for *The Naked and the Dead*. Indeed, Dos Passos' *Three Soldiers* depicted the situation imitated in countless war novels and films since: the hero is a sensitive individual whose identity is threatened by the dehumanizing process of turning men into soldiers. The idea is revealed in the titles of the main sections of the novel: "Making the Mould," "The Metal Cools," "Machines," "Rust," and "Under the Wheels." The major struggle is, then, not between conflicting ideologies represented by opposing armies but rather between the individual and the army as a total institution. "It seems to me," Dos Passos' hero remarks, "that human society has been always that, and perhaps will be always that: organizations growing and stifling individuals, and individuals revolting hopelessly against them, and at last forming new societies to crush the old societies and becoming slaves again in their turn."[3]

Thus while *Three Soldiers* describes the American army in Marxist terms as a microcosm of American society, it is with the individual that Dos Passos is really concerned. In an unequal contest, his hero must either succumb to the System and be exploited,

[3]John Dos Passos, *Three Soldiers* (Boston, 1964) , p. 421.

rebel against the System and be destroyed, or attempt, in Hemingway's evocative phrase, to make "a separate peace." For Dos Passos, however, there was no such peace: "Whichever won, tyranny from above, or spontaneous organization from below, there could be no individuals."[4] If one emphasizes Dos Passos' position here it is because there is a close correlation with Mailer's, particularly in *The Naked and the Dead*. Indeed, the "liberal" conservatism of the older writer, with its concern with the problem of individualism in a mass society, is remarkably close to the "left" conservatism of the younger. As Mailer describes himself, he is a "Left Conservative. So he had his own point of view. To himself he would suggest that he tried to think in the style of Marx in order to attain certain values suggested by Edmund Burke."[5]

In its indebtedness to Hemingway and Dos Passos as well as its concern for the propositions of biological and sociological determinism at the centre of the American naturalistic tradition, *The Naked and the Dead* would appear to be a most old-fashioned modern novel. And yet, closer study reveals that the novel is actually a radical departure, indeed, a new kind of war novel which marks the beginning of the post-modern era. How can this be?

Part of the answer lies in Mailer's decision to write a novel about the war in the Pacific. His reasons were a mixture of pragmatism (*"it was and is easier to write a war novel about the Pacific — you don't have to have a feeling for the culture of Europe and the collision of America upon it"*) and idealism (*"the Pacific war had a reactionary overtone which my young progressive-liberal nose smelled with the aid of PM editorials"*).[6] Beyond this was perhaps an intuitive perception that the external enemy was a "phantom" and the real enemy lurked within. In a footnote to his explanation of how he began to write about the Pacific war, Mailer reveals the buried element:

> The very last thing [at Harvard] was to try to start a novel about an insane asylum. I had worked in a state hospital for a week the summer before my senior year, and twelve months later, in the summer after graduation, I began real work on the novel which was finished nine

[4]*Ibid.*, p. 343.
[5]Norman Mailer, *The Armies of the Night* (New York, 1968) , p. 208.
[6]*Advertisements for Myself*, p. 28.

months and 600 pages later, just before I went into the Army. It was called *A Transit to Narcissus,* and it was based on a play I had written earlier about the same insane asylum called *The Naked and the Dead.* Yes.[7]

Mailer's first novel begins, then, as a conventional study of war which centres on the experiences of a representative infantry platoon involved in a campaign to capture a remote Pacific island. By showing how the campaign looks from the top and bottom of the military hierarchy, Mailer exposes the inadequacy of the traditional naturalistic explanations. The Japanese army turns out to be a "phantom" enemy; the real foe lurks elsewhere. The officers and men who comprise Mailer's microcosmic society are revealed to be victims of the same mechanisms of repression existing in both army and civilian life. As one G.I. observes, "Even if we do get back we'll get a fuggin. What did it matter if they ever got out of the army? It would be the same thing on the outside. Nothing ever turns out the way you want it."[8] Each man is driven to submit or dominate by more potent forces than mere economic considerations. As General Cummings explains to Mailer's hero, Lieutenant Hearn, "I've been trying to impress on you, Robert, that the only morality of the future is the power morality, and a man who cannot find his adjustment to it is doomed."[9] Behind politics there is psychology; beyond Marx and Darwin there are Freud and Nietzsche.

Thus *The Naked and the Dead* pursues a deeper insight into the relationship between self and society. Already Mailer understood what Norman O. Brown was to later write: "Without an understanding of the seamy side of sexuality there is no understanding of politics."[10] As Mailer polarizes the army into liberal and reactionary factions, the class war, in Ralph Ellison's pregnant expression, is turned into the ass war. Every significant character in the novel is possessed by a powerful irrational demon. The reactionaries, General Cummings and Sergeant Croft, are driven to seek power to compensate for their own felt sexual inadequacy while the liberals, Hearn and Red Valsen, are sexually adequate

[7]*Ibid.,* p. 27.
[8]Norman Mailer, *The Naked and the Dead* (New York, 1948) , p. 577.
[9]*Ibid.,* p. 323.
[10]Norman O. Brown, *Love's Body* (New York, 1966) , p. 11.

but emotionally paralysed, unable to commit themselves to any positive course of action, even love. The rest of the men are as sexually frustrated as they are politically oppressed. Perhaps, as Hearn muses, "the trouble with Americans is that they don't know how to screw";[11] in any event, they are screwed at every turn. The relationship between politics and sexuality is made explicit on the last page of the novel when Major Dalleson, the archetypal military mind, has an epiphany about the role of sex in war: "At this moment he got his idea. He could jazz up the map-reading class by having a full-sized colour photograph of Betty Grable in a bathing suit, with a coordinate grid laid over it. The instructor could point to different parts of her and say, 'Give me the coordinates.' "[12] No wonder that Mailer would later observe about the military mind that one minute in the mind of General Westmoreland was more obscene than all the dirty words in all the dirty novels written in America![13]

Now we can understand why Red Valsen observes bleakly that whatever happens, the men will "get a fuggin." But Mailer's concern lies beyond the realm of self and society in the relationship between man and (inner and outer) nature. As Melville used Moby Dick, so Mailer uses the awesome presence of Mount Anaka as an external focus for the internal confrontations of each of his characters. Like Ahab, Cummings and Croft are mesmerized by the mountain, feeling some kind of mystical identity with it at the same time as they seek the key to its mystery. Like Ishmael, on the other hand, both Hearn and Valsen are repelled by the mountain out of a combination of fear and awe. When Cummings sends Hearn and the platoon on a vain quixotic mission to climb the mountain, Croft transforms the assignment into a personal quest. When Hearn and Valsen refuse the challenge in different ways, the climactic confrontation is forged.

Thus the relation between the novel's structure and its title becomes clear. *The Naked and the Dead:* a process, as in Conrad, of transplanting man from civilization to nature where, stripped to the bone of his existential being, he ends up either naked or dead. In

<hr />

[11]*The Naked and the Dead,* p. 340.
[12]*Ibid.,* p. 721.
[13]Recorded in the film, *Will the Real Norman Mailer Please Stand Up?*

the confrontation with Mount Anaka, each man becomes his own Sisyphus: Hearn ends up dead while Valsen ends up spiritually broken; Croft's obsessive desire to climb the mountain is frustrated while Cummings' dream of using the assault on the mountain as a stepping stone to promotion is shattered. At this point, we may recall Mailer's use of Nietzsche's remark as the epigraph for this last part of the novel: "Even the wisest among you is only a disharmony and hybrid of plant or phantom. But do I bid you become phantoms or plants?"[14]

That polarization between the naked and the dead, between plant and phantom, is pursued on every level of the novel: in the conflict between the officers and enlisted men, between Croft and Valsen, and, most significantly, between Cummings and Hearn. But note that all of them are defeated, for, as Nietzsche said, even the wisest among them is a disharmony. As Red puts it, "Aaah, everybody loses. Red almost said this aloud. It was true. He knew it, they all knew it, everyone of them. He sighed again. They knew it, and yet they still were soft, still didn't get used to the idea."[15]

Everybody loses, but not in the same way. The liberals like Hearn and Valsen lose out to society while the reactionaries like Cummings and Croft lose out to nature — their own human nature. To pursue his personal vision, Croft must subvert the military hierarchy to which he has committed his life, while Cummings' confidence in his ability to control destiny is upset by a series of unexpected coincidences. Moreover, both come to recognize that they are actually dependent upon those they control. Croft realizes that he could not climb the mountain alone. "If he had gone alone, the fatigue of the other men would not have slowed him but he would not have had their company, and he realized suddenly that he could not have gone without them. The empty hills would have eroded any man's courage."[16] Cummings, too, acknowledges that his campaign to turn men into machines has failed. "The men resisted him, resisted change, with maddening inertia. No matter how you pushed them, they always gave ground sullenly, regrouped once the pressure was off. You could work on them, you could trick them,

---

[14]*The Naked and the Dead*, p. 431.
[15]*Ibid.*, p. 577.
[16]*Ibid.*, p. 709.

but there were times now when he doubted basically whether he could change them, really mold them."[17]

But while Mailer's sympathies lie with the liberals, it is the reactionaries who command his respect. Hearn and Valsen may share Mailer's political ideals, but Cummings and Croft reflect his fascination with psychism. Their ideas may be abhorrent but they are dangerous precisely because only they have a vision of transcendent heroism and the energy to carry it through. Thus Hearn identifies himself with Don Quixote and the "bourgeois liberals" of the past while he connects Cummings with Faust and the drive towards totalitarian control in the future. As Mailer remarked, "Beneath the ideology in *The Naked and the Dead* was an obsession with violence. The characters for whom I had the most secret admiration, like Croft, were violent people."[18]

To fathom the full implications of this paradox, we must understand the dilemma of the liberal-intellectual, Hearn, which stands at the centre of the novel. Hearn's problem is similar to that of other fictional heroes of the post-war decade. Like the adolescents of Capote, McCullers and Salinger, Hearn is a psychological orphan who is betrayed by the adult world — in this case, his father figure, General Cummings. And like those other adolescents, Hearn is trapped in an existential situation from which there seems to be "no exit." Even his most rebellious act — grinding out a cigarette on the floor of the General's tent — is a gratuitous adolescent gesture.

On the political level, Hearn is caught in a crossfire between the radical left and right in which he is labelled a hopeless "Bourgeois idealist" by both sides. Cummings says, "The only trouble is, one thing remains with you. Somewhere you picked it up so hard that you can't shake the idea 'liberal' means good and 'reactionary' means evil. That's your frame of reference, two words. That's why you don't know a damn thing."[19] Back in college a dedicated Communist had criticized him for being a "bourgeois intellectual": "You've reacted against the lies of the system, but it's a nebulous rebellion. You want perfection, you're a bourgeois idealist, and

[17]*Ibid.*, p. 717.
[18]Norman Mailer, *The Presidential Papers* (New York, 1963) , p. 136.
[19]*The Naked and the Dead*, p. 84.

therefore you're undependable."[20] Even Hearn recognizes the justice of these remarks:

> It disturbed Hearn deeply. He had been born in the aristocracy of the wealthy midwestern family, and although he had broken with them, had assumed ideas and concepts repugnant to them, he had never really discarded the emotional luggage of his first eighteen years. The guilts he made himself feel, the injustices which angered him were never genuine. He kept the sore alive by continually rubbing it, and he knew it. He knew also at this moment that out of all the reasons why he had begun to quarrel with Conn in officers' mess, one of the vital ones had been that he was afraid of not really caring enough about what Conn was saying. It was true of too many of his reactions. And since his direct self-interest could only move him back toward the ideas of his father, there was no other direction for him to turn, unless there was some other emotional basis for continuing in his particular isolated position on the Left. For a long time he had thought there was one, for even a longer period he had sustained his politics because his friends and acquaintances in New York assumed them as a matter of course, but now in the isolation of the Army, under the searching critique of the General's mind, his fingers were being pulled from the chinning bar.[21]

But Hearn's sense of isolation is exacerbated by his own disillusionment with liberal ideology. Confronted with an apocalyptic global war and with Cummings' prophecy of an imminent reactionary century, he realizes that the liberal imagination is too impoverished to fathom the new urge to power and too ambivalent to offer an heroic alternative. Cummings is right: "The root of all the liberals' ineffectiveness comes right spang out of the desperate suspension in which they have to hold their minds."[22] Thus Hearn recalls his friends, "all the American college intellectuals, . . . with their clear logical voices, their good manners, their kindness, their tact and their miserable, dreary and lucid intelligences" and how "they analyzed politics, sometimes hopefully, sometimes sadly, with a detached and helpless and intrinsically superior attitude. There was good wit, incisive but always peripheral information, and the dry dejuiced hopelessness of all of them with their rational dessicated minds and their wistful contemplation of lusts and evils they

[20]*Ibid.*, p. 343.
[21]*Ibid.*, p. 169.
[22]*Ibid.*, p. 174.

would never understand with their bodies. William Blake angels, gray and clear, hovering over horseshit."[23]

Hearn's rejection of his past closes the circle of alienation around him and brings him to the position of intellectual paralysis and irresolute leadership which finally leads to his own death. Faced with a hostile universe, Hearn says with the other post-romantic adolescents of the post-war decade, "The only thing to do is to get by on style."[24] But style, alas, is not enough in the world of power politics. Shortly before his death, Hearn rehearses the options left open to him and discovers that there is nothing left but a "skinny enough hope" that good will triumph:

> If the world turned Fascist, if Cummings had his century, there was a little thing he could do. There was always terrorism. But a neat terrorism with nothing sloppy about it, no machine guns, no grenades, no bombs, nothing messy, no indiscriminate killing. Merely the knife and the garrote, a few trained men, and a list of fifty bastards to be knocked off, and then another fifty.
>
> A plan for concerted action, comrades. He grinned sourly. There would always be another fifty, that wasn't the idea. It had no use. It was just something to keep you occupied, keep you happy. Tonight we strike at Generalissimo Cummings.
>
> Aaah, horseshit.
>
> There were no answers you could find, but perhaps there were epochs in history which had no answers. Rely on the blunder factor. Sit back and wait for the Fascists to louse it up. . . .
>
> Drought season for anarchists.[25]

Now we can see why Mailer had to kill off his hero in the end. Faced with the prospects of a totalitarian society, the individual can join the System and be exploited by it (like Croft); rebel against the System and be destroyed by it (like Pruett in *From Here to Eternity*); or make a separate peace outside the System (like Yossarian in *Catch-22*). But Hearn is finally too irresolute to do any of these. The ultimate revelation of *The Naked and the Dead* is the death of liberalism as a positive force in the modern world.

[23]*Ibid.*, p. 240.
[24]*Ibid.*, p. 326.
[25]*Ibid.*, pp. 585-6.

This opposition between a dying liberalism and a nascent fascism becomes the central dialectic in Mailer's work, from *The Naked and the Dead,* through his essays on "Hip" and "Square," to his vision of *Cannibals and Christians* and, finally, *The Armies of the Night.* But the more apocalyptic Mailer's vision of political reality becomes, the more intensely his fictive protagonists turn to alternatives of personal salvation. As Mailer transforms the terms of the dialectic, his heroes abandon politics for imagination, liberalism for hipsterism, and Marxism for existentialism. For Mailer, the way out of Hearn's paralysis becomes the way in — "up the upper Amazon of the inner eye."[26] Thus Mailer's work continues to reflect the same schizoid tendencies that Mailer had detected in American life:

> Since the First World War Americans have been leading a double life, and our history has moved on two rivers, one visible, the other underground; there has been the history of politics which is concrete, factual, practical and unbelievably dull if not for the consequences of the actions of some of these men; and there is a subterranean river of untapped, ferocious, lonely, and romantic desires, that concentration of ecstasy and violence which is the dream life of the nation.[27]

It is not surprising that all of his subsequent protagonists — all orphans and veterans, anonymous writers and divided men culminating in Mailer's finest creation, the author himself — develop out of Hearn and his dilemma. In each of the novels, from *Barbary Shore* through *Why Are We In Vietnam?*, we find the same obsessive situation: an unformed narrator, haunted by a memory of killing and crippled by a perception of the intimacy of violence and sexuality, dominated by a father figure whom he must either destroy or transcend, who must perform the existential act of making himself up from scratch. Lovett, the veteran suffering from amnesia in *Barbary Shore*; Sergius, the orphaned flyer psychologically maimed by his memory of napalm bombing Korean civilians in *The Deer Park;* Rojack, the war hero haunted by the face of a German soldier he shot who kills his wife and is thus "reborn" an outlaw in *An American Dream;* and D. J., the adolescent who comes of age during a brutal, mechanized bear hunt just in time to go to war in *Why*

---

[26]Norman Mailer, *Cannibals and Christians* (New York, 1966) , p. 128.
[27]*The Presidential Papers,* p. 38.

Are We In Vietnam?: each seeks an alternative to Hearn's paralysis in Mailer's perception that "a hero is a consecutive set of brave and witty self-creations."[28]

In other words, each protagonist asks the question put by the Princess Casimassima, "I want to know *à quoi m'en tenir*," and each discovers the key to identity in the commitment itself. Lovett finds his alternative in Trotskyite ideology, Sergius in art, Rojack in encouraging the "psychopath" in himself, and D. J. in the orgiastic release of nihilism. The development has been from revolution to rebellion, in Camus' terms, but, strangely enough, the last novel is written out of essentially the same elements as the first: the connection between politics and the seamy side of sexuality, the confrontation with nature as a device for confronting the self, an important literary model (this time, Faulkner), even another Asian war. Apparently, things have not changed very much in a quarter of a century. Throughout, as Sergius notes, the "real world" remains "underground — a tangle of wild caves where orphans burned orphans."[29]

Not surprisingly, one finds the same concerns in Mailer's nonfiction of this period: the increasing impossibility of American political life and the necessity for the individual to find an existential life style. *Advertisements for Myself*, as its name suggests, asserts the primacy of the artist by describing the stages of development in Mailer's presentation of the self. It is a curious kind of autobiography which uses the artist's work as a key to the development of the man. At the same time, in "The White Negro," he was creating an imaginative *alter ego* who "set out on that uncharted journey into the rebellious imperatives of the self"; "the American existentialist — the hipster"[30] who was to serve as the model for Rojack in *An American Dream*. In *The Presidential Papers,* Mailer attempted to unite imagination and politics in a new kind of "existential politics." Implicit in his argument is the assumption that the artist has a significant role to play in the political arena. Mailer sees himself as "a court wit, an amateur adviser"[31] who can act as a guide through the twisted *paysage moralisée* of contemporary *realpolitik.* "This

[28]*Ibid.*, p. 6.
[29]Norman Mailer, *The Deer Park* (New York, 1967), p. 192.
[30]*Advertisements for Myself*, p. 339.
[31]*The Presidential Papers*, p. 1.

book," he writes, "has an existential grasp of the nature of reality, and it is the unspoken thesis of these pages that no President can save America from a descent into Totalitarianism without shifting the mind of the American politician to existential styles of political thought."[32]

Mailer's attempts to inflate the figure of the artist on the political landscape are, curiously enough, disconcertingly close to Lionel Trilling's notion of *The Liberal Imagination*. Trilling wrote that we must "force into our definition of politics every human activity and every subtlety of every human activity." For, "unless we insist that politics is imagination and mind, we will learn that imagination and mind are politics, and a kind we will not like."[33] In an astonishingly naive open letter to Fidel Castro, Mailer makes a desperate attempt to reassert the Romantic primacy of imagination in politics by comparing the two one-dimensional superpowers and concluding, "There is one way in which we are a greater nation than Russia. Our creative artists are greater. Our writers, our poets, our painters, our jazz musicians. We have a life in all our private arts which they do not possess."[34]

By the time of *Cannibals and Christians,* it was clear that the life in all the private arts was having little impact on the life in the rest of the nation, particularly on life in the White House. The book is wryly dedicated "to Lyndon B. Johnson *whose name inspired young men to cheer for me in public,*" and it projects a growing awareness of the impossibility of American politics. The title suggests a further development of the old dialectic between reactionaries and liberals while the book itself proposes an artistic analogue to the kind of guerrilla warfare that Hearn had considered just before his death.

> There's that Godawful *Time* Magazine world out there, and one can make raids on it. There are palaces, and prisons to attack. One can even succeed now and again in blowing holes in the line of the world's communications. Sometimes I feel as if there's a vast guerrilla war going on for the mind of man, communist against communist, capitalist against capitalist, artist against artist. And the stakes are huge. Will we spoil the

[32]*Ibid.,* p. 5.
[33]Lionel Trilling, *The Liberal Imagination* (Garden City, 1954) , pp. 103-4.
[34]*The Presidential Papers,* p. 77.

best secrets of life or will we help to free a new kind of man? It's intoxicating to think of that. There's something rich waiting if one of us is brave enough to get there.[35]

The fruits of this guerrilla warfare are to be seen in Mailer's next novel, *Why Are We In Vietnam?*, in which obscenity is used as a weapon. Though some would argue that the weapon was a booby trap which had blown up in its maker's hands, one thing was clear: Mailer was desperately trying to deal with the moral surrealism in American life. What remained surprising in his fiction, however, was Mailer's inability to create a narrator as interesting as he was. Thus, side by side with his fictional creations, there grew in his nonfiction another *persona* who also seemed to be made up from scratch. This emerging *persona* was remarkably similar to the divided self of Lieutenant Hearn. Perhaps Mailer explained why when he commented on the influence of E. M. Forster on his style:

in some funny way Forster gave my notion of personality a sufficient shock that I could not manage to write in the third person. Forster, after all, had a developed view of the world. I did not. I think I must have felt at that time as if I would never be able to write in the third person until I developed a coherent view of life. I don't know that I've been able to altogether.[36]

The Armies of the Night may be seen as Mailer's attempt to resolve the inner contradictions of his previous fiction and non-fiction in a new form that is part-history and part-novel. The subject of the book is the March on the Pentagon in 1967 in which Mailer participated as a demonstrator against the Vietnam war. Thus the novelist plays a major role in the "History as a Novel" though he is described throughout in the third person. In this manner, Mailer attempts to unite the two roles of the artist — as performer and witness — and resolve the split between politics and imagination that had haunted his protagonists since *The Naked and the Dead*.

Appropriately, the primary metaphor that runs through the book is one of civil war. That civil war extends from the split in the nation over Vietnam through the split in the left over the limits of

[35]*Cannibals and Christians,* p. 221.
[36]*Ibid.,* p. 209.

dissent to the split between generations over the vision of the future. The conflict is once again between Cannibals ("All the healthy Marines, state troopers, professional athletes, movie stars, rednecks, sensuous life-loving Mafia, cops, mill workers, city officials, nice healthy-looking easy-grafting politicians") and Christians ("the Freud-ridden embers of Marxism, good old American anxiety strata — the urban middle-class with their poliferated momumental adenoidal resentments, their secret slavish love for the oncoming hegemony of the computer and the suburb, yes, they and their children . . . on a freak-out from the suburbs to a love-in on the Pentagon wall") .[37] But the dialectic which began in *The Naked and the Dead* has taken a new turn where, in Arnold's famous phrase, "ignorant armies clash by night."

> Mailer was haunted by the nightmare that the evils of the present not only exploited the present, but consumed the past, and gave every promise of demolishing whole territories of the future. The same villains who promiscuously, wantonly, heedlessly, had gorged on LSD and consumed God knows what essential marrows of history, wearing indeed the history of all eras on their back as trophies of this gluttony, were now going forth (conscience-struck?) to make war on those other villains, corporation-land villains, who were destroying the promise of the present in their self-righteousness and greed and secret lust (often unknown to themselves) for some sexo-technological variety of neo-fascism.[38]

Though "Mailer's final allegiance . . . was with the villains who were hippies,"[39] he remains isolated from the main battleground at "that lonely flag" of his Left Conservativism, remarking that "there was no one in America who had a position even remotely like his own."[40] For, at the same time, Mailer is experiencing his own civil war. As an individual he is caught between his desire to get arrested for the Cause and his desire to be released quickly so that he can make a particularly "wicked" party in New York that evening. As an artist he is caught between his belief that "his work was the real

[37]*The Armies of the Night*, pp. 46-7.
[38]*Ibid.*, p. 110.
[39]*Ibid.*
[40]*Ibid.*, p. 203.

answer to Vietnam"[41] and the realization that his work was not enough. Once again, Mailer portrays his hero's consciousness divided between politics and imagination: "stationed between [activist] Lens and [poet] Lowell he felt the separate halves of his nature well-represented, which gave little pleasure, for no American citizen likes to link arms with the two ends of his practical working-day good American schizophrenia."[42]

The outcome of the growing civil war is in doubt. There is a question whether it will be resolved by repression, reform, or revolution. Similarly, the character of Mailer's own civil war is ambiguous. Politics is constantly warring on imagination. " 'The essence of spirit was to choose that alternative which did not better your position, but made it worse.' Mailer was quoting himself again, but not with pleasure, for he was getting ready to go against his own maxims."[43] As he watches a group of college professors turning in their draft cards, Mailer is moved to review *his* alternatives in a new light. "For years he had envisioned himself in some final cataclysm, as an underground leader in the city, or a guerrilla with a gun in the hills, and had scorned the organizational aspects of revolution. . . ." But now he recognizes that his role will be a more modest one:

no gun in the hills, no taste for organization, no, he was a figure-head, and therefore he was expendable, said the new modesty — not a future leader but a future victim: *there* would be his real value. He could go to jail for protest, and spend some years if it came to it, possibly his life, for if the war went on, and America put its hot martial tongue across the Chinese border, well, jail was the probable perspective, detention camps, dissociation centers, liquidation alleys, that would be his portion, and it would come about the time he had learned how to live.[44]

We are back where we began, with Hearn on the eve of his death. The same reactionaries' century is on the horizon; the same tactics of guerrilla warfare are considered and rejected. As for Hearn, so for Mailer, "there was no escape. As if some final cherished rare innocence of childhood still preserved intact in him was brought finally

[41]*Ibid.*, p. 72.
[42]*Ibid.*, p. 125.
[43]*Ibid.*, pp. 217-8.
[44]*Ibid.*, p. 94.

to the surface and there expired, so he lost at that instant the last secret delight he retained in life as a game where finally you never got hurt if you played the game well enough."[45] All that is missing is Hearn's reliance on "the blunder factor." And that is provided in the closing lines in Mailer's next book, *Miami and the Siege of Chicago*: "We may yet win, the others are so stupid."[46]

Much earlier, Mailer had written, "As the years go by and I become a little more possible for Ph.D. mills, graduate students will begin to write about the slapping of my creative rage, of Mailer's vision of his rage as his shield, when what I was trying to say was simply. 'The shits are killing us.' "[47] Well, despite everything that Mailer has written since, the shits are still killing us. The problems in society remain the same; the dilemma in Mailer's work remains the same. And now, in a new book, Mailer has carried his ambivalences to the moon. In an ungracious moment we might agree with Marx that *revolution* is the poetry of the future. A second thought might argue that we are asking too much of the artist: there is no final resolution to the tension between politics and imagination. Perhaps Günter Grass is right, "Let us be conscious of this: A poem knows no compromises — but we live on compromises. He who actively sustains this tension is a fool and changes the world."[48]

[45]*Ibid*.
[46]Norman Mailer, *Miami and the Siege of Chicago* (New York, 1968) , p. 223.
[47]*Advertisements for Myself*, p. 19.
[48]Quoted in Kurt Lothar Tank, *Günter Grass* (New York, 1969) , p. 105.

Americans, Exiles and Canadians

Dennis Duffy

The weather would have seemed pleasant that summer in Lennox-ville had not its very breeze warned the exile of the oncoming bit-terness of winter. It was a time of trial, for the newly-released prison-er, by no means hale after the vicissitudes of captivity, had now to rethink what he was to do with a shattered life.

The men who lose a war hold one weapon of revenge, that of their memoirs. As Hitler's marshals were to show, the magic of lit-erary recollection transforms abject ruin into gallant surrender, the easy participation in cruel practices into a stoic devotion to national survival, an astute victor into a clumsy amateur blundering his way to triumph. This American exile yearned to undertake his campaign for vindication, but the physical and nervous strain he had endured prevented his beginning it then in Lennoxville. The documents and letters he had salvaged reposed undisturbed in the vaults of the Bank of Montreal, where they had been placed for safekeeping.

Rock Grove was a pleasant house, however, and the small colony of American exiles who had gathered around him strove to entertain each other as well as extend a mutual aid during this time of recov-ery and indecision. Thank God, his own children kept themselves amused. They had the offspring of good families — such as the Cum-mings and the Stotesburys — to play with. At times, their father would shoulder aside sufficient of his cares to allow room on his back for the children. There he would sing along with them and beat out with his foot the tunes of old times not forgotten, the gal-loping glees of his old country, sounds now of a lost world.

Within three months, the colony had dispersed and he and his family sailed for England, doubtful as they all were of his capabilities for surviving the Quebec winter. Lennoxville had been but a way station. The exile was to be lived out in the Old World. It was the autumn of Confederation, but neither Jefferson Davis nor his family possessed any interest in the new nation. For these American exiles, Canada was a place to pause in before moving onward.[1]

* * *

There are many varieties of the exilic experience. We begin by recalling that of Jefferson Davis because, strange as it may seem, it is in some ways akin in its motivations to those of present-day exiles. Not that these exiles are rootless wanderers planning to use Canada as a way station, for this is not the case.[2] The similarity lies in the fact that Davis and his kind came up against the might of America whose nature they had grossly misinterpreted. Their slaves had been escaping to Canada decades before a few of their one-time masters found it prudent to follow. The Confederates discovered that the centralizing thrust of American civilization was irresistible. They discovered that a world had changed within their very lifetime and that the pluralist society, based upon a doctrine of a concurrent majority, which they assumed themselves to have possessed as a matter of birth, had never existed beyond the theorizings of their own spokesmen. The basis of that system for which Davis lost nearly everything was abhorrent and wicked. Yet the United States of America had from its founding countenanced the existence within its borders of what it was later to brand a moral disgrace. It had granted the highest political offices to upholders of that system and even surrounded chattel slavery with a host of legal defences. In fact, so effective a job had been done that Southerners came to hold

[1]Information on Davis at Lennoxville: Ishbel Ross, *First Lady of the South, the Life of Varina Davis* (New York, 1958) , pp. 302-04.

[2]See "Amnesty — Who Needs It," editorial in *Amex: the American expatriate in Canada,* II (August-September, 1970) , 3.
My authority for any statement made in this attempt to speculate upon the implications of the fact of American exiles in Canada is slight. I am no longer an American citizen, nor can I be considered an exile. This is not a sociopolitical study, but merely the thoughts of a former American who has enjoyed some contact with American exiles.
The solidest American journalism I have come across on the tone and tenor of the American exile in Canada may be found in *Phoenix* (student newspaper at CUNY's Queens College campus) , XII (Nov. 10, 1970) , 9-15.

an altogether unrealistic view of the resilience and vigour of their culture, a way of life they imagined could survive trial by violence because it had been founded on violence.

Without transforming today's American exiles into neo-Confederates, it can be said that Vietnam made them aware of the existence of an America their education (except in very special circumstances) and official culture had conditioned them against ever knowing. What they had conceived to be a peaceful nation forced into a number of wars by the greed and savagery of predators in this hemisphere and the other came to appear a warlike empire devoted to military aggression as an acceptable — if taxing — method of resolving international conflicts and rivalries in favour of that empire. More specifically, the exiles here came to feel that the Selective Service System was not an equitable device by which a free society distributed justly the burdens of defence, but a class-biased method of social control that assured the means for the continuance of the warfare state without any gross disturbance to society.[3]

The vast majority of war resisters, themselves the majority of American exiles, were anything but radicalized when they came. It is doubtful that many of them, especially deserters, could even have been called politicized. The sense of alienation from their homeland has rarely been a process accomplished before the journey was undertaken. Many of the feelings outlined in the preceding paragraph arose in the actual coming to Canada, in the gut realization at the border crossing that for them their homeland was a place best left behind. It is as if a man were to learn that what he dismissed as the annoyances of frequent headaches were in fact the agonies of a brain tumour. The "first generation" of exiles, those who came in the summer of 1967 when their increase in numbers began to make an impact on the Canadian consciousness,[4] have be-

[3]The fact that the Vietnam War has destroyed the usefulness of the draft as a means of waging war-as-usual and made conscription cost more in social unrest than its military benefits warrant, the rise in America of the theory that colonial wars are best waged with professional armies, the easing of draft quotas: these developments came about too late to have affected the majority of the American exiles now here.

[4]It was in the September 1967 issue of *Saturday Night* that draft-dodgers first appeared on the cover of a Canadian magazine. And — a personal detail this, but of some significance — my wife and I were first contacted about putting up newly arrived draft-dodgers in the spring of '67.

come more radicalized, in at least a cultural sense, with every passing year. But then who in North America, from stock brokers to academics to teenie-boppers, has not, at least in appearance? We float on a culture where radical concepts and life-styles form the staple of the communications media. This has as much to do with radicalism as wearing a tiger skin with the Simple Life, but it appears as radicalism to the sort of people who are titillated or terrified by it. However, the rebel, the urban guerrilla, drops out either internally or externally; he prepares for war or declares a separate peace, often smoking a separate peace pipe. He does not take off. That is the action of the person who has been surprised.

Impelled by his surprise, the American exile (I repeat, I am creating an entity from experience and hunch which I believe corresponds to certain attitudes of the majority of American exiles) did not come seeking the Heavenly City. He came out of very concrete motives: to get out from under the weight of military service in a war he considered not his. He came to a society the Ontario Board of Tourism has aptly described as Friendly, Familiar, Foreign and Near. That society is North American, its land in a very short time wrested from a harsh wilderness and wrenched from its indigenous occupants, its ways with nature marked by careless exploitation and downright hostility. For the exile, Canada's colonial status offers many reminders — of varying degrees of reassurance — of the place he left behind. Brand names, business structures, modes of social intercourse, films and television, books and magazines all smell of home. Whatever differences do exist between There and Here are subtle and not to be discerned quickly or — so at times it appears — without evoking a mystique of muskeg. In an exercise typical of the Canadian colonial mentality, Robert Fulford attributed the inability of draft-dodgers ever to become fully Canadianized to the impossibility of their returning to the U.S.: "part of every Canadian's equipment is his ability to enter the United States at will. . . . What every native-born Canadian possesses, and what the dodgers lack, is a visa to the U.S."[5]

Unless the war resister takes the wings of the morning or dwells in the uttermost depths of the sea, unless he leaves the developed Western nations, he will dwell in countries akin to his native one. It

[5]"Draft Dodgers," *Saturday Night*, LXXXIII (Nov. 1968) , 11-12.

is not so much a matter of the Americanization of the globe as the universality in the West of technological society, closely identified with America as it is. In Canada he will find this technological society more integrated with America's than elsewhere, for at least in English Canada he will find the cultural centres more overt in their orientation toward New York and San Francisco than Paris or London would be.

Will he adapt, then, to his new country, or remain an undigested lump of gristle within it? He is joining a nation based theoretically upon a concept of a mosaic rather than that of a melting pot, a nation in which ethnic ties remain strong. Canadianization is not a magical process, and it happens to immigrants not merely because they desire it, but because it appears impossible for them to hold the kind of jobs and status they desire without altering the old ways of living. Nor is "Canadianization" always wanted: many occupants of the various squares on the national mosaic gladly retain their ethnic identity at some cost to their social standing and job opportunities. This is especially true in matters of marriage and child raising. For example, the degree of obedience a WASP Canadian banker demands from his adolescent daughter varies widely from that a Greek-Canadian shopkeeper exacts from his. Any change coming about in the attitudes of the latter person will be the result of a conviction of the "superiority" — since permissiveness is identified with the upper-middle class training — of this very clear-cut antithesis to the traditional way of governing children. But that alternative has to exist before it can be chosen.

When we speak of Canadianization, and of the fears that this may prove impossible with American exiles,[6] we must accept the

[6]These fears have been most sharply articulated on the Left by Professor Robin Mathews. While his strictures exemplify the ease with which Canadian nationalism becomes Canadian nativism, they serve to emphasize that there is no magic connected with radicalism, that American dissidents do not necessarily possess any greater affinity for Canadianism than American rightists. "The U.S. citizen in recent years has done an immense amount to divert Canadian attention from Canadian interests. In recent years U.S. citizens have increasingly taken over posts that should have gone to Canadians. That is where the U.S. draft dodger is today." Mathews, "The U.S. Draft Dodger in Canada is Part of U.S. Imperialism in Canada," *AMEX*, II (June, 1970) , 25. See also Mathews, "Draft Dodging", *Canadian Dimension*, VI (Feb.-March 1970) , 10-11. One finds the same sort of warning echoes by a student radical, editor of York University's student newspaper: "The point is . . . Americans in Canada are helping to

possibility that what is being viewed as a Canadian alternative may be in fact a matter of class rather than one of nationality. To offer a concrete instance of this: a friend, second-generation Italian-Canadian, had "Canadian" girls held up by her parents as examples of all the moral laxity her rearing had preserved her from. Now "Canadian" girls did not really stay out late because they weren't "Italian." It was a matter of the parents attributing to all Canadian girls the patterns of behaviour they had observed in upper-middle class ones. The many Canadian children reared as strictly as their European counterparts are not nearly so visible as the hell-raising, articulate children of the well-to-do.

We would be foolish to ignore the extent to which the signs of social class mould our perceptions of what we consider to be a national or cultural style. With considerable logic, the American urbanologist Edward Banfield argues in his *The Unheavenly City* that the "statistical Negro" is a body very different in kind from the living American black. The Negro pulling down a middle-class salary and leading what is seen as a middle-class existence differs only in pigmentation from his white associates and is slandered when lumped with underclass Negroes in statistics on crimes of violence, marital desertion and unemployment. There is enough truth in this to make one wary of attributing patterns of behaviour in American exiles to their national origin. We have the phenomenon of invisible draft-dodgers (Draft-dodger, like Whig and Tory, is a once-derogatory epithet which recipients have turned into a polite designation of themselves), and certain kinds of exiles and war resisters are as ghostly as the Canadian girls whose actions my friend's parents never noticed. Keep in mind two familiar, elementary facts: first, not every American exile has fled the draft or accompanied someone fleeing military service, a number are 'established' families or individuals who have decided to leave America and become Canadians; secondly, all dodgers do not affect the dress and manner

---

undermine the cultural identity necessary for any liberation struggle. Canadians on the left welcome Americans who have decided not to serve their country's military machine. But you must realize that you're not fighting imperialism in the heartland, but in the colony — a colony that hardly knows its own condition." Delores Broten, "Platform", *AMEX*, II (Oct.-Nov., 1970), 22.

However strange it may be for American draft-dodgers to hear themselves termed outside agitators by academics as well as bankers, they had better get used to it.

we associate with Youthcult. Consider three acquaintances who came to Canada to escape the draft: one was a computer specialist who "placed" himself immediately, another had his choice of jobs between the Royal Ontario Museum and the Addiction Research Foundation, and chose to ride the wave of the future rather than that of the past, while the third was the male half of a married couple, under-21, from small-town West Virginia, with no white collar qualifications beyond those for a file clerk. The first was New York Jewish in background, the second a Southern Negro born into poverty, a self-made man if ever one existed, the last purebred WASP. Virtually the sole common characteristic beyond that of age and national origin was their reluctance to be drafted into military service in the Vietnam War, for none of them were pacifist. As for their national origin, each one's experience of America appeared as remote as the movies to the other two, and about as unreal as the movies of America appear to anyone who knows the part of America that is being filmed. Yet we all know which of this group of three, none of them political persons, fits the common image of the draft-dodger: the husband with a year of junior college behind him, his wife a former dime-store clerk, overwhelmed by the urban hardness of Toronto. If they fit any pigeonhole, then it ought to be the one already occupied by the Maritimers in the film, *Goin' Down the Road*. Their small-town backwater origin was of far greater prominence in their attitudes and life-styles than their nationality. But because this couple quite sensibly gravitated to the semi-communal, no-steady-job existence possible in the drop-out community of any urban centre, we know the way they ought to be described if we want to get across their peculiar essence, their ineffaceable individuality: American Draft-Dodger Hippies. And it was the husband who, in fact, came to appear on a magazine cover in a piece on draft-dodgers.

You have only to glance at the communications media to appreciate that the draft-dodger is strongly identified with those elements in Canadian society that appear frightening and alien to many. He appears un-Canadian not only to radicals on the Left, but also to the Canadian counterparts of the folks back home who dismissed him as un-American. To the extent that American exiles are visible as a group they will be identified by such people with deviant strains in the national make-up. Youthcult, cultural radicalism, freaky clothes, communal living: these threats to the old ways make the term "draft-dodger" raise an image of long hair, blue jeans and battered pick-up trucks parked in the dusty front yards of crumbling, inner-city houses, "Oh Cannabis" instead of "Oh Canada."

The draft-dodger is not permitted to be just another New Canadian, since he attracts attention not for his own sake but for what Canadians think he tells them about themselves. Left alone, he would cease to be visible, but instead he is photographed and researched. He fascinates the media, and academics devote time to him at conferences. Clearly, his presence here is catalytic, activating a number of feelings Canadians have about their country in a manner that the presence of Texahoma gas-and-oil execs and Portuguese peasants does not. One hears that draft-dodgers now outnumber Eskimos in this country; Ukrainians outnumber both, yet fail to excite the kind of attention American exiles have. Why?

II

The palmy days of publicity are over for draft-dodgers. From roughly the summer of '67 to the summer of '69 they helped fill the media's appetite for new material. The media "take up" only what they sense can be made to interest their audience, and only so long as they sense the public to be able to absorb more opinion on a subject. The fact of the recent prominence of draft-dodgers in the media still fails to account for the intellectuals' interest in them.

It is hardly a coincidence that draft resistance in the United States and Canadian Nationalism both enjoyed an upsurge in the late Sixties. The involvement of the United States in another Asian war became an "issue," a proof of the rightness of the case for anti-Continentalism. The installation of nuclear missiles on Canadian soil by a Prime Minister who amused the young Caesar with his encyclopaedic knowledge of baseball averages, the growing awareness of the high costs of American investment in the Canadian economy, Expo 67: all these are milestones, of greater or lesser import, in the rise in Nationalist sentiment. Still, the single process which most united Canadian students and intellectuals in their distrust of American society has proved to be the War. As an international conflict, it has either brought about or reinforced the unease felt by many with a forward policy viewed as a natural outgrowth of America's international role since World War II, a role in which Canada has a minor but noticeable share. Within American society, the War exacerbated social unrest, making Canadians conscious, at times smugly assured, of the relative stability of their own society. While in Canada the moral impact of the War has fallen largely upon the educational community, it has also generated considerable unease about the U.S. and its omnipresence in Canadian life among all sections of the electorate. The intellectuals are more convinced of their rightness, naturally, and the divergence between their opinions and those of the rest of the country is particularly wide where draft-dodgers are concerned. Most Canadians are not Cold War Revisionists, and tend to dismiss draft-dodgers with the maxim that, "If they won't fight for their own country, they won't fight for ours." The War for Middle Canada is a tragic blunder, an obscene fluke and not the culmination of a decades-long surge in American aggressiveness. Opposition to that War, even to the extent of abandoning a homeland in order to stay out of the fighting, lacks a clear-cut moral authority to those who take no ideological posture toward the War. For those who do, and this now includes the majority of the educational community, the presence of draft-dodgers here confirms many of them in their view that America has reached its nadir in repudiating its best future in the youth it has compelled to flee.

The current American exiles are not, as we know, the first. The exilic Founding Fathers, the United Empire Loyalists, were the losers of the first American civil war, and provided for *English* Canadians a vision of their country as something more than another occupant of the North American continent. This vision is amply supported by a mass of historical evidence for Canada's adversary role, but that group of exiles and the myths which grew up around them played their part in strengthening Canadian awareness of this role. The United Empire Loyalists sought not just safety and relief from the exactions of what they viewed as a violent, intolerant society, they came also seeking stability within the specific context of the monarchical, British social system they had seen destroyed in the United States. They were bringing to Canada the very beliefs that were — from an English viewpoint — the moral justification for the existence of the colony. They were, if you will, reaffirming with

177

their feet the existence of the Great Chain of Being. Pioneers they became as well as exiles, building a society upon a tradition shattered by revolutionary violence which they determined to restore in a new land. Time was to prove, however, the impossibility of transplanting that tradition without severe modification, and thus they left their successors with a host of ambiguities and complexities, making this new society so difficult to explain, so taxing to delineate.

If the present-day American exiles came seeking the same abstract values as their predecessors, they have arrived without any longing for or knowledge of the political tradition in which these values have become reified. Nor in 1971, after decades of a chipping away at the British connection, are they likely to find very much in the tenor of Canadian life to confront them with the necessity for learning just what is owed to this British tradition. Does there exist some body of knowledge for them to learn, in however informal a manner, or is it instead a matter of a lesson their presence has to teach Canadians about the present state of Canada?

III

To the extent that Canadian Nationalism depends upon the conviction that we order our affairs better than America does hers, the presence of exiles would appear to offer some heartening evidence of the soundness of the Cause. To be a radical now in Canadian politics is to be Nationalist and anti-American, which is why the Canadian Left, however Nationalist, remains close in its thought and style to the American Left, also fiercely anti-American. The badness of American life is a persistent theme in Canadian intellectual history,[7] as well as a conversational staple of vacationers

---

[7] The hero of Sara Jeanette Duncan's *The Imperialist* (1904) describes America as "the daughter who left the old stock to be the light woman among nations, welcoming all comers, mingling her pure blood, polluting her lofty ideals until it is hard indeed to recognize the features and aims of her honourable youth . . ." (Toronto, 1961) , p. 233.

Kipling heard from, or put into the mouth of Canadians he encountered in 1892, a less elegant, perhaps more honest version of the same sentiments when he wrote of a Canadian having "a pronounced objection to having anything to do with a land rotten before it was ripe, a land with seven million negroes as yet unwelded into the population, their race-type unevolved, and rather more than

returning from Florida and New York. Even a stopped clock is correct twice daily, and this time our rusty mechanism may be banging out the hour of doom. It hasn't been that long ago that Canadians were rightly perturbed about the brain drain, responding to it by a "Motherhood" campaign to stay in Canada instead of proceeding to nationalize the American branch plants who refuse to underwrite or carry on intellectual work in this country. The thought of the legions of American youth, many with university educations, pouring into the country is gratifying, and would be even more delightful were university people less unsettling to the general public than at present. The new arrivals are a manifestation of the fact that America is in trouble. The sight of thousands of young Americans repudiating their country ought to destroy the Continentalist, powder-monkey ideology that formed the support of an earlier generation of Canadian intellectuals.

Of course, it is nice to know that Canada has become the "North Country Fair" to many young Americans, and among the pleasanter attributes of life here is that the nation is not at war. But were it a more repressive and violent society than it is, were English Canada a mosaic of Royalist WASPs, flogging, and black flies, it would still attract draft-dodgers if only because Canada is where it is. The nature of the Selective Service System determines that most of the draft-dodgers who arrive will not come from the best-educated segments of American society. The draft is class-oriented; the sort of people who get into university and do well there are not as subject to the draft's vagaries as are those from lower socio-economic levels, a fact which grows more widespread as the War smoulders down. Many American exiles have earned undergraduate degrees and some undertaken post-graduate training, but Canada is not

---

crude notions on murder, marriage, and honesty." "From Tideway to Tideway," in his *Letters of Travel, 1892-1913* (London, 1938), p. 24.

Sara Jeanette Duncan's novel sounds another theme to be repeated in years to come: "American enterprise, American capital, is taking rapid possession of our mines and our water power, our oil areas and our timber limits. . . . They approach us today with all the arts of peace, commercial missionaries to the ungathered harvests of neglected territories; but the day may come when they will menace our coasts to protect their markets — unless by firm, resolved, whole-hearted action now, we keep our opportunities for our own people." (Duncan, p. 232).

recruiting *gratis* from the U.S. a cadre of skilled managers, analysts and budding technocrats.

If it is in the interest of the Centre and Right in Canada to view draft-dodgers as bellwethers of social turbulence, some opinion on the Left benefits from viewing them as the flower of an aware generation. But neither Left nor Right practices this mythologizing with any great conviction because everyone knows that the Americans obliterating Canada as an independent nation are not the ones up here — exiles, academics or executives — but the ones Down There in the board rooms, energy lobbies and TV studios. As their novelty wears off, draft-dodgers as a group will become as photogenic as Finnish-Canadians.

That will be to the advantage of everyone, for if ever there existed a time for Canadian introspection, it is the present. America's desperate position (if it is really all that desperate; the rumours of Apocalypse are spread by interested parties on Left and Right) is on so grand a scale as to focus our attention upon it rather than the perils of our own nation. Furthermore, the penalties of economic domination are difficult to dramatize. How do you convince people, many of whom are living better than their fathers ever did, that they might in time lose even that benefit of their colonial status? Easier to dramatize than economic domination is the threat to the existence of an indigenous culture, yet how miniscule appears the death of a magazine or the takeover of a textbook company when placed alongside the erosion of the economic basis for a culture. The problem is, not what will draft-dodgers contribute to Canada, it is, instead, will there be a Canada to strengthen?

IV

Draft-dodgers are the product of one of the most unpopular wars America has ever waged. Their presence here, along with the fact of that War, brings home to Canadians the confusions of their own situation. Here is a nation founded and nurtured in the shadow of one empire now attempting to resist absorption into another empire it once whole-heartedly embraced. Here is a nation linked in military alliance with America, a nation whose "star" branch of military service is integrated wholly with the defence needs of the United States, and whose economy benefits from the contributions it makes to the American war effort. This same nation welcomes, or at least admits, American draft-dodgers. The point is not to achieve consistency in the RCMP fashion, by casually passing a few of the shaggier ones along to the FBI. The need is instead to recognize the moral weakness — to put it mildly — of the Canadian position. It is difficult to be convinced that the admission of draft-dodgers is much more than a sop to an uneasy conscience, however humane the results of that gesture may be. An awareness on the part of Canadian intellectuals of the existence here of draft-dodging Americans and other exiles ought not to result in self-congratulation, but in an agonized insight into just how close to disaster this nation now stumbles. The draft-dodgers proclaim to us not how independent we are, but how little of our social being there is that neglects to serve the aims and interests of the American Empire.

The dangers of equating public with personal morality are manifold. More than one cool thinker has warned us of them, without telling how to avoid the grosser delinquencies of double-think and numbness concerning matters of public morality. It hardly requires the moral acuity of an Augustine to survey our reasonably free, reasonably humane, reasonably prosperous society (for so it is to academics and intellectuals) and to sense that it is shot through with mendacity and humane only when it costs little. But it would require a spiritual tenacity beyond the reach of pragmatic liberalism to avoid using this knowledge as an excuse for guilt-laden impotence.

Allow me to make a vast assumption. Let us, like the fellow who talked the girl into sleeping with him for a million dollars only to have her balk when he finally offered five, take the principle for granted and haggle only over details. The day has dawned when Canada has purchased itself back from the United States. Decisions about Halifax and Winnipeg are made in the boardrooms of Toronto rather than New York. Canadian energy resources are very carefully marketed in the U.S. on a small, short-term, expensive basis, thereby instructing the profligate Americans in the virtues of husbanding one's wealth and refraining from inordinate growth. A few matters still remain before the New Jerusalem can be proclaimed: the economy is still based largely on extractive and raw-material industries, thereby necessitating a heavy dependence upon the fluctuations in world markets; Eastern and Western Canada continue to consider themselves to be in bondage to Central Canada; the Caribbean peoples find the exactions of mini-imperialists no less galling than those of the Americans; crime rates continue to inch upward; students bitch about the educational system and liberals suffer agonies of guilt; government grows more remote and Parliament weakens; the wear and tear of urban life scratches deeper, and the French in Quebec remain dissatisfied. In other words, the gruelling fight to realise the objectives of economic nationalism will be but the beginning of our attempts to grapple with the problems besetting us. Perhaps some of the problems in education and urban life will decline as the fascination with American problems and models lessens, though getting out from under America will not roll away the twentieth century for us. The odds favour our continuing to wreck a dying planet with a way of life whose basic, unannounced premise is the infinite resilience and inexhaustibility of the non-manmade environment. Viewed from this perspective, the questions raised by the presence of American exiles in Canada come to possess a very small degree of interest. I have tried to consider some of these questions, but even as I write I am made aware of the scholiastic, Byzantine nature of the subject I am considering. Just as Carlyle's *Frederick the Great* is said to have praised the virtues of silence in fourteen volumes, so the object of my treatment is finally to shift attention away from the subject it purportedly attempts to analyze. For Canadians today, a concern over the presence and Canadianization of American exiles takes on the characteristics of a man living in a polluted city, smoking two packs of cigarettes daily, but wondering if he oughtn't to lay off char-broiled burgers.

The interest of Canadian intellectuals in draft-dodgers stems from their own involvement in a moral exile, in an estrangement from what they view as the Americanization of the basic institutions of their country. There is more to this estrangement than Americanization, but this is one fact that serves to unite Canadians of varying political persuasions in a way that economic radicalism cannot. The fact of a North American polity different in tone and history — whether for better or for worse — from that of the United States becomes less real with every day. It is *the* fact of life for any Canadian contemplating the state of his country and culture. His discovery of American exiles denotes his perception of his own perilous state and the brevity of the time remaining for redemption. There may have been a time when the American exile could have entered a different culture and could have worked with Canadians to raise that culture from dourness and complacency. How frustrating to sense that the battle cannot even be joined until another, a battle all but lost, is won! This, surely, is frustration, this certainly exile, wherever one may be dwelling.

Canada and the Vietnam War

John Holmes

In February 1966, the Hon. Paul Martin said there were "fundamental differences" between Canadian and United States policy
over Vietnam. These differences have not been obvious to critics.
Fundamental differences do not mean, however, that policy is
diametrically opposed. It can just be based on different premises.
Mr. Martin in the mid-sixties came close on occasions to full support
of the American premises, but he was defending them against the
charge of evil intentions more than endorsing their basic approach.
There were variations over the years in emphasis and attitudes by
Canadian spokesmen during the Liberal and Conservative administrations, but one can detect a certain consensus.

The recurrent theme in official Canadian statements is that the
issues in Indochina are complex and cannot be solved by military
means — a theme which sounds sometimes profound and sometimes
like a pious evasion of harsh reality. Canadians were not ingenuous
about the difficulties involved in making the Geneva Agreements
stick. They were aware of the attitude of communist countries and
of Mr. Dulles to the concept of neutrality, but they thought there
was a better chance of maintaining equilibrium in the area, the
inviolability of the plate glass window, if outside powers recognized
that it was safer to accept neutrality than to provoke interference.
They deplored Mr. Dulles's denying moral support to the Geneva
Agreements, his rounding up a paper alliance which alienated the
more influential non-communist Asians and justified a cynical

attitude to the Geneva bargain by the communists. They thought that forces loosed in Asia could not be traced solely to communist provocation. Canadians, by reason of the Commonwealth experience, had more sympathy for anti-imperialist forces than had the traditionally anti-imperialist Americans, no doubt because Canadians had less reason to feel betrayed by those whom they had helped.[1]

Differences over Vietnam have been concealed by the refusal of Canadian spokesmen to denounce United States policy. There were many reasons for this. The currency of international discourse is such that statesmen do not denounce each other with the freedom of private citizens. General de Gaulle expressed his disagreement indirectly and in terms which in the mouth of an editor would seem mild indeed. Whether or not one approves of this *politesse*, it is a convention and therefore official Canadian attitudes in Vietnam cannot be judged by the decibels of public statements. A diplomatic reason for tact was that public denunciation could undermine whatever influence Canada might have on United States policy. When Mr. Pearson gently suggested in Philadelphia in 1965 that the United States stop bombing the North, he drew the ire of President Johnson and forfeited the position of influence he had acquired. It is not only Canadians who resent criticism. The argument for loud diplomacy is that denunciation from Ottawa would have a shock effect on the United States government and public. It can be neither dismissed nor accepted without calculation. But one has to guard against inflation. Canadian advice has too often been written off in Washington because Ottawa was regarded as a tiresome and self-righteous nag. Canadian rhetoric on Indochina was also cautious (with certain notable exceptions) because of the requirements of impartiality of a Commission member. The United States was not denounced for its role in Vietnam, but neither was China. It would be silly to claim that public positions on Vietnam were determined entirely by Vietnamese issues. There have been practical economic reasons for treating both the United States and China with kid gloves, one case being, of course, stronger than the other.

[1]Official Canadians believed, of course, a lot of contradictory things about Indochina and United States policy. The attitude defined here is an oversimplification of the guiding assumptions.

It would be wrong to attribute the cautious Canadian attitudes on Vietnam to United States pressure. Naturally, the United States expressed its views in no uncertain terms. That is what diplomacy is all about. How much of a threat is involved thereby is for Canadian governments to calculate. There is no solid evidence of "blackmail." When Mr. Martin and others were defending United States motives they were expressing their own convictions, not acting as hired agents. In spite of doubts about the wisdom of United States policy Canadian spokesmen have been sympathetic to the United States reaction to communist provocation as they saw it. They recognize a dilemma for the Americans and one which involved the fate of an international security system in which Canada had a large stake. This attitude is largely shared by other allies of the United States, both in NATO and in SEATO. For Canadians, however, the attitude has been to a considerable extent the product of their unique experience in Indochina. To put it briefly, this has been an experience of the blundering, ineffectual and uncooperative government of South Vietnam, careless of the provisions of the Geneva agreement; the United States which grudgingly observed the terms of the Geneva armistices until they had become a farce; the North Vietnamese government which, from the beginning, thwarted and defied the efforts of the international control commissions in both Vietnam and Laos. When by the end of the 'fifties both sides were openly disregarding the truces, Ottawa had seen enough on the spot to regard the American intervention as a response to violation rather than as calculated imperialist expansion.

There has been, of course, an evolution over two decades in official Canadian attitudes. During the 'fifties the Americans did learn to see the value of the Geneva Agreements and the Commissions, and the differences between the two countries narrowed. Canadians had no reason to feel affection for the South Vietnamese government, which treated the Commission with scant respect, but by the late 'fifties there were increasing expectations that the Diem government would be able to make a go of it and create a state which, if hardly democratic in the Western sense, would, with massive American help, be the best hope of stability in a ravaged country. They saw with dismay the terrorist policies launched by the Viet Cong to upset the South Vietnamese experiment. It is clear from Canadian official statements, up until the mid-sixties at least, that this was seen as an operation directed from Hanoi and therefore an aggressive violation of the Geneva Agreements. That there were strong endemic revolutionary forces in the South was never denied. First-hand acquaintance with North Vietnam, however, discouraged regard for it as the democratic alternative.

The high tide of support of the United States — rhetorically at least — came in the early years of the new Liberal administration, 1963-1965, when the government looked upon the United States rush to the defence of the South Vietnamese government as being, on balance, justified. Then came a shift back towards the middle of the road. There were many reasons for this shift, including the intensification of articulate criticism of United States policy in Canada and the storm in the United States itself. Canadian leaders also wanted to make use of the Canadian access to Hanoi and Saigon to effect another armistice. The government knew that neither the United States nor the North Vietnam government would stop fighting because Ottawa told them to do so, and they concentrated on seeing if they alone or in collaboration with others might find some formula of agreement. Whether their chances of doing so had been spoiled, as has been charged, by the Minister's defence of American motives is a question hard to answer. When parties are angling for a truce, couriers are needed to convey to one side what the other is prepared to concede and they are likely to make use of the courier most convenient at the moment. Suspicion that the Canadian Commissioner was acting for the Americans could strengthen rather than weaken his credibility as a courier, although it might discredit his advice. It is possible that the messages which Canadian interlocutors carried back and forth during these years were, although not decisive, part of the process of reaching positions when both sides could go to Paris. The mediatory process is usually a maze.

By the late 'sixties it was hard for Ottawa to maintain positions which even United States Republicans were abandoning — although occasionally one wondered if hawks had flown north. Canadian spokesmen, however, had been defending United States ends, and the means now seemed to be fashioning different ends. The persistent Canadian belief that the issues could not be solved by military means was strengthened by the very escalation of the war. The bombing of the North was at first regarded as understandable, but the conviction grew that talks would never be possible unless it was stopped. This opinion crept more and more into public statements, and by 1968 the government seemed to have concluded that on this subject the time for unquiet diplomacy had come. So too had the other NATO allies, and the chorus was more effective than another yap from the tiresome neighbour.

The change in Canadian attitudes is most notable since the spring of 1968. Mr. Trudeau brought different preconceptions about Vietnam from those acquired in office by his predecessors. Neither he nor Mr. Sharp, however, has shifted to public criticism. On Vietnam they are cool, and largely silent.[2] The situation has, of course, changed. The bombing of the North has ceased, the United States has come to the conference table and the withdrawal of troops has started. Intermediaries are less obviously needed now that the two sides are in contact in Paris, and there has been a diminution of enthusiasm for the mediatory role in general on the part of the new government.

THE INTERNATIONAL CONTROL COMMISSIONS

Central to the Canadian experience of Vietnam is the part played in the International Control Commissions for Vietnam, Laos, and Cambodia. The obligation was to be judicious and impartial rather than neutral. This was not a UN supervisory body of the usual kind but a troika on which there was to be a representative communist country, a representative Western country, with a neutral chairman. Canadians were prepared on many occasions to find the South Vietnamese guilty, but the Poles could not do likewise with respect to North Vietnam. Canadian impartiality was, of course, conditioned by Western perspectives and prejudices, and the record was not impeccable. Nevertheless the single-minded advocacy of one party by the Poles pushed the Canadians into protecting the rights of the other. Since its first year, when it accomplished its most important mission by adjudicating many differences between the belligerents in the difficult post-hostilities period, the Commission in Vietnam has been humiliated and frustrated but maintained

[2]In the *Monthly Report on Canadian External Relations* for 1967 there were 63 entries on Vietnam; in 1968, 15; and in 1969, 7.

188

because no one wanted to destroy a last symbol of the Geneva Agreements. The Canadian Commissioner has not denied, as has been claimed, that the United States is acting contrary to the Geneva armistice. He has insisted, however, that this had to be seen in the context of violations by the other side. In 1962 a majority report of the Commission, from which the Poles dissented, established this principle. However, Canada dissented a few years later from a report in which the Poles and the Indians criticized only the United States and South Vietnam for violation and refused to make public evidence in the Commission's hands concerning North Vietnamese actions in the South.

Over sixteen years a large number of Canadian Foreign Service and Army Officers have served in Indochina. They have had an enlightening experience of Asia at the grass roots, but it has been a particular kind of experience. The time has been largely spent combatting the knavish tricks of the North Vietnamese, not only in Vietnam but in Laos as well. Virtually all Canadian veterans of Indochina have returned with more hawkish attitudes than prevail at home. One can agree or disagree with them or discount their special cause for prejudice, but it is not easy to write them off. It is hard for anyone who has honestly looked at the record to deny the consistent deceit and tendentiousness in Hanoi's attitude towards the Commissions and the terms of the agreement. The issues in Vietnam are, however, broader and deeper than the truce and have to be judged in an historical framework longer than that during which Canada has been involved. Canadian officials may have seen Vietnam up too close and in a special context.

THE EFFECT ON CANADIAN FOREIGN POLICY

Mackenzie King had argued, with considerable support, that Canada ought not to become involved in distant continents because it had no interests there. In 1954 Canada was obliged to accept a nasty obligation to help maintain the peace in Southeast Asia — an invitation issued prècisely because Canada had no interests in the area. The assumption had to be discarded that Canada led a sheltered existence and its youth and underdevelopment excused it from far-flung obligations. Mr. King had been dead four years. Canadian zeal in NATO, in Korea, and in the United Nations had

189

already set Canadian policy on a new course, but the Indochina requirement forced the country into a foreign policy involvement more exotic and less collective than had previously been contemplated. Canada found itself in an exposed position in the centre of world conflict. There were advantages for a country eager to make its mark in world politics. With responsibility came some degree of influence. Canada learned, for one thing, that to have influence in world politics it is an advantage to have special knowledge. Canadians scattered throughout these countries had access to areas denied to other peoples, Eastern or Western. Their deductions were listened to with respect in London, Paris, Delhi, even Washington. Canadian critics who have accused their government of "passing information" to the Americans ignore the function of political intelligence in persuasion. It is not easy to persuade Washington when it thinks it has a monopoly of the facts. Since the war began to rage throughout the area and the Commission lost its significance, this special advantage diminished — although the access to Hanoi and its leaders still gives Canadians special status.

Our role in Indochina was the classic case of middlepowermanship. There was not, before 1954, much theorizing about the role of a middle power. That came after the Suez crisis, when this phase of Canadian policy had reached its crest. The Indochina experience of the 'fifties confirmed the view of many Canadians and of our friends that this was our special destiny and our best contribution to international order. It satisfied our desire to do our own thing, complementary to that of the great powers but by no means that of a handmaiden. It enabled us to differ from the United States without opposing the interests of the United States as we saw them. It took some courage for the government in 1954 to accept an assignment in which we had no expectation of help or even moral support from our large ally, but of course it was not the audacity required to oppose the Americans directly. We had to suffer American scorn more than American hostility.

Then we had to pay for this heady experience. The role of the middleman is not simply that of the fairy godmother beloved by all. Powerful interests and passions were involved. Our role was useful but peripheral, and this was no peripheral quarrel. At times Canadian good judgment gained respect, at least in foreign offices, but we also gained enemies and disparagers. Relations with friends and allies may have suffered more than relations with antagonists. The Poles and the Russians had no reason to feel disappointed in our performance. This close association may not have been good for Canadian-Indian relations which by the mid-fifties had become close. Different perspectives encouraged mutual exasperation. At the same time personal associations developed between Indians and Canadians and with Poles as well which, because of the insights they provided and the lasting contacts they afforded, had their own reward. Our diplomacy was honed. But whatever was gained in the 'fifties may have been lost in the 'sixties when a confrontation became a war.

Among the casualties has been the Canadian belief in its role as a middle power. To this Vietnam has been only one contributing factor. The expulsion of UNEF was more important. The present scepticism is bred of disillusion bred of exaggeration. The function of the intermediary was mistaken for that of the international policeman and found wanting. As the war in Indochina has become more immoderate, there has been a revulsion in Canada against the approach to peace through moderate international action. On the one hand it is regarded as gratuitous do-goodism which interferes with our commerce. In the eyes of other critics this commitment to mediation has tied Canada to an ineffective policy of quiet diplomacy which has had no effect on the parties, in particular the United States, and been bad for our soul.

Has this thankless assignment in Asia turned Canada away from that continent? The recent White Paper with its Pacific orientation suggests not, but the emphasis in the White Paper is commercial and cultural, with little concern for security. Vietnam has certainly not encouraged us to seek a partnership with the Americans in Pacific security which we had never sought earlier. There is no clamouring for an extended "role" in Indochina. The government, it is implied, would not refuse useful service in a further commission but it wants to have a good look at the terms first. Over the years the Indochina assignment has kept the eyes of both our External Affairs and National Defence departments distracted from Europe to Asia, and made it harder for the government to slide back into the North Atlantic womb. It revealed to the government with a shock that so long as we assert our interest in world-wide "stability" and world-wide freedom of commerce, we are vulnerable to service farther away from home than Mr. King would have liked.

THE EFFECT ON DEFENCE POLICY

The ICC assignment was unwelcome to the defence authorities, although they did it well. There was at that time little disposition to regard peacekeeping as an acceptable or accepted role for armed forces. Vietnam had a hand in changing all that. Indochina was not an easy assignment, but it was often interesting and always challenging. In the first year there was a real sense of accomplishment. It was an exotic assignment for the permanent forces and a road to promotion. It was gradually built into the regular program of the services and helped prepare them, after UN assignments in the Middle East and Africa, to look upon peacekeeping as one of the continuing functions of the Canadian forces.

The most important impact of the Vietnam War on Canadian defence policy, however, may have been its effect on the alliance in general and in particular on our relations with the United States. Twenty years ago few Canadians doubted that when the United States was at war, Canada would be at war whether we liked it or not. Now we have got used to the idea that the United States is at war, as it has been in a *de facto* way for almost a decade, and Canada is not only not at war, it has never considered such a course. Our commitment to the ICCs has given us a valid excuse, but even without such a commitment it is doubtful that a majority of Canadians would have been disposed to join the Americans in battle. What is more, there has been no evidence of any undue pressure by the United States government to induce us to do so — although requests for support of South Vietnam have been made in general terms to the NATO allies. And we have suffered no sanctions. The consciousness of alliance obligations has been modified. The opposition to involvement has not been entirely idealistic. A "silent majority" of Canadians probably just think that Indochina is a good area for us to keep out of, especially as the United States has no pressing need of military assistance. Because of the Vietnam war, however, there is now an opposition to fighting as an ally of the United States sufficiently articulated to make the government sensitive. It has been a factor in the debate over a continuing commitment to NORAD and NATO, although not decisive. Before Vietnam, it was assumed that the United States would always be on the side of the angels and that, although we reserved our right to limit our contribution to the heavenly hosts, we would be on that side too. That the United States would be on the side of the angels, or at any rate on the side where our interests lie, is probably still the basic assumption of most Canadians, but it is not taken for granted as it once was.

This change is reflected in attitudes to the Defence Production Sharing Agreements. Up until the mid-sixties these were seen not as the harnessing by the United States of our resources to its war machine but rather as Canada demanding its rightful share in the alliance armaments business. Because of the circumstances of Vietnam and Canada's commitment to the Geneva agreements, Canadians have become aware of the ambiguity of their position consequent upon this pooling of continental resources. The assumption that the pooling of allied resources was inevitable because we were all involved in a common effort has been questioned because we are not all involved in the American effort in Vietnam. There has been no change of government policy but a change in the climate in which government policy is formulated. The case has at least been recognized for making ourselves less dependent in future on this profitable trade if we want to strengthen our independent hand in world politics.

This diminished sense of partnership may be the most important result of Vietnam on the relations between Canada and the United States. There is evidence that it is felt on both sides. Canadian defence officials have suspected an exclusion of Canadians from military intelligence they had previously shared.[3] On the Right Wing of American politics there is some husky criticism of Canada, but Canadian policy on Cuba, China, NATO, and sealhunting attract more comment than Vietnam — except that the latter is associated with the lively subject of deserters and draft-dodgers. On the whole Canada's non-belligerent position in Vietnam has created remarkably little antipathy in the United States, one of the blessings

[3]See, for example, testimony of Dr. G.R. Lindsey at the Commons sub-committee on maritime forces, January 28th, 1970.

of being rarely noticed whatever we do. Americans do not seem to have changed their view of the principle of continental defence as inviolable and, what is more, sensible. It is hard for them to see that for Canadians the disconcerting realization that we could differ in our choice of enemies raises fundamental questions about joint defence. Who discerns — or provokes — the attacker? The implications for Canadians are unclear. For some, the obvious conclusion is disengagement from military association with an "imperialist power." For other Canadians the logic of joint defence, on the grounds both of efficacy and cheapness, remains so convincing that differences about policy in a distant part of the world can be disregarded. The climate of opinion has shifted to the extent that further commitments to continental defence on Canada's part, such as, for example, joining in an ABM or AWACS system, would be expected to rouse louder hostility than in the past. The Canadian hope seems to be that we can carry on avoiding new decisions until something has been resolved in Vietnam. Vietnam may simply have frozen joint defence. It is a question, however, whether a posture of not getting out of it and not getting on with it can be sustained in a decade when there is likely to be rapid technological and political change in the United States.

The horror of Vietnam has strengthened the desire of Canadians to search for non-military ways of making their contribution to international security — a disposition clearly evident in the underplaying of security issues in the recent White Paper on foreign policy. Such choices may not be open to great and super-powers — and it may only be an illusion that they are open to lesser powers. For the time being, however, Canadians have become less restless in their present status, less ambitious for a role in international security. Vietnam may have witnessed — and promoted — the rise and fall of Canada's affair with the middle power as a role, but it has also encouraged a sense of thanksgiving at not being a great power.

SOCIAL AND CULTURAL FACTORS

Much of the impact on Canada of the Vietnam war is a spill-over or a mirror image of its impact on the United States. One must be careful in one's deductions because the Vietnam war is only one, although perhaps the major, element in the transformation of American society and attitudes in the past decade, and it is part of a world-wide movement, not just a North American phenomenon. It would be hard to say how much the increasing "anti-Americanism" in Canada is attributable to the Vietnam war and how much to the racial issue, United States policy in Latin America, or its heavy investment in Canada. It is the exercise of great military force in another continent, however, which especially seems to confirm the diagnosis of "imperialism."

The effect on Canadian attitudes to the United States has been ambivalent; the Vietnam war has stimulated in Canada both alienation and identification. In spite of the articulateness and the passion of the critics, probably just as many Canadians regard the US endeavour to "resist aggression" in other parts of the world as justified and worthy of moral support — even though they may increasingly consider it a losing cause.[4] Vietnam has raised the level of anti-American feeling in Canada and it has also tended to polarize attitudes towards the United States. For the majority, however, it may just have stimulated Canadianism, both of the affirmative and perverse varieties. It could once be assumed that all Canadians, with the exception of a few last-ditch Loyalists, regarded the United States as a frequently arrogant, not particularly lovable, but essentially benevolent power and, provided one was not expected to say so loudly, a good friend to have on our side. Few doubted that the United States was a good deed in a naughty world. For a large number of less articulate Canadians there was also a strong urge to share the higher standard of living in the United States or to make it in the big time. Now that the higher standard of living includes the possibility of compulsory military service in the Indochinese jungles and a much higher liability to municipal violence,

[4]As late as 1966, according to polls of the Canadian Institute of Public Opinion (Gallup) only 31% of Canadians thought the United States should withdraw its troops from Vietnam whereas 18% favoured carrying on at the present level and 27% were for increasing the attacks. By 1967 these figures had shifted to 41%, 16% and 23%. In 1968, 35% of Canadians said they were grateful to the Americans for their efforts in Vietnam and 37% disassociated themselves from what the Americans were doing there. In May 1970, 36% said their opinion of the United States would go up if they withdrew all their troops from Vietnam and the same per cent said it would have no effect on their view of the great neighbour.

calculations have shifted. Fewer Canadians are moving to the United States and more Americans are moving to Canada.[5] It is hard to say whether this trend will outlast the Vietnam war, because the motivation is ecological and romantic as well as political — or whether calculations will be altered by the threat of civil commotion in Canada.

Resistance to the United States, as a Canadian mood, has shifted leftwards. Canadian intellectuals are affected by the mood of American liberals, an apparent state of despair about American civilization. The Canadians do not know whether to respond by rejecting the United States and finding their own way or by wallowing in sin with the Americans. This dilemma is attributable to one virtue, fairmindedness — the realization that we share the horrid bourgeois civilization and the Cold War and it is not decent to attribute the wickedness to the United States and the virtue to Canada. It is attributable also to the hair-shirt hangup which makes it impossible for some Canadians to accept more fortunate circumstances when they have them. Out of a laudable effort to avoid hypocrisy, Canadian critics of United States policy in Vietnam have been anxious to blame their own government for complicity. They have got things out of proportion. They ignore the detachment from the war in Indochina which the Canadian government has maintained and the part it has tried to play in keeping peace in that area and they centre their attention on the less important fact that Canada has not denounced the United States or broken off its defence-production sharing agreements. The latter are legitimate criticisms but they are not central. Identification with the United States and its conflicts is found most notably on the extreme Left and the extreme Right — although it is probably the Lumpen Middle, brain-washed by television, that is least aware of the fact that Canada is not itself at war in Vietnam. Canadian radicals join anti-Vietnam parades in the streets of Washington and other Canadians assume an identity of interest with the United States government by calling for the exclusion of draft-dodgers and deserters. The Right and the Left do not worry about consistency. They both regard the United States and Canadian governments as linked

[5]Since 1964 the annual immigration of Americans to Canada has doubled from 11,000 to 22,000 whereas the number of Canadians believed to have moved to the United States has declined from 50,000 to 30,000.

inseparably in defence of the "capitalist system," and they must be destroyed together or preserved together in accordance with values more important than the preservation of national identity. The dilemma is for the pragmatic Canadian nationalist. The Vietnam war, which has given a strong stimulus to Canadian nationalism, could in the end contribute to the erosion of Canadian sovereignty or at least the idea of Canada, not by American intervention, but by the refusal of Canadians to accept their condition as non-Americans.

Finally, what impact has the Vietnam war had on Canada's view of itself, of its place in the world and on the view other people, including the Americans, have of Canada? How much of the increase in nationalism and self-confidence in Canada in the past sixteen years is attributable to the expansion of our economic growth to near great power figures and how much to our neighbour's misfortunes? Canadians have suffered in the past not from an inferiority complex *vis-à-vis* the United States but from a consciousness of smallness or perhaps of small-townness. Like small-towners they felt poorer and less sophisticated but had no doubt of their moral superiority. The Vietnam war may have encouraged smugness, but it is a question whether it has aggravated our sense of moral superiority. Those Canadians most convinced of the immorality of American policy are those most determined to associate Canada with the crime. Other Canadians think we are letting the Americans fight our crusade and they, therefore, feel morally inferior. What has shifted may be the Canadian view as to who has the luck — at least up until October, 1970. The comforts of a quieter life and in particular the freedom from the terrible obligations to keep the peace in all parts of the world have become more obvious. We seem to be in a period of retreat from the ambitions for world influence which characterized us at the time of the Geneva Conference of 1954. Whether this is a renunciation of world responsibility or a seeking after a different or more appropriate responsibility for a country economically rather than militarily strong remains to be seen. Strengthening of the yearning for independence or neutrality, for a non-military role, has certainly been encouraged by the Vietnam war, partly by the desire to keep out of something so messy and partly because of the apparent demonstration of the futility of military force.

The Vietnam war still rages and the results are uncertain. If it ended in a new Geneva agreement with a responsible part for Canada, an adjustment to reasonably independent régimes in Indochina, and an American withdrawal without too great a loss of face, we might all resume our active and constructive role in the building of a strong United Nations by experience. On the other hand an American withdrawal in disarray accompanied, or perhaps preceded, by upheavals in the United States would drive us into a frantic effort to isolate ourselves from contagion or, impelled by the death wish which plagues many Canadians, to jump into the flames in order not to be unlike the Americans. Whatever the shape of events, we are likely to feel a cold chill from a collapse of the *Pax Americana*. Whether we have liked it or not, and it is far from the ideal way to keep the peace, we have regarded it as a bulwark. *Sub specie aeternitatis* we may regard the disintegration of the American empire as a good thing, but at the moment it would leave Canada more exposed and vulnerable than it has ever been part of our philosophy to regard ourselves. The shock waves alone could be devastating. This is not an argument to join the Americans in the way they are going; it is simply to underline our vital interest in their fate. Canadian calculations about our own situation in the world, whether they are neutralist or alliance-minded, for the most part assume a strong and internationally active United States — as well as a strong Soviet Union in counterpoise. A shift in the capacity, stability, or disposition of either superpower would bring us hard up against the brute facts of survival as an over-resourced and underpopulated entity. Our present obsession with independence as the principal theme of foreign and defence policy may then seem to ourselves as heedless as it now does to most foreigners.

Preoccupation with Canada has never been an American obsession, but there is evidence of a changing attitude to us in the age of Vietnam. Persistent in American mythology, although never high in profile, has been the vision of Canada as the tranquil frontier and second childhood. It is a view which may be destroyed by recent events in Quebec, but Canada is a vast country. It is disconcerting to find Canada regarded as an oversized Walden Pond, a bucolic vision which Canadians have been anxious to cast off, but it is not unattractive to be a haven where brilliant and attractive Americans come to find rest and help fight our expressways. Most sober Canadians realize that we face many of the issues of American society and would like to avoid American mistakes. Many of the American immigrants, especially the intellectuals, see their mission in helping us do this. But we are not just the United States in the days of its innocence and we need different cures for different illnesses. Desegregation or school bussing is no panacea for our ethnic differences, and as for Vietnam, our national sin is under- rather than over-involvement in the affairs of other states. We must some time shake that paralyzing conviction that Canada's national purpose is catching up with the United States. Vietnam may have helped.

One is tempted to conclude, trying to avoid smugness, that the Vietnam war and all it has done to the United States, its soul and its image, has given Canadians more confidence in the quality of their own country or at least made them value more their habitat. But has it? Our liberation will not come through any form of obsession with the United States, even if it is hostile. Our artists and writers remain infatuated by the excitement and drama of Vietnam and the race riots — all of which they vividly deplore. The most successful English-Canadian play of the year is about the Chicago trials, a phenomenon which one critic described as "the ultimate US cultural invasion of our country." The expatriate actor, Donald Sutherland, whose views, if he were in Canada, would be called anti-American, says, "America is the most exciting country in the world because it is so volatile." Canadians have always been more attracted by its excitement than its republican virtue. The US has always been better theatre. The Vietnam war and the American tragedies it has provoked have fascinated Canadians and drawn their attention away from the incipient tragedy in their own country. And so the Canadian radicals — the Anglophones at least — have studied foreign remedies for domestic maladies which are unique. If it continues, that would be a sell-out by English-Canadian reformers with consequences as threatening to the Canadian survival as the sell-out of our physical resources with which they are preoccupied.